C000252591

PRAISE FOR
DISINTEGRATION

"Martyanov shows that America's disintegration is irreversible because the ruling elites are an organic part of the calamitous sources of dysfunction that have destroyed the country."

—PAUL CRAIG ROBERTS

"Andrei Martyanov's third book discussing the collapse of the U.S. Empire looks into the social and economic phenomena which all contribute to that collapse. *Disintegration* is a multi-level analysis of the crisis which is now so clearly plaguing the USA of 2021. I consider *Disintegration* a "must read" for every U.S. patriot who wants his country to overcome its current difficulties and for every person on the planet who wants to avoid a full-scale war between Russia and/or China and the USA. Indeed, if you want to get a superb summation of what is really going on in the United States—read all of Martyanov's books."

—THE VINEYARD SAKER

DISINTEGRATION

INDICATORS OF THE COMING AMERICAN COLLAPSE

Andrei Martyanov

Clarity Press, Inc.

© 2021 Andrei Martyanov
ISBN: 978-1-949762-34-1
EBOOK ISBN: 978-1-949762-35-8

In-house editor: Diana G. Collier
Cover design: R. Jordan Santos

Library of Congress Control Number: 2021932295

Clarity Press, Inc.
2625 Piedmont Rd. NE, Suite 56
Atlanta, GA. 30324
http://www.claritypress.com

CONTENTS

INTRODUCTION

When in June of 2020 the U.S. media connected to the Democratic Party, such as *Huffington Post* among many others, ran yet another bizarre, and ultimately untrue, story of some Russian intelligence "unit" paying bounties to the Taliban for killing U.S. soldiers in Afghanistan, it became plain that the American fourth estate had reached bottom.[1] Even when it first emerged from the dark recesses of the *New York Times*' lie machine, and was spread by the massive DNC propaganda network, it was patently clear that the U.S. media and intelligence "community," which served as a source for this story, had failed to come up with an even remotely believable lie. Not only did the Trump Administration, including though its military and intelligence representatives, flatly deny those allegations, but even the public comments in various profoundly anti-Trump media were putting the whole premise in serious doubt.

No less than Suhail Shaheen, the representative of a political office of the Taliban, in his interview to Russia's Ria, directly pointed to the U.S.-supported Kabul regime's Department of National Security as the source of the "leak" to U.S. media.[2] It was *Russiagate* and the *Skripal Affair* all over again—a hack job by what has become known as "the deep state," in reality primarily a Democratic Party-connected cabal of bureaucrats hellbent on removing Donald Trump from office by any means, including the most preposterous and grossly unprofessional fantasies. In the "Taliban bounties" story one aspect which stood out in its sheer idiocy and lack of military or, for that matter, clandestine operations sense was the fact that no sane professional in Moscow could have come up with such a ridiculous way of promoting the "killing" of U.S. servicemen in Afghanistan. Should the Russians have decided on serious bloodletting of the

U.S. in Afghanistan they could have provided the Taliban—which is designated a terrorist organization in Russia—with appropriate military assistance to dramatically increase U.S. casualties while providing Russia with enough plausible deniability to dismiss any American claims of their interference.

But Russia wouldn't do so, including for obvious geopolitical reasons, since it is in Russia's national interest to keep the U.S. bogged down in Afghanistan, while preoccupying the Taliban and the other jihadist parties with Afghanistan's mess rather than looking northward towards the former Soviet middle Asian republics, now independent Muslim-populated states, which flank Russia's soft Asian underbelly. Russians have always been on record about their stance on Afghanistan:

> How long would the Afghan government endure today if it were left alone to face the Taliban? A rapid slide into chaos awaits Afghanistan and its neighbors if NATO pulls out, pretending to have achieved its goals. A pullout would give a tremendous boost to Islamic militants, destabilize the Central Asian republics and set off flows of refugees, including many thousands to Europe and Russia. It would also give a huge boost to the illegal drug trade. Opium production in Afghanistan in 2008 came to 7,700 tons, more than 40 times that of 2001, when international forces arrived. If even the ISAF presence could not prevent the explosive growth of Taliban drug dealing, then it is not difficult to understand what a NATO pull-out would lead to. As people in the West count the coffins of NATO soldiers from Afghanistan, let them not forget to include the coffins of Americans and Europeans who were killed by Taliban heroin in their own countries. A "successful end" to the operation in Afghanistan will not come simply with the death of Osama bin Laden. The minimum that we require from NATO is consolidating a stable political

regime in the country and preventing Talibanization of the entire region.[3]

Eventually, as was the case with the multitude of stories in the Russiagate narrative, this particular story faded away but not the conclusions which might independently be derived from it—that the United States was on its way towards the complete dysfunction of its political institutions, which were exhibiting peculiar, abnormal responses to a changing world, both externally and internally. Those responses, from making up primitive, if not altogether laughable, narratives such as those populating Russiagate as a whole, or the Taliban bounties story in particular, to the present hysteria in social media, the much more serious deliberate obliteration of their own country's history, and the again deliberate collapse of law and order by Democratic Party operatives and elected officials from states' governors to cities' mayors, such as the defunding of Police Departments and excusing violent protest—all these are signs not only of general collapse—America's collapse has been in the progress for some time now, and has been predicted by a number of observers—but in actuality the utter, historically unprecedented degeneration of America's so-called elites, which have exhibited a level of malfeasance, incompetence, cowardice and betrayal of their own people on such a scale that it beggars belief. Where is the precedent for such a historic occasion where a country, having no external factors pressing it into a geopolitical corner, self-obliterates with such a speed and ferocity that even the collapse of the Soviet Union begins to fail in comparison.

Anyone in America who bothered in the last few years to open their eyes would have easily noticed a dangerous trend. More than three years ago, I wrote:

If the United States has any future as a stable and relatively well-working Republic it must start a really serious nationwide discussion on the competence or rather lack thereof, and indeed the malice, of the Washington lobbies and corrupt politicians, many of whom, far from serving people, as they claim, should be serving serious prison terms for precisely *not* serving Americans but rather their own financial and power interest. Will such a discussion be sustainable on a nation-wide scale in the Orwellian world of the U.S. mass media? President Trump ran on a "Drain the Swamp" agenda. Today, it becomes increasingly evident that the so-called "swamp" will stop at nothing to preserve its own power. The more the American general public is educated on that, the higher are the chances for a recovery, even if it takes a long time.[4]

As it turned out, I was too optimistic, because there will be no recovery. It will be something else altogether, because what will emerge will not be the United States we used to know. If the United States preserves itself as a unified state—a doubtful proposition in itself, once one considers the speed with which a complete and severe systemic dysfunction has afflicted the country—everything we knew about the United States will be gone and the world will face an unstable third world geopolitical entity armed with nuclear weapons, placed in the middle of an internal power struggle, which may take an extremely violent form, with the ever declining institutions of the American state unable to mitigate the unfolding catastrophe threatening to evolve into a full blown civil war, which will tear the United States apart and threaten the designation, and indeed the very existence, of those we commonly identify today as Americans.

This book is not about predictions of America's possible fates—albeit some will inevitably be made as a result of elaborating on the fundamental driving forces behind America's dramatic departure from the status, granted self-proclaimed, of a global hegemon and her manifest political, ideological, economic, cultural and military decline. These latter are the forces whose long-term effects are the focus of this study, because it is they that are driving the United States into chaos. Not only have America's elites failed to recognize and counter those calamitous forces— they have become an organic part of them.

What, then, are those forces, which drive current American crisis? We already identified one such force: America's power media-intellectual elites. It is these elites who, by virtue of their low and constantly declining quality, provide the necessary force for America's existential crisis to evolve from bad to worse. They drive this crisis but they are certainly not the only factor. An elaboration on the role of the elites is expedient because elites are a reflection and a product of those other forces.

Those other forces range from economic to military to moral forces, which define the severity of America's crisis and with it, the shape of the emerging new world which already sees a greatly diminished role of the United States, which has largely lost its competitive economic and scientific edge. This crisis also saw U.S. actual military power shrinking dramatically despite its ballooning budget, and this is just a start. Moral and cultural decay is a self-reproducing calamity. The interaction and interplay of all those forces is what matters for the fate of America.

And then there is an issue of the existence of the nation as a people, which Americans never actually became, being increasingly separated by racial and ethnic loyalties which already threatened a partial Balkanization of the United States of which many, such as Robert Bork, warned as early as 25-30 years ago, and now by political loyalties. Multicultural societies, no matter what ideology or political creed they follow, are always threatened by impulses towards separatism and dissolution.

It is thus important to look at the interplay of those forces in order for us to see not only the shapes of things to come but to learn proper lessons in order to either do all we can to stave them off or, at least get ready to mitigate the tragedy which will unfold before our very eyes. It is an American tragedy, and with it the tragedy of Western civilization, which has finally reached its limits and struggles to face an internal and global reality it influenced in the most profound way. Because of its willful failure to recognize obvious causes and effects, it has rejected a fundamental principle which defined Western Civilization—reason and rational thought.

Endnotes

1 Erick Beech, "Russia Offered Afghan Militants Bounties to Kill U.S. Troops: Reports," *Huffington Post,* June 29, 2020.

2 *"Сухейль Шахин: в слухах о подкупе Россией талибов нет ни слова правды"* (Suhail Shaheen: there is not a word of truth in rumors about Russia buying of Taliban), *Ria.ru,* August 8, 2020, https://ria.ru/20200808/1575484836.html.

3 Boris Gromov and Dmitry Rogozin, "Russian Advice on Afghanistan," *New York Times,* January 11, 2010.

4 Andrei Martyanov, *Losing Military Supremacy. The Myopia of American Strategic Planning* (Atlanta: Clarity Press, Inc., 2018), 215.

1. CONSUMPTION

Access to Food

Any real productive economy could be defined for laymen in a few very simple words—as a matrix or pattern of human production and consumption. Humanity currently defines itself primarily through states, with most states comprised of one or more nations or peoples of different races, cultures and ethnicities, and having different consumer patterns. Despite their multinational composition, states' cultures tend to be regarded as that of the dominant majority. Hence, as an instance, we have distinct Italian, French, Arab, Indian, and Chinese cuisine. Cuisine is a marker and a derivative of a culture of a nation or even a civilization. It also denotes differences in national economies. While milk and bread are common throughout the world as food staples, the American agricultural staple is beef—so this makes American cuisine distinct and well-recognized around the world, as a cuisine which provides for an astonishing variety of beef dishes ranging from simple hamburgers and barbeque to the most exquisite cuts such as steaks. This also denotes an American consumer pattern.

While Americans eat all kinds of things, Japanese Sushi is not regarded as part of an American consumer pattern, despite its being very popular both in the U.S. and around the world, whereas Sushi and Japan are inseparable not only in the cultural but also in the economic and metaphysical senses. Remove sushi from American daily ration and many people will be upset, but they will learn to live without sushi. Remove beef from American cuisine and a huge political problem arises, even if you offer Americans all kinds of compensatory delicacies instead of beef. The United States and beef are inseparable. But where, as a famous commercial once headlined, is the beef? Is it en route to disappearing from general access? The more economically

7

developed a nation is, the larger is the variety of foods it offers to its people. Truly economically developed nations offer an easier access and a larger, sometimes astonishing, variety of foods. Generally speaking, visiting a grocery store in any nation can give an initial impression of its level of economic development. But that impression will, indeed, be a first one.

By far the most important indicator of national economic development is the ease, or otherwise, of access to food by the majority of the population. Shelves packed with a variety of foods in and of themselves do not, however, tell the full story. In the United States it has always been accepted as common knowledge that food on the shelves of America's grocery stores is available and easily accessible to everyone. So much so, that the image of the American abundance of food even made it into Hollywood, not just as a background of an American film against which the main plot of the story developed but as a specific focused representation of abundance, and of not food only. In Oliver Stone's 1993 Vietnam war flick, *Heaven & Earth*, the Vietnamese wife of the main character, ably played by Tommy Lee Jones, is overwhelmed by the abundance when taken for the first time to the American supermarket and tries to hoard food, such as rice, only to hear her American husband's one-liner: "This is America, baby, stores stay open 24 hours." This epitomized America's agricultural abundance and the reliability of her supply chains.

Things have changed, though, both since the 1970s portrayed in the movie and since the 1990s when the movie was made. The change was profound. Today, in 2020, shelves in any grocery store in Ho Chi Minh City, Moscow, Krasnodar, or Beijing, or, for that matter, Jakarta, can give American grocery stores a run for their money, or indeed any store in what is commonly referred to as a developed world, be that Canada, Netherlands or Japan. Food is available. It is the ever-important issue of access to it, which hides behind the images of abundance on the shelves. It was this image from the Western world which played a crucial propaganda role in the ideological struggle between what seemed then as a well fed West and permanent deficit-afflicted Soviet Union. While the West was developing a whole food abundance by-product industry ranging from "stay in shape" movements to armies of dietitians, Soviet people stood in lines, or used all kinds of irregular distribution systems, such as "gift sets" (*podarochnye nabory*) for employees of companies and organizations, to get access to high demand items varying from canned crab meat to even canned green peas and high-end cold cuts.

This all changed long ago. The Soviet Union is no more, and Russia's grocery stores look like temples of food abundance. But what also has changed is the image of American food abundance, as access to it becomes increasingly difficult. The Covid-19 pandemic definitely made Tommy Lee Jones' character one-liner obsolete—stores in America do not stay open anymore 24 hours. But while this could be blamed on the paranoia which engulfed the country, certain facts started to emerge as the grossly over-sold pandemic exposed some truths, which the image of an American economy of plenty had been hiding for a long time.

A May 2020 study by the Brookings Institution on food insecurity in the United States due to Covid-19 pandemic revealed terrifying facts about hunger in the U.S. The study defined "food insecurity" as:

- The food we bought just didn't last and we didn't have enough money to get more.
- The children in my household were not eating enough because we just couldn't afford enough food.[1]

The numbers are damning for a country which, at least outwardly, enjoys a global reputation of being the next best thing after the horn of plenty. Food insecurity for every social group in America is literally skyrocketing.

> The Survey of Mothers with Young Children found that 40.9 percent of mothers with children ages 12 and under reported household food insecurity since the onset of the COVID-19 pandemic. This is higher than the rate reported by all respondents with children under twelve in the COVID Impact Survey

(34.4 percent) but the same as women 18–59 living with a child 12 and under (39.2 percent.) In 2018, 15.1 percent of mothers with children ages 12 and under affirmatively answered this question in the FSS, slightly more than the 14.5 percent that were food insecure by the complete survey. The share of mothers with children 12 and under reporting that the food that they bought did not last has increased 170 percent.[2]

This news didn't make headlines in the U.S. mainstream media which continued to report on the state of the stock market and the other irrelevant-to-real-economy subject of financial markets and hedge funds. The fact that America cannot feed vast numbers of her children and in terms of food security could be defined as a third world nation is certainly not something U.S. media punditry wants to discuss publicly. While one might assume that the majority of hungry children in this survey are those of minorities, which might have been somewhat true few years ago, today food insecurity doesn't discriminate. Children of all races and ethnicities are affected by this real food insecurity pandemic, a much more dangerous one than Covid-19. The study by Brookings points out that the estimates are very "conservative" and concludes that:

High levels of food insecurity are not just a problem of households with children. Prior to the crisis, in 2018, 11.1 percent of households were food insecure and 12.2 percent of households answered the single question in the battery affirmatively. The Urban Institute's Health Reform Monitoring Survey, in the field from March 25 to April 10, used the six-question short form food insecurity module and found that 21.9 percent of households with nonelderly adults were food insecure. By late April 2020, 22.7 percent of households reported in the COVID Impact Survey not having sufficient resources to buy more food when the food that they purchased didn't last. Overall rates of household food insecurity have effectively doubled.[3]

At this stage it is no longer about consumer patterns it is merely about having enough to eat to avoid going hungry. America's "last resort" food supply, her vast network of food banks, was overwhelmed with the events which followed Covid-19 pandemic getting a hold of America's economy. As *Yahoo news* reported in August 2020:

> "The best way to describe it is, we were very active through Hurricane Harvey, which devastated Houston and the surrounding area, and this is way worse than that," said Mark Brown of the West Houston Assistance Ministries, a large food pantry in the area. "I've never seen this level of community-wide desperation at such an extended level."[4]

The real scale of food insecurity, a fancy term for what amounts to various stages of severity of hunger, is difficult to measure. Some numbers, even in the country which loves to exaggerate, defy imagination and shatter the image of American affluence which was projected outward for decades. When even in such well-off states as Colorado, more than 30% of population struggle with getting food, it raises the question about not just the lack of effectiveness of the food delivery system as a whole but of its efficiency in the latest iteration of American capitalism, where food insecurity becomes commonplace.[5] Much of the dramatically increased demand for food from food banks came from people and households who are new to food insecurity.[6] Already in 2010, way before Covid-19 pandemic. *The National Geographic* took a note of a changing face of the American hunger when concluded that:

> Chances are good that if you picture what hunger looks like, you don't summon an image of someone like Christina Dreier: white, married, clothed, and

housed, even a bit overweight. The image of hunger in America today differs markedly from Depression-era images of the gaunt-faced unemployed scavenging for food on urban streets. "This is not your grandmother's hunger," says Janet Poppendieck, a sociologist at the City University of New York. "Today more working people and their families are hungry because wages have declined."[7]

Today, for tens of millions of Americans, wages have not just declined, they are about to simply disappear, their disappearance being contingent on the termination of unemployment benefits, for those who qualify. After that, many will face either permanent unemployment or low-paying jobs in the service sector. That will hardly be conducive for exercising a gourmand's taste in food. Food would become a question of survival. Nor, in America, at least in some significant segments of her population experiencing food situation similar to that of the Great Depression days, will food be forthcoming. For people who saw what happened in the 1990s to Russia's population as a result of its "free market reforms" and liberal economic policies based on the same laissez faire principles extolled in the United States as foundational to the existence of the American nation, the sight of people scavenging dumpsters for food could be in store. America's food future is at best foggy, at worst—grim.

The current, both latent and manifest, food insecurity crisis in the U.S. cannot be blamed on Covid-19 pandemic which was a trigger, but not the cause of the steadily deteriorating condition of the American white middle class. A 2015 study by Angus Deaton and Anne Case on white non-Hispanic mortality in the U.S. had the effect of an exploding bomb, when it established the alarming trend of the American white middle-class simply dying at a younger age, including through a dramatic rise in suicides and poisonings, not to mention liver diseases—all solid indicators of a much deeper problem than merely declining or stagnating wages or, for that matter, food insecurity.[8] In the end, food insecurity problem was not acute in 2015 while it is becoming a nation-wide calamity in 2020. Other factors were at play, albeit most of them, fundamentally, of the economic nature, which, inevitably, shaped the moral and metaphysical outlook for people. People started losing their faith and will to live.

The Illusion of Affluence

For any Russian traveling to the West or the United States in the late 1980s or early 1990s after the Iron Curtain fell, the reaction to Western abundance could be somewhat reminiscent of Le Li's reaction to the variety of groceries in the first American supermarket her husband took her to in Oliver Stone's flick *Heaven & Earth*. The Soviet Union's constant shortage of consumer goods and delicacies, and sometimes of staples, compared to the abundance and perceived affluence of the combined West was inevitably a primary detractor as it concerned the largely misconstrued material "wealth" Soviet communist ideology promised but never delivered. Few in the USSR, or for that matter, elsewhere in the world, wanted to delve into the intricacies of Marx's impersonal debate with late Lasalle, or read, let alone fully grasp, the essence of Marxism's arguably second most important work after the *Communist Manifesto*, the *Critique of the Gotha Program. Marginal Notes to the Program of the German Workers' Party.* Not many really wanted get back into that neck of the woods of Soviet ideology which foresaw not just the development of the proverbial productive forces which would lead to the transition to communism, but of the new man, who would be largely ascetic. Obviously, the small font, the caveat, of the main propaganda slogan of the Marxism, a communist ideology one of the main sacraments, misattributed to Marx, "from each according to his ability, to each *according to his needs*" was ignored by the majority.[9]

This was the Catch-22 of consumerism, a cognitive dissonance of sorts for affluence, set up beautifully by Marxism. Yes, everyone would get what they needed in communist system, but it was all predicated on the extremely specific needs attributable only to a person of the highest cultural level and scientific mind. A man or a woman of the future would be distinguished by his or her altruism and higher callings. In this world of a new man, the particulars of accumulation and affluence differed dramatically from the consumption-based tradition of Western post-WW II developed industrial capitalism—in such a world there would be no Rolls-Royces, or private jets, or 10,000 square foot gilded palaces with hundreds of acres of property, nor for that matter, brothels or drugs. The new social organization and the elimination of physical labor together with a dramatic increase in productivity would—so the theory went—allow people to concentrate on self-improvement and creative labor. Under these circumstances the new man would need decent transportation, decent housing, decent clothing, just to name a few other things, and it was due to this definition of "decent" or "good" that the issue of a future consumption pattern arose. Of course, this point made by Marx has unleashed many passions since 1917, and remains contentious:

> If the material conditions of production are the cooperative property of the workers themselves, then there likewise results a distribution of the means of consumption different from the present one. Vulgar socialism (and from it in turn a section of the democrats) has taken over from the bourgeois economists the consideration and treatment of distribution as independent of the mode of production and hence the presentation of socialism as turning principally on distribution. After the real relation has long been made clear, why retrogress again?[10]

But the discussion on what the definition of good is and how the distribution of wealth should be organized still rages on even today. The historically latest talking points on this issue could be defined as "What, then, instead of the possibility of acquiring a Rolls-Royce and a private jet should a system offer?" The systemic crisis of the West and of liberalism, a euphemism for 21st century capitalism, again raises the issue of a "good life" and how it is defined or rather, how it is difficult to do so.[11] Is high consumption a necessary part of a good life and of its definition? Irving Kristol, for one, doubted that.[12]

But in order to avoid the countless unnecessary and dubious primarily Western liberal narratives that are detached from reality, we may safely assume that an expanding level of consumption is a part of a good life. After all, even Marxism was about consumption albeit by what it declared to be the fairest distribution of wealth based on the input of labor. Hence a famous Soviet slogan taken directly from the Bible, and turned into a proverb: who doesn't work, does not eat.[13] This is how consumption was seen more than 2000 years ago, its level determined by primitive plows and primitive tastes. Humans consume: from food, to clothing to machinery and much else. That is why humanity develops industries and an economy and there is nothing wrong with consumption as long as it is done within common sense bounds. And as the human economy has changed dramatically since biblical times, so has consumption.

Yet, the difference between consumption for basic survival, or for that matter moderation in consumption, and excess consumption has certainly remained as profound as ever throughout human history. As Jeremy Rifkin notes:

> The term "consumption" has both English and French roots. In its original form, to consume meant to destroy, to pillage, to subdue, to exhaust. It is a word steeped in violence and until the present century had only negative connotation... The metamorphosis of consumption from vice to virtue is one of the most important yet least examined phenomena of the twentieth century.[14]

This is not to say that attempts to study consumption have not been undertaken, they certainly have, but if one would try to define a good life in material terms, what would be considered sufficient or satisfactory? Marxism tried to answer this question by moving consumption into the utopian field of a presumed human rationality and desire to improve in moral and cognitive terms, arresting desires for consumption due to humanity's new outlook on life. In other words, Marxism wanted to create a new non-acquisitive man by obliterating class divisions in the society that stimulate the desire to have more than that had by others. It was an enticing idea for its time but it couldn't work, because changing human nature has turned out to be even more difficult than unleashing a revolution, or building advanced productive economies. Humanity has always wanted, quite simply, more. Marxism failed because human nature remained static, even when embellished by advanced university degrees and an allegedly broad enlightened view of the world. Humans, naturally, continued to want what Marxism couldn't provide—an access to the very kind of consumer pattern that the United States had no inhibitions against promoting around the world in the aftermath of World War Two.

The United States provided more than just a comfortable level of consumption for the majority, it provided a miniature version, a consumer path of sorts, to what was eventually defined as an ultimate objective of human life—the consumption pattern of a leisure class, which Thorstein Veblen by 1899 had defined as conspicuous consumption.

> The quasi-peaceable gentleman of leisure, then, not only consumes of the stuff of life beyond the minimum required for subsistence and physical efficiency, but his consumption also undergoes a specialization as regards the quality of the goods consumed. He consumes freely and of the best, in food, drink, narcotics, shelter, services, ornaments, apparel, weapons and accoutrements, amusements, amulets, and idols or divinities. In the process of gradual amelioration which takes place in the articles of his consumption, the motive principle and proximate aim of innovation is no doubt the higher efficiency of the improved and more elaborate products for personal comfort and well-being. But that does not remain the sole purpose of their consumption. The

canon of reputability is at hand and seizes upon such innovations as are, according to its standard, fit to survive. Since the consumption of these more excellent goods is an evidence of wealth, it becomes honorific; and conversely, the failure to consume in due quantity and quality becomes a mark of inferiority and demerit.[15]

Consumption, far from satisfying actual human needs, became a broader social and cultural phenomenon and that is how it continues to exist till the present day. Huge numbers of people consume not because they need to do so, but because they want and are driven to this consumption to avoid a "mark of inferiority and demerit." In Soviet post–World War Two times, upon completion of the initial restoration of the country from the rubble of the Axis invasion, once the economy started to gain steam and the improvement of life became undeniable, new Soviet consumer wants began to emerge. It was one thing to want a personal car, which in 1950s was an unheard-of luxury, and another to want one in the 1970s when car ownership became commonplace—that was understandable, albeit while the ownership of a car was certainly a sign of some sort of being well-off, it wasn't an instance of conspicuous consumption per se, insofar as it had acquired some degree of social necessity. But acquiring the latest fashions in clothing and other everyday items, ranging from cigarettes to alcohol, were.

No matter how the ideological department of the Communist Party tried to explain the consumer goods deficits in the USSR, in the era of exploding electronic means of mass communications, especially of television, it was impossible to conceal Western fashion trends and just about everyone in USSR wanted a pair of American denim jeans, French perfumes, or Japanese consumer electronics in the 1970s. A popular saying of the day in the USSR was: "They tell us that capitalism stinks, but what a delightful smell." Any Soviet person who wore American denims, Seiko or Omega watches and drove a car was often looked at with envy. In a country with a consumer goods deficit, being privy to Western

consumer patterns was becoming an honorific thing. The Soviet
diplomatic corps, journalists stationed in foreign, especially
Western, countries, sportsmen or professionals working abroad
were considered to be holding highly desirable occupations since
they were giving an access to what, wrongly, was perceived as a
consumer paradise in the West.

The 1982 phenomenal success of the album by the famous
and tremendously influential Soviet rock band, *Urfin Juice,* hailing
from what today is the city of Yekaterinburg (formerly Sverdlovsk)
contained a song titled *World on the Wall*, which perfectly captured
the Soviet obsession with Western consumerism and grossly
idealized and misconstrued the image of the West in general.
The song demonstrated Soviet youth's increasing disillusionment
with, primarily, the consumption realities of the USSR. Parts of
song's lyrics were both satirical and profound:

Каждый плакат словно окно.
Смотришь ты жадно через стекло.
Каждый плакат запечатлел
В мире мечтаний высший предел.
Песни звучат те, что тебе
Помогут попасть в мир на стене.

И взгляд твой как телевизор.
Программы разнообразны.
Ты любишь думать о вечерах
где-то в Майами-Бич,
утро на Плас-Конкорд,
ночь на Сансет-Бульвар.
Заочно!
Ты любишь Гиндзу в ночных огнях
и ранчо на Йелоу-Крик,
мартини в Сан-Тропе,
и звуки Корнеги-Холл.
Hi-Fi!

В мыслях этих все желанья
Темных уголков сознанья
Разом ты исполнишь, потому что
В самодельном мире все легко.
Я уверен, ты не стал бы
Лезть в те джунгли, если б лучше знал их.
И не стал бы слушать эти песни,
Если б их перевели тебе.

Every poster on your wall is like a window
You are looking insatiably through the glass
Each poster captured
In the world of desires a highest limit
The songs are playing which will help you
To get into the world on the wall

Your glance is like a TV
With a variety of the programs
You love to think about evenings
Somewhere in Miami-beach
Morning on Place de la Concorde
Night at the Sunset Boulevard
All of it, remotely.
You love Ginza in night lights
Yellow Creek Ranch
Martini in San Tropez
And sounds of Carnegie-hall
Hi-Fi!

In all these thoughts are desires
From the dark corners of mind
You will fulfill at once because
Everything is easy in make-believe world
I am sure you wouldn't
Go into those jungles if you would know them better
You wouldn't listen to those songs
If somebody would have translated them for you.

It was a prophetic piece of music which foresaw the Soviet demise which happened not because NATO armies were stronger than the Soviet Armed Forces—they were not. Nor was Western education better than the Soviet one. The paradox of the collapse of the Soviet Union, apart from largely internal problems with ethnic nationalisms and rot in the party elites, lay in the fact that in the USSR, the majority of its population was beginning to live better than at any point in the history of Russia and her geographic fringes and huge masses of people, either openly or privately, wanted what they saw as the primary advantage of Western capitalism—material affluence. It was, in the end, the Western phenomenon of affluenza which played an important role in the toppling of an already largely dead Soviet version of Marxism and led to a collapse of what was known then as World Socialist System.

Endnotes

1 Lauren Bauer, "The COVID-19 crisis has already left too many children hungry in America," Brookings Institution, *Up Front,* May 6, 2020. https://www.brookings.edu/blog/up-front/2020/05/06/the-covid-19-crisis-has-already-left-too-many-children-hungry-in-america/

2 Ibid.

3 Ibid.

4 Christopher Wilson, "Out of work and with families to feed, some Americans are lining up at food banks for the first time in their lives," *Yahoo News,* August 7, 2020, https://news.yahoo.com/food-banks-increased-demand-newcomers-unemployment-expiring-090006421.html.

5 Saja Hindi, "1 in 3 are struggling to eat in Colorado: 'It would be impossible without the food banks,'" *The Denver Post,* August 8, 2020, https://www.denverpost.com/2020/08/08/food-banks-help-coronavirus-covid-colorado/.

6 Mackenzie Koch, "Food banks soar in demand amid pandemic," 13 WOWK TV, August 7, 2020, https://www.wowktv.com/news/food-banks-soar-in-demand-amid-pandemic/.

7 Tracie McMillan, "The New Face of Hunger," *The National Geographic,* August 2014, https://www.nationalgeographic.com/foodfeatures/hunger/.

8 Anne Case and Angus Deaton, "Rising morbidity and mortality in midlife among white non-Hispanic Americans in the 21st century," Woodrow Wilson School of Public and International Affairs and Department of Economics, Princeton University, *PNAS,* October 29, 2015, p. 2, https://www.pnas.org/content/pnas/early/2015/10/29/1518393112.full.pdf.

9 Karl Marx, "Critique of the Gotha Program," *Marginal Notes to the Program of the German Workers' Party,* 1875, https://www.marxists.org/archive/marx/works/1875/gotha/ch01.htm.

10 Ibid.

11 John. J. Mearsheimer, *The Great Delusion: Liberal Dreams and International Realities* (Yale University Press, 2018), 27.

12 Ibid.

13 "For even when we were with you, we commanded you this: If anyone will not work, neither shall he eat," 2 Thessalonians 3:10, *The Orthodox Study Bible* (Nashville, Tennessee: Thomas Nelson Publishers, 1993), 481.

14 Jeremy Rifkin, *The End of Work. The Decline of the Global Labor Force and the Dawn of the Post-Market Era* (New York: G.P. Putnam Sons, 1995), 19.

15 Thorstein Veblen, "Chapter 4: Conspicuous Consumption," *The Theory of the Leisure Class* (Macmillan Co., 1899; EBook released by Project Guttenberg, updated February 7, 2013), http://www.gutenberg.org/files/833/833-h/833-h.htm#link2HCH0004.

2. AFFLUENZA

The Politics of Prosperity

Consumer patterns are based on an intricate balance between need and want. The Soviet version of communism emphasized primarily the need; Western post-World War II capitalism was driven, if not over-driven altogether, by the want, no matter how trivial or even detrimental it was. It was the victory of want over need, or using a more refined definition of the need—a *reasonable* want—that created a serious economic and mental illness in the West, which was titled Affluenza and was defined as "a painful, contagious, socially transmitted condition of overload debt, anxiety and waste resulting from the dogged pursuit of more."[1] Progress was inevitable, but so was the growth of consumption because the concept of the betterment of human life, or the good life in general, was primarily described as and built around material productive forces. Material productive forces in the West in the post-World War II period were impressive due to the United States benefiting from insulation from the catastrophic events of World War II. Capitalism and what was promoted as "free enterprise" achieved an astonishing success in providing a standard of living for the majority of the population without parallel in human history.

The late Samuel Huntington lamented, justifiably, that "the West won the world not by the superiority of its ideas or values or religion (to which few members of other civilizations were converted) but rather by its superiority in applying organized violence."[2] But this statement hardly drew the full picture, which was much more complex. The Western contribution to the world was immense, ranging from the arts to the sciences, and was much more nuanced than mere military conquests. The immediate post-World War II period was the United States' moment to shine, reflected in its attempt to offset the military triumph of the nominally Marxist Soviet Union over Nazism[3] through projecting an image, not entirely untrue, of America's prosperity and wide array of products available for consumption by its citizens. If the Marshal Plan provided a demonstration of its prosperity, and was billed as designed primarily to fight communism, in actuality, as Michael Hudson describes, it was a whole other game altogether:

> Under the aegis of the U.S. Government, American investors and creditors would accumulate a growing volume of claims on foreign economies, ultimately securing control over the non-Communist world's political as well as economic processes.[4]

Later, what transpired during the famous, or infamous for some, "Kitchen Debate" in July of 1959 between then U.S. Vice President Richard Nixon and Nikita Khrushchev framed the whole economic debate between American capitalism and Soviet Marxist views, and in turn the Cold War, as well as its outcome.

> Nixon: *I want to show you this kitchen. It is like those of our houses in California.* [Nixon points to dishwasher.]
> Khrushchev: *We have such things.*
> Nixon: *This is our newest model. This is the kind which is built in thousands of units for direct installations in the houses. In America, we like to make life easier for women...*
> Khrushchev: *Your capitalistic attitude toward women does not occur under Communism.*
> Nixon: *I think that this attitude towards women is universal. What we want to do, is make life more easy for our housewives....*[5]

Viewed in retrospect, this debate, apart from Khrushchev's obvious lie that Soviet Union housewives had access to dishwashers, comes across as rather comical but it did contain, nevertheless, an important element which played the role of the proverbial 800-pound gorilla in the room. This gorilla was revealed in Nixon's description of a mortgage:

> This house can be bought for $14,000, and most American [veterans from World War II] can buy a home in the bracket of $10,000 to $15,000. Let me give you an example that you can appreciate. Our steel workers as you know, are now on strike. But any steel worker could buy this house. They earn $3 an hour. This house costs about $100 a month to buy on a contract running 25 to 30 years.[6]

The gorilla was credit and its obverse side—debt—which would play a destructive role for both the United States and global economy later on.

It was precisely on Nixon's watch as POTUS, in August 1971 that the U.S. took its currency off the gold standard, and what was effectively a gold embargo became official. As Ralph Benko wrote in 2011:

> Today we celebrate, or, actually, mourn the 40th anniversary of President Richard Nixon's taking America, and the world, off the gold standard, making many promises that were promptly broken. (For instance, President Nixon promised that the dollar would retain its full value. It only is worth about 19 cents today of what it was worth in 1971.)[7]

This event marked the establishment of a system in which the United States was enabled to borrow automatically from foreign central banks simply by running a payments deficit. The larger the U.S. payments deficit grew, the more dollars ended up in foreign central banks, which then lent them to the U.S. Government by investing them in Treasury obligations of varying degrees of liquidity and marketability.[8]

Suddenly the United States, which was having rather serious problems both economically and militarily in Vietnam, was enabled to, in effect, tax other nations for however the United States wanted to spend its growing budget deficit, be that on U.S. Cold War expenditures or social programs of the guns-and-butter economy.[9]

The United States as a whole went from the economy of need to the economy of pure want and conspicuous consumption. There was nothing in this system not to America's liking, since this system allowed it to control the non-Communist world by exporting inflation to it, while maintaining a flow of cheap raw materials and goods into the U.S. In effect, the United States didn't really have to work or produce much if it didn't want to, and this is exactly what happened. The party started with the emergence of the FIRE (Finance, Insurance, Real Estate) economy and the radical deindustrialization of the United States. It drove consumption to unprecedented heights—and it drove not just consumer debt, but also government debt into the stratosphere.

And that was just the beginning.

Some estimated that by mid-2010s, up to 71% of the U.S. economy was spent on consumer goods.[10] This all became possible due to the U.S. being able to "issue" as much debt as it wanted, because that debt would have been, in the end, converted to U.S. T-bills, one way or another. The world was having to pay for America's party. And pay it did, further fueling American consumption, which for many Americans had become honorific and conspicuous on the road to affluence, which was now seemingly opened. A famous, and utterly false, myth still circulating in the U.S. has it that the Soviet government didn't allow the release of the Hollywood 1940 adaptation of John Steinbeck's *The Grapes of Wrath* in the USSR due to concerns that Soviet citizens would realize that even destitute Americans, during the times of Great Depression, had in their possession a whole truck and could travel. But this film was never forbidden in the Soviet Union, let alone personally by Stalin as some alleged, and in 1948 saw a limited club release there, with Russian subtitles, as *The Road of Calamities*. This film, together with many other Hollywood and European, including German, flicks, were captured by the Red

Army from the German Reich's Archive, and became known in the USSR as Trophy Movies.[11]

Yet, the persistence of this crude myth about "how they had trucks" being stuck in the Soviet public's mind rather than *The Grapes of Wrath*'s portrayal of the devastating impact on masses of Americans of an economic depression revealed something peculiar about American consumerism. It demonstrated the diversion of the focus of Americans' and world attention to America's always very materialistic projection of its success, in which consumption mattered greatly, far more than a proper balance between need and want would require.

This consumerism was also a major constituent part of Americans' exceptionalist view of themselves, which, from the time of Alexis De Tocqueville, who documented Americans' "garrulous patriotism,"[12] bloomed into full-blown condescension toward the rest of the world, whose standard of living did not compare with America's level of consumption. No matter what the Soviet, or later, Russian achievements were, there seemed to be always a card trumping that—the American standard of living and the level of satisfaction of the American "want," be that construction of mammoth aircraft carriers or better cars. And it worked.

Myths akin to *The Grapes of Wrath* trucks' cultural impact on the Soviets continue to exist in the American cultural milieu to this day. There was and is very little doubt that Nixon did beat Khrushchev in Kitchen Debate—precisely because any American kitchen was better than any Soviet one and the dishwasher was in mass production, unlike many Soviet consumer goods, many of which remained in the chronic deficit category till the Soviet collapse. Indeed, dishwasher machines, inter alia, were an extremely rare sight in Soviet kitchens, to say the least. Much of the production of Western consumerism in general, and American in particular, and its projection into what then was called the Eastern Bloc remained built around a few important categories of consumer goods, among which cars, consumer electronics and, of course, food products, or rather, the variety of them, were the most important. The impact, however, was much broader. It came not only from movies, including movies from Europe, which by the 1960s and 1970s also showed a rather affluent lifestyle enjoyed by the Italians or French, but through such a powerful tool as exhibitions. There were many American, not to mention European or Japanese, exhibitions sent to the Soviet Union.

In my personal memory as a preschooler, the *Education USA* 1969-70 exhibition in Baku (it was a multicity exhibit) was a gigantic success, as were most U.S. exhibitions to the USSR.[13] For kids it was great adventure to get to the center where the exhibition was held. Free nicely printed magazines, plastic bags and pins were provided for each visitor. The same was the case with Baku's portion of the 1976 exhibition, *Technology for the American Home*. Adults, however, could not conceal their marveling at America's classrooms, the use of advanced electronics and other teaching aids, and even on their furniture. American homes looked futuristic, affluent, and they stirred desires in others, those same proverbial wants and ideas. Millions upon millions of Soviet citizens attended American exhibitions whose themes ranged from education and recreation to industrial and household design.[14]

There was no denying that the Americans, as it seemed then, lived better, much better, than average Soviet citizens, and both sides knew it. This fact was admitted *sotto voce* in the USSR and no amount of often reasonable and literate rationales for the USSR lagging in its standard of living behind the U.S. could convince the average street Ivan that free education, free health care and, albeit not as good as in the U.S. but still free housing were the things which really mattered. As Keith Suter observed: "The Red Army could resist a NATO invasion into Eastern Europe but not the televised transmission of Dallas and Dynasty."[15] While there were no transmissions of Dallas and Dynasty in 1970s USSR— both would be shown after 1991, after the Soviet collapse—the consensus about the American, and Western in general, standard of living and consumption patterns had already emerged by the early 1970s. Russians knew the difference by then between the palaces of the rich and famous, and the lifestyles of employed professional Americans, or Germans, or French for that matter, or what generally became known as "the middle class," and they wanted just that. Most Soviets, or Americans for that matter, then in the 1970s or 80s, let alone the Americans in the 1990s, wouldn't even listen to the rumblings of the approaching economic catastrophe. Life was good and, as James H. Kunstler aptly summarized it: "History will probably record that America's Baby Boom generation threw one helluva party; Gen X was left with the sorry task of cleanup crew; and the Millennials ended up squatting in the repossessed haunted party-house when it was all over."[16]

The Reality of Debt

The party and the American Dream, a euphemism for consumption, started coming crashing down in 2007. By that time America's biggest pastime after baseball—obsessive shopping— was becoming a bit tedious and wasn't bringing as much excitement as it once had. By then, the United States was pretty much done with transferring its industries to China and elsewhere and financializing its economy. While actual industrial output in the U.S. was falling, the U.S. was producing more and more debt. This didn't go unnoticed. It was becoming clear already in the 1980s that American affluence was being sustained primarily by debt. It was becoming also clear that the United States, both as a state and as a society, was living beyond its means. While in the 1980s, talking about U.S. national debt was becoming fashionable, the real storm was brewing within America's ever- growing consumer debt. It was very easy for just about anyone to get credit in the 1990s and 2000s, and the verb "to afford" started to take on a very different meaning than it had in 1960s or even in 1970s. Affordability meant the ability to get financing, to get into debt, that is.

It is well-known truism that hindsight is 20/20 but the trend on America's debt enslavement became apparent a long time ago. Charging purchases and taking out loans became as American as the flag and apple pie. Since 2003, U.S. household debt went from bad to worse and reached, even in the pre-Covid-19 pandemic period, levels which were simply unsustainable. Even before Covid-19 mass hysteria afflicted America, its March 2020 debt reached $14.3 trillion, a 1.1% increase from the previous quarter.[17] The majority of this debt was in mortgages, very many of which were unsustainable due to the ongoing de-industrialization of the United States which had removed well-paid and high skills jobs from the U.S. and shipped many of them abroad, while simultaneously remaking the U.S. economy into the FIRE economy where real jobs contributing to value added production were becoming increasingly difficult to come by. Rifkin, quoting Paul Samuelson, saw increased government spending as the only viable way of cheating the devil of "ineffective demand."[18]

Ineffective demand was already, in the mid-1990s, American society's initial response to Affluenza and the loss of non-debt driven, actual purchasing power. This all went hand in hand with a deliberate hiding of the actual numbers of the unemployed, which realistically were much larger than the government reported.[19] The practice of misreporting actual unemployment numbers since the 1990s and 2000s has been "improved" even more, and often requires clarifications from even the most ardent supporters of America's present economic "model." As CNBC reported on the appalling numbers of unemployed in the U.S. in June 2020:

> The unemployment rate doesn't include the share of workers who may have dropped out of the workforce, perhaps due to feeling pessimistic about the chances of finding a job in the current economy. More than 6 million workers have dropped out of the labor force since February. In fact, the unemployment rate is a much-higher 21.2% as judged by another metric. This metric, which the BLS calls U-6, includes people "marginally attached to the labor force." These are people who aren't currently working or looking for work but are available for work, as well as part-time employees who want and are available for full-time work but have had to settle for part-time employment.[20]

In fact, "bending" economic data to fit the affluence narrative, if not altogether cooking the books on the national and international levels, is an American tradition which goes back precisely to the start of America's deindustrialization and financialization of her economy. One could reasonably accurately count cars, refrigerators and tons of beef or chicken produced by the national economy. This count would give an accurate impression of the nation's economy and would constitute its real Gross Domestic Product (GDP). But not in the new American "economic" paradigm, which turned everything upside down because the financialized American economy was still supposed to remain largest in the world while simultaneously producing less and less. This was a larger issue than merely obscure and unreliable economic data and vanity, it was and is a metaphysical one—only by remaining the world's "largest" economy could the United States still claim its status as a "shining city on the hill."

As Investopedia defined it, real GDP

> is a macroeconomic statistic that measures the value of the goods and services produced by an economy in a specific period, adjusted for inflation. Essentially, it measures a country's total economic output, adjusted for price changes. Governments use both nominal and real GDP as metrics for analyzing economic growth and purchasing power over time.[21]

It is a very vague definition because the value of anything, as economic theory tells us, is defined as a measure of benefits to an economic "agent," or the maximum amount of money one is willing to pay for good or service, while market value is defined by a minimum amount an agent is willing to pay. Here is where the consumer pattern reared its ugly head. Obviously, market forces influence value, but *ineffective demand* was a direct result of America's deindustrialization, stagnating or altogether declining wages, and trying to overcome consumer demand oversaturation with offerings. This was because people started to see less and less value in conspicuous consumption, apart from not being realistically able to afford it. It may have been good to dream about a brand new, and extremely expensive, Chevy Corvette or Louis Vuitton products, but under the circumstances of the actual economy shrinking, those purchases were of a dubious value for any "economic agents" who worked 8 to 5 jobs, had mortgages or ever increasing rent to pay and went to shop for food at the nearest Safeway or Walmart. On the surface, it seemed American consumption remained high, but American affluence became a euphemism for drowning in debt, even when trying to pay for necessities, especially food and filling the tank with gas to drive to jobs which increasingly paid less and less in real terms.

The events which originated with the fraud of the Covid-19 pandemic and then of the DNC and media dogs instigating the nationwide riots of Black Lives Matter and Antifa, demonstrated how skin deep American affluence was for the majority and how fast the value and consumer pattern could change. Far from having a run on iPhones or Tesla cars, the United States as a whole has demonstrated what products were truly economically valuable. As former CIA officer Philip Giraldi noted, while describing a huge and still growing demand for firearms and ammunition:

> Another thing one is now having difficulty in buying is alcohol. People are depressed and are drinking a hell of a lot more than normal, which can, of course, result in impulsive behavior. I live in Virginia and our state store is constantly running out of everything. A cashier told me that they are selling 300% more booze than normal for this time of year. Last week I went into a large and well-known liquor store in Washington D.C. and bought the last few bottles of our favorite scotch *The Famous Grouse*. They had run out and didn't know when they would get more. ... Finally, a family member owns a construction company. He recently said that business is unexpectedly booming, in part because people are building panic rooms, safe havens and even 1960s style fallout shelters in and behind their houses. But unlike the threat of nuclear

war in the sixties, the current fear is that with the wreckers being given a free hand by the authorities, organized home invasions penetrating prosperous neighborhoods cannot be that far away."[22]

Many Americans may have enough money to increase their alcohol consumption threefold to deal with psychological stresses of their disintegrating political system, the crushing economy and an atmosphere of constant paranoia and fear, but alcohol consumption is hardly an indicator of purchasing power or real prosperity. Apart from food insecurity for tens of millions of Americans, an unfolding homelessness crisis is ominous in its scale. As ABC Channel 10 News in San Diego reported:

As many as 3.5 million Americans are homeless, according to the Department of Housing and Urban Development. It says most of those people live on the streets or in a shelter. That's just one definition. It doesn't count the 7.5 million Americans who live with others because of high housing costs. The newest data shows the homeless population is mostly male, white and middle-aged. But the crisis goes far beyond that. More Americans are homeless today compared to before the Great Recession.[23]

These are terrifying numbers made even more dramatic by the fact of the United States making its standard of living and consumption one of the pivots of its mythology. When Brazil, with a population of 210 million, that is, two thirds the size of the U.S. population, has five times fewer people living in the streets in 2017 than the United States, one has to question the U.S. claim to be a first world country.[24] Of course, one may question the statistical methods behind those astonishing numbers, but there is a purely subjective factor which plays here—people do notice signs of a dramatic deterioration of life all around them and at some point a consensus begins to emerge.

Even openly biased, if not altogether lying, media such as Seattle's very own KOMO News couldn't ignore the fact of the once beautiful, safe and clean Seattle turning into a mecca for the homeless, drug addicts and criminals. *In* March of 2019, KOMO News produced a documentary with the telling title, *"Seattle is Dying."* As the creator of this documentary expressed it, himself:

> It's called, Seattle is Dying, and I believe the title to be true. But it's not a hopeless program. There are ideas and concepts in the show that could start conversations about change. I hope. Mostly, I want it to be a reminder that this is not normal. This is not the way it has to be. This is not right.[25]

Of course, it wasn't and isn't right, but it didn't matter. Lack of normality was already even then becoming a norm in America. In the end, as the events of the Spring of 2020 so vividly demonstrated, the situation in Seattle was just warming up and ultimately turned into one of several, such as were happening in New York, San Francisco and Portland, Oregon. These became American capitals of bizarre social experiments and the breakdown of law and order, as was manifested by the creation of a totally lawless and radically anti-law and order, and anti-white racist entity (which included a large number of whites) that the whole world knew as a Capitol Hill Occupied Protest / Capitol Hill Organized Protest (CHAZ/CHOP) zone. It was there, in Seattle's Capitol Hill, where for many people around the globe, who observed America's self-immolation and self-humiliation live on TV and the Internet, the true scale of America's material and political ills became evident. The rest of the world's media had a field day not only viewing the impotence of Seattle's law enforcement, which had its hands tied by the political lunacy of its City Council and mayor, but also the fact that the whole area looked like a war zone. It also looked dirt poor.

If the modern world knew about horrific state of such American cities as Detroit or Chicago, seeing cities once presented to the world as centers of American prosperity, innovation and the new economy, such as Seattle, San Francisco or Portland, turning into real dumpsters was something new. If America was as wealthy as it was constantly declared to be to the world, the revelation to the world of America's numerous communities which looked like third world slums, with their dilapidation, dirt, lawlessness, drug usage and homelessness, somehow didn't fit this picture. Cognitive dissonance was inevitable. The stock market continued to rise, while California resumed its rolling outages due to a heat wave.[26] While positive macroeconomic indicators grew, so did the lines to food banks. The growth of capitalization of such companies as Apple continued, together with ongoing dying out of whole industries in the United States whose return was anything but guaranteed, even before the irresponsible shutting down of the economy due to Covid-19. That translated directly into tens of millions of unemployed from the service industries, especially tourism, hospitality and financial services, to even the aerospace industry, which was severely mauled by dropping demand for air travel.

While one may see an eventual rebound of sorts in aerospace, there will be no recovery for a bulk of the service industries. Those tens of millions of unemployed Americans will need somehow to survive, which leaves no place for Affluenza or conspicuous consumption. It doesn't leave any place for anything even remotely defined as prosperity—that simply is not there, if it ever realistically was for the majority of Americans who never made it into the top 10 percent, to say nothing of the even more exclusive 1 percent where honorific and conspicuous consumption as a way of life still continues.

A simulacrum of American prosperity turned out to be just that—a simulacrum, a reference to something which in reality doesn't exist except in image. Many tried to warn that the once decent standard of living, which emerged primarily in the 1950s through the 1990s, which had created the famous American middle class was on its way out, together with this middle class, but they were either ignored or laughed at. In the end, America's post-World War II economic supremacy had primarily been due to the United States remaining fully unscathed by that war and becoming the world's main manufacturing hub and owner of the world's reserve currency.

But even this advantage didn't hold for long in historic terms. As Pat Buchanan bitterly quoted Arthur Hermann of the Hudson Institute:

> In the 1960s, manufacturing made up 25% of U.S. gross domestic product. It's barely 11% today. More than five million American manufacturing jobs have been lost since 2000.[27]

The scale of this catastrophe is not understood until one considers the fact that a single manufacturing job on average generates 3.4 employees elsewhere in non-manufacturing sectors.[28] Of course, stockbrokers and financial analysts, together with political scientists, may want to contest this universally agreed upon assertion, but nothing can obscure the simple fact of America's long lost prosperity, which was the envy of the world in the 1950s and 1960s and even into the early 1990s, being a direct result of the American manufacturing capacity, which could fill the internal market with virtually every consumer good ranging from medicine to cars to complex machines. It was this manufacturing capacity which employed a vast army of well-paid American productive workers who generated enough employment and wealth, which allowed America to experience an acute case of Affluenza until Nixon's decoupling the U.S. dollar from the gold standard and the debt rush hitting America with unparallel force, which in the end finished off both the U.S. manufacturing base and America's middle class, the direct offspring of this manufacturing capacity.

In 2020 the Bank of America estimated that "in 1985 it took 30 weeks at the median wage to pay for big fixed costs like housing, health care, a car, and education; fast forward to today when it takes a mathematically impossible 53 weeks of a 52-week year to buy those things."[29] America is accelerating towards its fate of becoming a poor country and nothing can be done about

it in the middle, let alone the short term other than printing
more money, which simply makes the problem much worse, not
even marginally better. Today, when walking along the shelves
in Walmart or even looking at the sale of farmers' equipment at
Coastal, one is seeing tags from around the world, all of which
spell out that "This item is NOT made in USA."

Once, a long time ago, New York City served as a showcase
of American grandeur and prosperity with its shining upscale
shops' windows and displays signaling American consumer and
standard of living exceptionalism. This is all gone today and
not only shiny displays. America's Premier City itself is fading
into the new grim American reality. As one proud New Yorker,
a best-selling author, and symptomatically a former hedge-fund
manager, blood-chillingly admitted recently:

> I love NYC. When I first moved to NYC, it was a
> dream come true. Every corner was like a theater
> production happening right in front of me. So much
> personality, so many stories. Every subculture I loved
> was in NYC. I could play chess all day and night. I
> could go to comedy clubs. I could start any type of
> business. I could meet people. I had family, friends,
> opportunities. No matter what happened to me,
> NYC was a net I could fall back on and bounce back
> up. Now it's completely dead.
>
> "But NYC always, always bounces back." No. Not
> this time.
>
> "But NYC is the center of the financial universe.
> Opportunities will flourish here again." Not this time.
>
> "NYC has experienced worse." No it hasn't.[30]

The author of this grim statement, James Altucher, blames
NYC decline on the broadband internet, which makes so many
industries related to travel and meetings irrelevant. He couldn't be
more wrong, which one might expect from a financial manager.
The name of New York City in his eulogy to his beloved city could
now easily be substituted with that of the United States of America

and the diagnosis would still be the same. America IS becoming a poor country and as such she sees her national power, always exaggerated to start with, abandoning her in the midst of a historic change of tectonic scale and it remains to be seen if the United States will pull itself through these events intact—forget about prosperity which is long gone and Affluenza and consumerism fast become a distant memory.

Endnotes

1 John De Graaf, David Wann, Thomas Naylor, *Affluenza: How Overconsumption Is Killing Us—and How to Fight Back* (San Francisco: Bernett-Koehler Publishers, Inc., 2014), 1.

2 Samuel Huntington, *The Clash of Civilizations and the Remaking of World Order* (New York: Simon & Schuster Paperbacks, 2003), 51.

3 See Andrei Martyanov, *Losing Military Supremacy: The Myopia of American Strategic Planning* (Atlanta: Clarity Press, Inc., 2018).

4 Michael Hudson, *Super Imperialism. The Origin and Fundamentals of U.S. World Dominance* (London-Sterling, Virginia: Pluto Press, 2003), 11.

5 Vice President Richard Nixon and Soviet Premier Nikita Khrushchev, *The Kitchen Debate* (transcript), July 24, 1959.

https://www.cia.gov/library/readingroom/docs/1959-07-24.pdf.

6 Ibid.

7 Ralph Benko, "Forty Years Ago Today Nixon Took Us Off the Gold Standard," *Fox News,* August 15, 2011, https://www.foxnews.com/opinion/forty-years-ago-today-nixon-took-us-off-the-gold-standard.

8 Hudson, *Super Imperialism,* 17.

9 Ibid.

10 De Graaf et al., *Affluenza,* 15.

11 *Первые в Кино* (First in the Cinema). Nikolai Mayorov. Unpublished Book. http://cinemafirst.ru/zarubezhnye-filmy-v-sovetskom-i-rossi/.

12 Alexis de Tocqueville, tr. Henry Reeve, *Democracy in America* (first edition 1838), Chapter 16.

13 "Chronology: American Exhibits to the U.S.S.R.," *US Department of State. Diplomacy in Action* (Archived content: Information released online from January 20, 2009 to January 20, 2017), https://2009-2017.state.gov/p/eur/ci/rs/c26473.htm: "This exhibit toured six major cities—Leningrad, Kiev, Moscow, Baku, Tashkent, and Novosibirsk. This was the first American exhibit to tour a Siberian city. Attracting nearly a million visitors, the exhibition portrayed the techniques and technologies provided by diverse private sector educational resources used in the American educational system."

14 Ibid.

15 Ralph Summy and Michael E. Salla, eds., *Why the Cold War Ended: A Range of Interpretations* (Westport, Connecticut: Greenwood Press, 1995), 191.

16 James Howard Kunstler, "Boomer Elegy," *Clusterfuck Nation blog,* April 3, 2020,
https://kunstler.com/clusterfuck-nation/boomer-elegy/.

17 Jeff Cox, "Consumer debt hits new record of $14.3 trillion, *CNBC News,* May 5, 2020, https://www.cnbc.com/2020/05/05/consumer-debt-hits-new-record-of-14point3-trillion.html.

18 Jeremy Rifkin, *The End of Work: The Decline of the Global Labor Force and the Dawn of the Post-Market Era* (New York: G.P. Putnam Sons, New York, 1995), 37.

19 Ibid., 167.

20 Greg Lacurci, Here's why the real unemployment rate may be higher than reported. CNBC, June 5, 2020, https://www.cnbc.com/2020/06/05/heres-why-the-real-unemployment-rate-may-be-higher-than-reported.html.

21 Akhilesh Ganti, "What is Real Gross Domestic Product (GDP)?" Investopedia, May 28, 2020, https://www.investopedia.com/terms/r/realgdp.asp.

22 Philipp Giraldi, "A Nation Falling Apart. Piece by piece," *Unz Review,* July 21, 2020, https://www.unz.com/pgiraldi/a-nation-falling-apart/.

23 Chaas Toborg, "When it comes to homelessness in America, there is no single cause," *Channel 10 ABC News San-Diego,* January 10, 2020, https://www.10news.com/news/national-politics/the-race-2020/when-it-comes-to-homelessness-in-america-there-is-no-single-cause.

24 Alexandre Guerra, "Pesquisa estima que 101.854 pessoas vivem em situação de rua no Brasil" (Research estimates that 101,854 people live on the streets in Brazil), *Fundação Perseu Abramo,* May 30, 2017, https://fpabramo. org.br/2017/05/30/pesquisa-estima-que-101-pessoas-vivem-em-situacao-de-rua-no-brasil/.

25 Eric Johnson, KOMO News Special: "Seattle is Dying," *KOMO News,* March 14, 2019, https://komonews.com/news/local/komo-news-special-seattle-is-dying.

26 "PG&E Implements Outages for Up to 220k Customers Amid California Heat Wave," *CBS Channel 13 Sacramento,* August 14, 2020, https://sacramento. cbslocal.com/2020/08/15/pge-warns-of-more-rolling-outages-amid-california-heat-wave/.

27 Pat Buchanan, "Stress Test of a Straining Superpower, *Unz Review,* July 24, 2020, https://www.unz.com/pbuchanan/stress-test-of-a-straining-superpower/.

28 "How Important Is U.S. Manufacturing Today?" *MAPI Foundation,* September 13, 2016, https://mapifoundation.org/manufacturing-facts/2016/9/13/how-important-is-us-manufacturing-today.

29 Tyler Durden, "The Devastation of The Middle Class: It Now Takes 53

Weeks Of Median Wages Every Year To Pay For Basic Needs," *ZeroHedge,* August 19, 2020, https://www.zerohedge.com/markets/devastation-middle-class-it-now-takes-53-weeks-median-wages-year-pay-basic-needs.

30 James Altucher, "NYC Is Dead Forever… Here's Why," *James Altucher blog,* https://jamesaltucher.com/blog/nyc-is-dead-forever-heres-why/.

3. GEOECONOMICS

The Crystal Palace was a cast iron and glass structure which was erected in Hyde Park in London to house the 1851 *Great Exhibition*, a forerunner of international Expo events, which would serve as a place to showcase the achievements of participant nations. The Queen opened this 1851 exhibition, emphasizing that it was above all a "peace festival" intended to promote friendly competition between nations.[1] But as Alan Palmer noted:

> But Victoria and (prince) Albert were out of touch with the public mood, for the thousands who flocked to Crystal palace delighted in specifically British achievements and were content to cast curious glances of patronizing approval on what had come from overseas...[2]

The exhibition was also marked with growing Russophobia, which was spurred by Tories and Whig businessmen who deplored the incursion of Russian traders into the areas which Britain considered her traditional markets, specifically in the Far East and Eastern Mediterranean, among others. In the end, British suspicions and displeasures with Russia, sublimations of their imperial policies, resulted in the Crimean War, which initiated a sequence of events which inextricably contributed to the Russian revolution and influenced the outcome of World War II—a defining event of both the 20th and to a large degree the early 21st centuries.

Initially Marxists, and later larger swaths of the educated public who were not Marxists at all, called the phenomenon imperialism—the constant great capitalist powers' rivalry for acquisition of colonies to exploit and markets' metropoles to sell their produced goods. Later, the ever-evolving imperialism would receive the fancy title of geoeconomics and would become a part of a geopolitics, which, as a fully evolved field of study, would encompass much more than just geography, as envisioned initially by Mackinder, but the overall state of economic, political and military affairs in the world. It also accounted for the passions which such a state of the affairs could or would unleash, as was the case with the profound British Russophobia becoming a political factor on the road to the Crimean War. or as was the case with one of the fathers of German geopolitics, Karl Haushofer.

Haushofer, often characterized as the brain behind the geopolitics of the Third Reich, is a case in point where a moral and emotional factor plays a decisive role in forming highly consequential and influential views and theories. This, in the case of Haushofer, concerned his love-hate relations with Britain. During Haushofer's formative voyage around half the world in 1909 on board the steamer *Goeben*, he was afforded a tour of Britain's colonial possessions, culminating in his reception by Horatio Herbert, Viscount Kitchener, at Fort William in Calcutta. The facility radiated British colonial grandeur and power, and later Haushofer would abhor the British subjugation of India in one of his poems titled "England in India," where the British were called a "miserable people of robbers," and Albion was defined as "perfidious."[3] Haushofer's passions and love-hate attitudes towards British Empire may have played some role in the Nazi approach to geopolitics, as one of Haushofer's geopolitics' key postulates was *Lebensraum*, a key tenet of the Third Reich's strategy, which resulted in World War II in general and Barbarossa, in particular. For Nazi Germany's attempts to acquire *Lebensraum*, the Slavic people paid a price in tens of millions killed, maimed, enslaved and traumatized for the rest of their lives, not to mention the physical destruction of their countries, especially the USSR. But behind all geopolitical rationales for slaughter and destruction in the East one couldn't fail to recognize not just the military but the economic motivation.

After all, the Third Reich's objectives in the East, while driven to a large degree by racial and ethnic hatred for the Eastern

Slavic *Untermensch*, were primarily economic ones. *Lebensraum* was more than just a geographic, that is to say, geopolitical idea, it was an economic one too. As Clausewitz might have rephrased his own famous dictum, Barbarossa was a continuation of economics by other, violent, means. It was an act of geoeconomics, which went in a wrong, by a 180 degrees direction, due to the absence at that time of such mitigating and limiting factors as nuclear weapons, which later would make economic conquests leading to a direct military confrontation between major powers unlikely. The Soviets viewed the expansionism of German National-Socialism as the highest form of imperialism, which, as the theory went, was a highest form of capitalism.[4] Needless to say, they had a point, at least on economic merit. Economic expansion and the acquisition of new markets, albeit often accompanied by extreme violence, in the end was primarily a conquest motivated by economic interests. It was part of geopolitics in a larger sense, and remains today the statecraft directly related to a conflict. An economic one. But still, it was war all over again, which, the same as its military-driven cousin, would produce not just economic destruction and dislocation for those it was waged against, but also extensive casualties, very real and human ones.

In 2016 a book with an appropriate title, *War by Other Means: Geoeconomics and Statecraft,* saw the light in the United States. The title couldn't have been more appropriate for 2016. This is not to say that, prior to this work by former U.S. Ambassador to India Robert D. Blackwill and Jennifer M. Harris, both of them members of the Council on Foreign Relations, geoeconomics wasn't viewed as anything other than war, or in a broader sense, a study of economic conflict. Though it was. It was Edward Luttwak who singled out geoeconomics into a study separate from geopolitics, when he noted in 1990 that:

> Everyone, it appears, now agrees that the methods of commerce are displacing military methods—with disposable capital in lieu of firepower, civilian innovation in lieu of military-technical advancement and market penetration in lieu of garrisons and bases.

But these are all tools, not purposes.[5]

It was distinction without a difference. While many economic activities in history could, and some should, be construed as geoeconomic activities, in many respects geoeconomics as a field separate from conflict, warfare and geopolitics was yet another instance, multiplied through the activity of political "scientists," of trying to obfuscate the issue. As the same Luttwak notes in the chapter symptomatically titled *Warfare by Other Means: Geoeconomics*, "This new version of the ancient rivalry of states, I have called 'Geo-economics.'"[6]

No matter how Luttwak or later, Blackwill and Harris, defined geoeconomics and its tools, it was still good old conflict wrapped in the thin shroud of political science's shallow intellectualism, the same type of a fallacy which produced simulacra of *The End of History*, *The Clash of Civilizations* and *The Grand Chessboard*, among many other concoctions, cooked up in the deep recesses of the primarily American think-tankdom, none of which panned out. But if geoeconomics is warfare by other means and, as Luttwak posited, is a conflict in a broader sense, then geoeconomics must obey the metaphysics of any conflict, be that military, cultural or economic. If geoeconomics, being warfare, envisions as a final result a triumph of one state's economy over all others, or, rephrasing Clausewitz—compelling the enemy to do our will—then, as with any conflict, an exact assessment of the capabilities of the warring sides is in order. But this is a precise field in which Western proponents of geoeconomics in general, and especially American ones, fail miserably, because of their systemic inability to operate with facts "on the ground," exhibiting ideological rigidity which increasingly comes across as a fanatical religious belief.

The opening sentence of Blackwill and Harris' treatise on geoeconomics is important in the sense of being an exhibit A of a delusion which afflicts contemporary American elites who, hiding behind scholastic rhetoric, failed to recognize America's catastrophic economic, military, political and cultural decline, whose roots are in the systemic crisis of liberalism. Blackwill and Harris state that:

Despite having the most powerful economy on earth, the United States too often reaches for the gun instead of the purse in its international conduct. America has hardly outgrown its need for military force, which will remain a central component of U.S. foreign policy. But Washington in the past several decades has increasingly forgotten a tradition that stretches back to the founding of the nation—the systematic use of economic instruments to accomplish geopolitical objectives, what we in this book term geoeconomics. This large-scale failure of collective strategic memory denies Washington potent tools to accomplish its foreign policy objectives.[7]

The book was awarded *Foreign Affairs* Best Book of 2016, and received many accolades by U.S. foreign policy and economic luminaries, ranging from Henry Kissinger to Lawrence Summers, despite the obvious fact that the initial assumptions of the authors were already patently untrue in 2016. By 2020 these assumptions, if not for their being dangerous, should be perceived as comical. For one—the United States doesn't have the most powerful economy on earth. It didn't have it in 2016, while in 2020 the United States finds itself in the deepest economic and political crisis in its modern history and, once the real American economy is revealed beneath the bubble-wrap of Wall-Street pseudo-economics and financial indices, one can easily see America's precipitous decline and departure from the mostly self-proclaimed status of hegemon.

Now, having lost the arms race and every single war it unleashed in the 21st century, geoeconomics—a euphemism for America's non-stop sanctions and attempts to sabotage the economies of any nation capable of competing with the United States—increasingly becomes not only a tool of choice, but the *only* tool the United States is using globally to try to arrest its obvious decline. A realistic assessment of the United States economically today provides a definitive forecast as to the ultimate outcome for the American Empire as a whole, and the United States as a hologram or an illusion of a nation-state in particular, which has lost its ability to compete economically with the rest of the world, thus showing a critical lack of talent in developing a clear geoeconomics vision, a term whose very authorship belongs to the United States.

* * *

Many contemporary geopolitical and economic observers, one way or another related to the reality-based community, noted on many occasions that American economic statistics is not in reality economic statistics, per se. It has for sure a financial statistic, but finances, while extremely important together with the financial system which provides a flow of money for the economy to operate properly, is by far not the only factor defining the economy. In fact, finances are a mere reflection, a derivative, of an exchange process which becomes possible only due to interaction of the productive forces. In other words, only production of material tangibles, of real wealth, that is, from food to furniture, to cars and computers with aircraft, provides the reason for the finances and, by definition, services to exist. This also constitutes the main engine behind any real geoeconomics, which is based on the ability of the goods of one nation to compete with and displace the goods of a competitor in any given market.

Evidently this is not how economics is taught in the United States, which reflects a rationalization of its severe deindustrialization. Behind this deindustrialization and America's economic decline were passions similar to those of Haushofer, who sought *Lebensraum* for Germany. American geoeconomics' version of the source of Haushofer's ideas is based on Americans' fanatical belief in finance, debt and American exceptionalism, in which even economic suicide through financialization and manufacturing of debt didn't matter as long as it was done by the exceptional United States which, as the thinking goes even today, is impervious to the ruthless laws of the real economy and national power. That, of course, has been proven wrong with disastrous consequences. Michael Hudson is on record with the description of the dominant views of America's elite, which continues to think that money is the measure of economy, writing: "My point was that the way the economy is described in the press and in University courses has very little to do with how the economy really works. The press and journalistic reports use a terminology made of well-crafted euphemisms to confuse understanding of how the economy works."[8]

The most obvious example of a complete decoupling of modern economic theory, or rather its nauseating monetarist iterations, from reality is, of course, the purportedly "healthy" behavior of the stock market, which grew despite the growth of the stream of appalling economic news from the U.S., which sees today unprecedented unemployment rates, with sectors such as manufacturing, mining, logging and goods production showing no signs of any serious recovery, remaining static in employment while recovery, which as is totally expected in the modern United States, comes primarily by way of the service sector.[9]

Yet, the slaughter of American productive forces is nothing new. In fact, it is now an established tradition of a parasitic American financial capitalism, quoting Hudson, to continue on "killing the host." Or, as he succinctly puts it: "Insurance companies, stockbrokers and underwriters join bankers in aiming to erase the economy's ability to distinguish financial claims on wealth, such as a fraud of capitalization, with, as an example, Facebook having higher capitalization than companies which produce actual tangible value, from real wealth creation."[10] The state of the American economy today is being reported on by entities that are its parasites, and as a result it looks good on paper, albeit even this image is increasingly difficult to project outwards, when in reality it is turning into a third world economy in a front of our own eyes. It has been more than a quarter century since Jeffrey R. Barnett came up with a list of criteria which defined, at that time, the West's superiority.[11] Out of 14 criteria listed by Barnett, only two, that is less than 15%, had anything to do with control over currencies and global finances; the remaining 12 criteria, including even a moral leadership one, which is a derivative of other 11, had everything to do with productive capacity and real wealth creation. The primary difference between the situation in

1994 when Barnett's thesis came out in the U.S. Army War College Quarterly, *Parameters,* and today is the astonishing fact of the United States losing leading positions in practically all criteria, from finished goods to high tech weaponry, to aerospace industry, in this list. Not only has the United States stopped producing real wealth, it finds itself today in a position in which it is prevented from addressing the issue on any serious level.

In September 2018 a report to President Donald Trump titled *Assessing and Strengthening the Manufacturing and Defense Industrial Base and Supply Chain Resiliency of the United States* was published by the Interagency Task Force, following the President's *Executive Order 13806,* which sought to take stock of the decades-long deindustrialization and the status of America's industrial base as related to defense.[12] The findings of the Report were shocking for both domestic and international observers, and could hardly be any more contradictory to the claims of American proponents of geoeconomics. These claims, in the end, required that the U.S. have more than just finances in order to be able to economically compete—that is to say, conduct war by other means—against nations who justifiably viewed the United States as an enemy, not as a mere competitor. The United States, certainly, could impose sanctions on China or Russia but in the larger scheme of things, these were nothing more than rearguard actions, because economically the United States increasingly couldn't compete in the international arena where tangibles are exchanged or traded, with the exception of a very few industries, such as commercial aerospace prior to its collapse in 2020, microchips, and cars, and a few other items from the shrinking American real economy and, especially, the shrinking machine-building complex.

While Hollywood could still produce entertainment, which it was selling abroad, and Microsoft can still produce software, the United States can no longer produce reliable, affordable cars or persevere with the feel-good myth of stickers that proclaim "proudly assembled in the USA" on household appliances sold in Home Depot or Lowe's. Even when a "proudly assembled in the USA" sticker is present, one has to ask a question about the parts from which those appliances are proudly assembled, because as the experience of agricultural attachments at Coastal (Farm and Ranch) stores shows, most of it is still produced in China. The 2018 Interagency Report to President Trump revealed some terrifying economic truths for the United States which seldom make it into the 24/7 economic news cycle as front-page news. Ultimately, the main message of the Report was correct in principle:

> To provide for our national security, America's manufacturing and defense industrial base must be secure, robust, resilient, and ready. To ensure taxpayer dollars are frugally and wisely spent, the defense industrial base must be cost-effective, cost-efficient, highly productive, and not unduly subsidized. In the event of contingencies, the industrial base must possess sufficient surge capabilities. Above all, America's manufacturing and defense industrial base must support economic prosperity, be globally competitive, and have the capabilities and capacity to rapidly innovate and arm our military with the lethality and dominance necessary to prevail in any conflict."[13]

The Report was also correct in warning about very real threats to achieving those stated goals from America's "competitors" and framed the issue in geoeconomics terms:

> Decreases in key production capabilities and declines in manufacturing employment, relative to the last time the U.S. faced a great power competition, left key weaknesses that threaten the nation's manufacturing capabilities. The industrial policies of foreign competitors have diminished American manufacturing's global competitiveness–sometimes as collateral damage of globalization, but also due to specific targeting by great powers like China. Finally, emerging gaps in our skilled workforce, both in terms of STEM as well as core trade skills (e.g., welding,

computer numeric control operation, etc.) pose increasing risk to industrial base capabilities.[14]

The United States could still sell its main export, U.S. T-bills, a.k.a. treasuries, which were crucial for financing America's infatuation with consumerism and making money, but T-bills, like the service economy, were not creating real wealth and haven't done so in decades, while on the other hand, being the main driver behind America's deindustrialization. T-bills could still be sold internationally; American-made cars, however, were running into problems competing on the international markets. President Trump's aggressive promoting of U.S.-made products on the international markets eventually ran into stern opposition. In his interview to one of the news outlets, Donald Trump threatened to impose 35% tariffs on German-made cars if they were to be assembled in Mexico. Trump also lamented the fact that U.S.-made cars were not selling well in Europe. The response from Germany's Vice-Chancellor, Sigmar Gabriel, was humiliating: "The U.S. needs to build better cars."[15]

The United Sates could, certainly, complain about the unfair trade practices of Germany, or Japan, where the United States has had very limited success with its cars, to put it mildly, but even in Russia, U.S. automakers ran into trouble. Ford was the first American car brand which came to the Russian market in 2000 with a vengeance, with the second generation Ford Focus becoming a best-seller in Russia. Ford was the second car-manufacturing company after Volkswagen to locate its production in Russia, and for years enjoyed what it seemed would be a very long-term romance with the Russians. But it only seemed so. On 27 March 2019 Ford announced that it was stopping production in Russia. As a popular Russian automobile monthly *Za Rulyom (At the Steering Wheel)* reported, the reasons for that were multiple but the main one was the fact that Ford had lost its competitive edge against Korean, Japanese, European and Russian-made cars. Ford's operation in Russia simply became unsustainable, with a catastrophic decline in sales starting in 2016.[16] Not only had Ford models remained fairly expensive, they started to lose out to the much more affordable Russian cars and to other competitors on technical merits, even including such a metric as the size of the cabin.

The pattern was pretty obvious, occurring not just in Germany or Japan where American-made cars were losing competition. But if Ford at least had had some success in Russia, Chevrolet never got off the ground there at all.[17] The time when the world would look at American-made products with curiosity and envy has long since passed. Why the United Sates was steadily losing its competitive edge is pretty obvious, once one begins to consider the fact that the world, devastated by World War II, was not going to lie in ruins forever and that eventually industrial capacity and competence would return. But even in the 1980s the United States could still boast the largest economy in the world, and unlike the United States' economy of the 2010s, it was a real economy with a massive production capacity. The American-made cars of the 1970s and 1980s may not have been the best cars in the world, but they were produced in the U.S., and they involved massive supply and logistical chains, which also provided employment to millions of people and that is what mattered in the end. Paul Verhoeven may have been sarcastic towards U.S.-made cars in his *Robocop* blockbuster, when satirizing a fictitious 6000 SUX getting 8.2 miles per gallon, but everyone could see that the police in the movie were driving the new beautiful American-made Ford Taurus, which certainly looked like—and was—an extremely competitive car. It even sold in Japan, where it was considered a luxury car.

Today, one can hardly recall any American-made sedan of truly global repute comparable to the Toyota Camry or Honda Accord. Unless one discusses a fairly narrow segment of sports cars, luxury cars, and especially trucks, where the United States remains competitive, U.S. automakers are simply no longer in the position to challenge passenger car imports domestically, let alone mount a serious competition internationally. But if the fate of the U.S. automotive industry remains on public display and in focus due to its obvious market implications, some industries in the United States have simply quietly disappeared without much ado, with the public taking little notice of that important strategic fact. While former Chief of Naval Operations Admiral Elmo Zumwalt defined the United States as a "world island" a direct reference to the seafaring character of the American nation,[18] the state of its commercial shipbuilding, for a seafaring nation, is dismal.

As the Report to President Trump on the U.S. Industrial base concluded:

> The primary cause decreasing competition in shipbuilding is the small comparative size of the U.S. commercial shipbuilding industry compared to the foreign shipbuilding industry, coupled with the Navy's unique military requirements. Products and services that lack competition are at a higher risk of being offered by a single or sole source supplier. Examples of lack of competition can be seen in many products critical to shipbuilding such as high voltage cable, propulsor raw material, valves, and fittings.[19]

This dry assessment, which also mentions such factors as the loss of skills and competencies, is an understatement in terms of an actual comparison of the shipbuilding industries of the United States with those of the rest of the world. In geoeconomics terms, shipping capacity is a must because geoeconomics and delivery of goods to the markets are two sides of the same coin. The commercial shipping industry remains a backbone of the global economy since it is responsible for up to 90% of the trade being done by waterways.[20] Currently, while the United States has the largest navy in the world, its commercial shipbuilding industry is dwarfed by those of China, the Republic of Korea, Japan and Russia.

In a statement before the Committee on Transportation and Infrastructure Subcommittee on Coast Guard and Maritime Transportation of the U.S. House of Representatives, Mark H. Buzby, administrator, maritime administration, U.S. Department of Transportation, revealed the actual depth of the disaster:

While the United States remains a global leader in naval shipbuilding, which represents the majority of the Nation's shipbuilding revenue, our large commercial shipyards are struggling to remain afloat. U.S. commercial shipbuilding of large merchant-type ships has been locked into a downward spiral of decreasing demand and an increased divergence between domestic and foreign shipbuilding productivity and pricing. In the case of large self-propelled oceangoing vessels, U.S. shipyards still lack the scale, technology, and the large volume "series building" order books needed to compete effectively with shipyards in other countries. The five largest U.S. commercial shipyards construct limited numbers of large cargo vessels for domestic use, averaging five such vessels per year over the last five years, with a peak of ten such vessels in 2016. This production is small, however, relative to the worldwide production of 1,408 such ships in 2016.[21]

Buzby's use of the term *small* is a cautious attempt to avoid the embarrassing truth of the United States having nowhere near the scale of commercial shipbuilding required for a nation which sees itself as a geoeconomics entity, ready to fight for economic dominance globally. The numbers simply do not support such American claims. One such number, which is at the foundation of the shipbuilding industry is the volume of steel produced by a nation. Ships are made of steel and it takes a lot of it to produce a good size commercial fleet that is truly competitive in a global economy. Given the size of its economy, which it claims without any substance is around $23 trillion, the United States level of steel production is surprising—insofar as China outproduces the United States by a factor of 11, while Russia, which has a population less than half the size of that of the United States, produces around 81% of U.S. steel output. Japan, which is also a seafaring nation, produces more steel than the United States.[22]

Of course, the United States has a large navy, with many large capital ships, especially the fleet of U.S. aircraft carriers, but the U.S. does not produce those ships every year. Commercial shipbuilding globally, however, produces all kinds of commercial vessels, including many large ones, every year. Many of those vessels are as large, or larger still than the U.S. Navy's aircraft carriers. Even a brief review of commercial shipbuilding in terms of tonnage of vessels leaves no doubt which nations are ready, or getting ready, for economic war. As the *e-Handbook of Statistics* states drily, 90% of all the world's shipbuilding in 2018 occurred in three nations: China, Japan and the Republic of Korea.[23] Once one considers the fact that in 2018 the deadweight (that is, the weight of an empty vessel) of the world's commercial fleet alone grew by 52 million tons[24] and puts it against the actual steel production in the United States, which is roughly 88 million tons, one gets a sense of America's relatively insignificant role globally in steel production and its absolutely inconsequential one in commercial shipbuilding. To add insult to injury, Russia, the U.S. "rival," or existential threat as declared by American exceptionalists, not only competes with the United States in steel production, which is one of the major indicators of a Composite Index of National Capability (CINC), but surpassed the U.S. in commercial shipbuilding.

Obviously, the United States tries to make its presence in the commercial shipbuilding felt. The latest commercial vessel, christened *Matsonia,* one of two *Kanaloa-class* container (Con-Ro) ships which will serve Hawaii with deliveries from the mainland, is one such attempt. It is a large vessel with a displacement of 50,000 tons and it is built at NASSCO shipyard.[25] The United States also managed to produce three 50,000 ton tankers for SEACOR between 2013 and 2017 and a few other similar ships of the same deadweight, including two LNG-powered *Marlin-class* containerships. While a seafaring nation itself, Russia has its trade done primarily by ground transport, ranging from rail to pipelines, and managed nonetheless in few short years to complete a turnaround in her shipbuilding industry, reaching a planned workload for its numerous shipyards of 800 vessels through 2035.

Russia's newest Far Eastern mega shipyard *Zvezda,* while still only partially operational, found its portfolio consisting of 118 vessels.[26] Russia's oil giant *Rosneft* alone had ordered 12 *Arc6* and *Arc7* ice-class tankers, 4 ice-class multi-purpose support vessels, and 10 *Aframax* tankers by 2019.[27] Most of those vessels, some of which are already afloat or under construction, are gigantic high-tech vessels ranging in displacement from between 115,000 to 129,000 tons and being as long as the U.S. Navy's aircraft carriers.

This all is happening against the background of Russia simply dominating the global market of ice-breakers, with the latest one, a *Lider-class* nuclear ice-breaker, at 70,000 tons of displacement being by far the largest ice-breaker in the world—no small feat, once one considers the fact that presently the largest ice-breaker in the world, project 22220, is displacing 33,000 tons. The first of three *Lider-class* ice-breakers was laid down at *Zvezda* shipyard in September of 2020. If the United States really planned to follow its own geoeconomic concepts, it appears that it never went beyond laying out hollow doctrines or ivory tower political science theories. The U.S. economic posture, which it alleges makes the United States economically the most powerful nation in the world, contradicts dramatically with truly geoeconomic, economically competitive postures—that is, the postures of America's so-called existential rivals, China and Russia.

If the Chinese economic miracle and export-oriented economy has been the focus of many American pundits for decades now, the fact of Russia getting into the geoeconomics game only relatively recently has started to attract the attention of Western punditry. One of the Western theorists on geoeconomics and Eurasian integration, Glen Diesen, even dedicated a large chapter in his treatise on the matter to what he termed the development of "strategic industries."[28] Yet Diesen, as well as Luttwak or, for that matter, any other proponent of geoeconomics as a distinct study field, is always inevitably dragged back to the discussion table of good old geopolitics, or rather its more comprehensive modern iteration, in which the power of a nation rests on its economic and military resources, which, in the end trickles down to form that nation's geoeconomic capability—which is nothing more than a fancy term for global economic competitiveness and the ability to defend itself by all necessary means, including military ones.

The pathetic state of America's commercial shipbuilding is the obverse side of U.S. naval power, which at this stage of its relation to the global economy and international relations exists primarily for the sake of defending the sanctity of the Shipping Lanes Of Communications (SLOC) crucial for the America's existence and equally so for interruption of the trade by others. Luttwak may have defined geoeconomics as *a war by other means*, but these have long been original means of war. Those very non-economic garrisons, military bases and weapons never disappeared and, in fact, are becoming increasingly the main tool in America's attempts to enforce its rules on what, by the declaration of its scholars and statesmen, it is committed to—economic warfare. Just economic warfare it is not, because the United States has already lost that. Accordingly, "warfare" increasingly becomes a competition across the full spectrum of human activities, ranging from military, economic, cultural and ideological, which has already taken the form of a Cold War, and which threatens to grow into a very real hot one—precisely for the reason that, as is the case with many political science constructs cooked up in the increasingly chaotic American strategies kitchen, most of those strategies never produced new ideas and concepts which never could alter the trajectory of facts on the ground.

Today, the United States suffers not only from intellectual collapse, which we will address in the following chapters, it also has increasingly less and less to offer economically, especially after losing its war on the major front of energy—a strategic industry in Diesen's words, who then gives a ruthless definition of the state of America's economy:

> The conviction that the U.S. developed a sustainable post-modern economy less reliant on traditional manufacturing jobs has been sustained by inflated asset prices masquerading as economic growth. The collapse of the tech bubble in the 1990s indicated that

the U.S. would need to accept a diminished position in the global economy.[29]

Today the United States faces an economic monster and fully self-sustained market in Eurasia and no amount of statistical tinkering, including by applying meaningless dollar numbers to something the United States is no longer capable of either producing or procuring, will change that reality. As the dramatic events in the hydrocarbon and aerospace markets demonstrated in the last 18 months, and as they continue to demonstrate in communications and high-end weapons markets, the United States has already lost or is losing fast its positions as a global competitor. Depending on the internal political and economic dynamics within the United States in the next couple of years, the turning of the United States into a large but regional and even third world nation is not such a far-fetched scenario. Granted, Russia's military might is able to deter the U.S. from unleashing a global thermonuclear conflict in its desperate attempt to preserve an imaginary status quo that many in Washington still think exists. But it does not, has not for a long time—and it is about time somebody in Washington got the message.

London's Crystal Palace, once the place for exhibiting British industrial and military prowess, and for scoffing condescendingly at others, is no more. It was demolished in 1936 after a catastrophic fire, symptomatically on the eve of the world war which would see a departure from greatness of the Empire on which the sun never sets. The Football Club Crystal Palace is all that is left today of the once proud Crystal Palace. The memory of a historically ironic negotiation between then mayor of London Boris Johnson and the Chinese, who wanted to invest in restoration of this important landmark, has also passed into oblivion. The negotiations failed and the world moved on. It always does.

Endnotes

1 Alan Palmer, *The Crimean War* (New York: Dorset Press, 1987), 10.

2 Ibid.

3 Holger H. Herwing, *The Demon of Geopolitics: How Karl Haushofer "Educated" Hitler and Hess* (Rowman & Littlefield Publishers, March 10, 2016), 18.

4 Vladimir Ilyich Lenin, "Imperialism as a special stage of capitalism," Chapter VII in, *Imperialism, the Highest Stage of Capitalism: A Popular Outline,* Marxists.org,

https://www.marxists.org/ archive/lenin/works/1916/imp-hsc/ch07.htm.

5 Edward N. Luttwak, "From Geopolitics to Geo-economics: Logic of Conflict, Grammar of Commerce," *National Interest,* No. 20 (Summer 1990), 17.

6 Edward N. Luttwak, "The Theory and Practice of Geo-Economics," in Armand Clesse, ed., *The International System after the Collapse of the East-West Order* (Leiden and Boston: Martin Nijhoff Publishers, 1994), 128.

7 Robert D. Blackwill and Jennifer M. Harris, *War by Other Means: Geoeconomics and Statecraft* (The Belknap Press of Harvard University Press, 2016), 1.

8 Michael Hudson and Sharmini Peires, "The Fictitious Economy, Hiding How the Economy Really Works" *The Unz Review,* February 28, 2017.

9 *Current Employment Statistics—CES (National),* 6-months CES chart, U.S. Bureau of Labor Statistics, July, 2020, https://www.bls.gov/ces/

10 Michael Hudson. *Killing the Host: How Financial Parasites and Debt Bondage Destroy the Global Economy* (Counterpunch Books. Electronic Edition, 2015), 18.

11 Jeffrey R. Barnett, *Exclusion as National Security Policy. Parameters 24,* no. 1 (1994), electronic version, 3-4, https://press.armywarcollege.edu/parameters/vol24/iss1/19/

12 *Executive Order 13806,* Federal Register, July 21, 2017, Section 2, https://www.federalregister.gov/documents/2017/07/26/2017-15860/assessing-and-strengthening-the-manufacturing-and-defense-industrial-base-and-supply-chain.

13 Interagency Task Force, *Assessing and Strengthening the Manufacturing and Defense Industrial Base and Supply Chain Resiliency of the United States,* report to President Donald J. Trump in Fulfillment of Executive Order 13806, September, 2018, 7-8.

14 Ibid.

15 "Germany to the US after Trump remarks: 'Build better cars,'" Associated Press as reported by *Business Insider,* January, 16, 2017, https://www.businessinsider.com/ap-german-vice-chancellor-rejects-trumps-german-car-remarks-2017-1.

16 Za Rulyom, "*10 причин развода: почему Форд нас оставил*" *(10 reasons for divorce: why Ford abandoned us),* https://www.zr.ru/content/articles/916956-10-prichin-i-sledstvij-ukhoda-fo/.

17 Ibid.

18 Elmo R Zumwalt, Jr., *On Watch* (New York: Quadrangle, The New York Times Book Co.,1976), 60.

19 Interagency Task Force, op cit., 80.

20 *Types of Transport Modes used in the Import-Export Trade*, Corpiness, November 8, 2019, https://www.corpiness.com/info/types-of-transport-modes-used-in-the-import-export-trade/.

21 Maritime Administration, U.S. Department of Transportation, *U.S. Maritime and Shipbuilding Industries: Strategies to Improve Regulation, Economic Opportunities and Competitiveness*, statement before the Committee on Transportation and Infrastructure Subcommittee on Coast Guard and Maritime Transportation of the U.S. House of Representatives, by Mark H. Buzby, Administrator, March 6, 2019, https://www.transportation.gov/testimony/us-maritime-and-shipbuilding-industries-strategies-improve-regulation-economic.

22 World Steel Association, "Global crude steel output increases by 3.4% in 2019" January 27, 2020, https://www.worldsteel.org/media-centre/press-releases/2020/Global-crude-steel-output-increases-by-3.4--in-2019.html.

23 UNCTAD, *Maritime Transport*, e-Handbook of Statistics 2019, https://stats.unctad.org/handbook/MaritimeTransport/MerchantFleet.html.

24 Ibid.

25 Matson Christens, "Matsonia," *PR Newswire,* July 6, 2020, https://www.yahoo.com/news/matson-christens-matsonia-200100140.html.

26 *В портфеле заказов ССК «Звезда» 118 судов* (Zvezda's portfolio of orders consists of 118 vessels), *Primpress,* July 27, 2018, https://primpress.ru/article/28720

27 "Zvezda Shipyard Increases Portfolio of orders by 42%," *Rosneft,* January 14, 2019, https://www.rosneft.com/press/news/item/193531/.

28 Glen Diesen, *Russia's Geoeconomic Strategy for a Greater Eurasia: Rethinking Asia and International Relations* (Routledge Taylor and Francis Group, 2018), 17.

29 Ibid., 39.

4. ENERGY

Modern civilization and energy are the two sides of the same coin. There is no civilization without energy production because there is no civilization without energy consumption. As with any human being, the process of expenditure and replenishment of energy is constant, even when we, humans, sleep. This applies even more so to modern societies whose existence without energy—be that gasoline for the cars, kerosene for jet engines, electricity for lighting and powering civilization's industrial machines—is inconceivable. In the end, the history of humanity's progress is a history of energy extraction and utilization, from primitive fires in the caves to the International Space Station and nuclear power stations, and, not to be forgotten, weapons of such an immense power that they can spell doom for human civilization as a whole.

Today, contemporary geopolitics and geoeconomics could be defined properly only within a framework which takes account of energy. Energy is not only the single most consequential economic factor; it is also a massive geopolitical one. For me personally, being a native of the city of Baku, now the capital of an independent Azerbaijan, from birth, the production of energy had a very specific smell which I absorbed from my childhood. Baku, and Apsheron Peninsula where Baku is located, smelled of crude. This smell became a constant sensory feature due to crude being pumped non-stop on Apsheron since 1846 when the first oil well was drilled there, long before American oil fields development.[1] The rest is history, with both Dmitry Mendeleev and the Nobel brothers playing a key role in the development of the Apsheron oil fields and of the petrochemical industry there. By the early 20th Century Azerbaijan, then part of the Russian Empire, was producing more than half of the world's oil.[2] Azerbaijan in general, and Baku in particular, became the crucible of Russia's oil industry.

By the Soviet time Apsheron was one huge oilfield and the crude was pumped near Baku, in Baku suburbs and inside Baku itself. The first Polytechnical Institute in Eurasia fully dedicated to education of oil engineers was founded there early in the 20th century. Apsheron oil was also literally the fuel that enabled the Soviet Union's victory in World War II. Off-shore exploration was also developing with astonishing speed and by the 1950s Baku had become the bona-fide oil and petrochemical capitol of the Soviet Union. It also was becoming increasingly a very beautiful and picturesque city. While the smell of crude persisted, often mixed with the smell of oleanders and rhododendrons, it didn't really bother most Baku natives. Even for purely Baku's iteration of the game of airborne curling, nylon—generally known by its trademark title Capron—lids from 3-liter jars were filled with a substance called kir, from which kerosene was distilled and which was used for asphalt.

Anyone born in Baku in the 20th century was automatically born into the world of the extraction and processing of the most important substance in modern humanity's history—crude oil. Crude and everything associated with it, from technology to people, was and still is a primary engine which drives the economy of not only Baku but the Caucasus region as a whole. Of course, since the collapse of the Soviet Union, Azerbaijan's role in crude production dropped precipitously in the former Soviet Union's space, with Russia producing in May of 2020 almost 14 times more crude oil than Azerbaijan.[3] This has led to a dramatic decline in the relative importance of Azerbaijan in an era when the economic, military and energy giants are back at what many in the West dubbed a great power competition or rivalry, much of which is built around energy. Crude oil and another hydrocarbon—natural gas—remain at the core of modern geopolitics and geoeconomics, if one is inclined to use that latter term for competition, or using Luttwak's definition—war by other means.

Overall energy production in the world often is expressed in the *MTOE* metric, which stands for *Millions of Tonnes Oil*

Equivalent—which defines a total energy output ranging from actual crude oil to gas and expresses in the number of Joules (a standard energy metric) obtained by burning one ton of crude oil. By 2019 the balance of energy production expressed in *MTOE* was telling. China was leading the world with 2,684 *MTOE*, with the U.S. and Russia following with 2,303 and 1,506 *MTOE* respectively.[4] Another crucial index of economic development, the production of electricity from all sources, ranging from oil, to hydro, to coal, to nuclear, saw China leading the world dramatically with 7,482 (*TWh*) Terawatts/hour production, with the United States being distant second with 4,385, with India at 1,614 and Russia at 1,122 *TWh*.[5] These numbers are crucial in understanding the formation of not just a new economic but a new geopolitical reality, in which the United States finds itself increasingly not just being challenged or overtaken economically—a reality which America's elites try to deny—but in terms of overall national power. Energy in this geopolitical and geoeconomic reality plays a crucial role and will continue to play and expand it in the future.

Anyone who read the economic headlines in March 2020 regarding the OPEC+ meeting in Vienna might as well have read the reports on a diplomatic negotiation breakdown, which precedes most wars. OPEC+ was a modification of the original OPEC (Organization of Petroleum Exporting Countries) founded in 1960, by the addition to it of Russia, Mexico, Azerbaijan and a few other crude producing nations in 2016. Bloomberg described the breakdown in Vienna in these terms:

> The breakdown is the biggest crisis since Saudi Arabia, Russia and more than 20 other nations created the OPEC+ alliance in 2016. The group, controlling more than half of the world's oil production, has underpinned prices and reshaped the geopolitics of the Middle East—increasing President Vladimir Putin's clout in the region. But it's come under increasing strain over the past year.[6]

The breakdown of the Vienna negotiations between two of the biggest players, Saudi Arabia and Russia alleged by Western media as "allies," was due to Russia's refusal to continue with her cuts in crude production in order to maintain crude prices at comfortable levels for producers. Russia, in essence, rejected all OPEC+ limitations on production of crude. Russian Energy Minister Alexander Novak explicitly stated that Russia's oil companies were free to ramp up production starting from April 1.[7] Western media and punditry immediately framed the collapse of the OPEC+ production limits as an oil war between Russia and Saudi Arabia. They couldn't have been more wrong, even considering the always very low standard of Western punditry when discussing anything Russia-related. In the end, they would be taught a cruel and humiliating lesson. Russia, refusing any production cuts for crude, was not fighting Saudi Arabia, she was fighting the United States. Namely the American shale oil and fracking industry. And effectively Saudi Arabia, by then turning around and boosting its own production contrary to the cuts it had at first demanded, was doing likewise.

America's emergence on the international oil market is a story of technology winning over common economic sense and also one of outright fraud. U.S. oil production between 2000 and 2011 was fluctuating in the corridor of 5-6 million barrels of crude a day. But by 2012 things had changed—the output started to grow at an increasing rate and by 2019 hit more than 12 million barrels a day.[8] By January of 2020, the United States was producing almost 13 million barrels of crude a day.[9] This massive growth in crude production was due to primarily what then was described as a shale boom. Of course, shale oil extraction technology, which has been around since the mid-20th century, had continued to improve as the years passed by. But shale oil production was always expensive and throughout the 20th century shale oil could not compete with the cheap crude extracted by classic vertical drilling, which often defined the skylines of such oil-rich places as the Apsheron Peninsula in general and Baku in particular, dominated by oil towers and, later, the sea, sprinkled with easily visible oil platforms.

A dramatic change for shale oil came with the improvement in fracking technology in the United States and the availability of cheap credit—debt, that is—for many independent oil companies, which rushed to even unproven shale oil fields in mid-2000s and eventually drove nearly all of the oil industry's growth, by 2019 accounting for almost two thirds of U.S. oil production. All that growth was achieved as financial analyst David Deckelbaum put it: "This is an industry that for every dollar that they brought in, they would spend two."[10] In plain language the industry wasn't viable economically no matter how one looked at it, even when one considered fairly high prices for crude. However, with crude prices going down, as they started to do in 2019, while the industry was requiring prices of between $55 and $65 per barrel in 2020 to break even, the prospects for U.S. shale oil were becoming increasingly dire.[11] But two factors of, as geoeconomics purists would say, geoeconomics, played against U.S. oil and its prematurely U.S. declared energy independence and notion of America becoming a net exporter of oil:

1. U.S. shale oil was financially non-viable;
2. U.S. oil exports were possible primarily due to the U.S. "picking up" quotas freed chiefly as a result of Russia and Saudi Arabia's earlier cuts within OPEC+ in an attempt to balance the world's oil market, which was facing sinking prices due to a glut in production.

Of course, there was a third factor which was in play here, and which was crucial for U.S. shale oil—it was Russia's costs. The cost of Saudi oil officially declared as low as $2.80 per barrel wasn't a factor.[12] It was simply regarded as a given that the Saudis would remain extremely competitive with just about any cost of oil. Saudi's problem lay in its backward political system, in its mono-economy and the tremendous weight of social and welfare obligations being dispensed to a vast network of Saudi royals and its general population, which couldn't have been revised without creating severe political instability in Riyadh. While never disclosing officially her costs, Russia went on record on a number of occasions, stating that Russia is comfortable with an oil price of around $40.[13] Russia's budget, in which oil was one of the main revenue contributors, albeit by far not the only one, had this number as a base price for a balanced budget. Russia's tiring of U.S. shale taking the market share of its production cuts was the main reason for the collapse of the February 2020 Vienna OPEC+ negotiations seeking production cuts, and had very little to do with any Saudi-Russian oil "alliance" on the other hand, or for that matter, any irreconcilable contradictions within it, but rather a lot to do with U.S. shale oil, in layman's lingo, not having any economic right to elbow out well-established oil-producers who were ready to negotiate and compromise, as they had on many occasions before, to keep the boat from rocking.

Economically and financially, U.S. shale oil was an anomaly, or as one reporter questioned it: "Do U.S. Shale Drillers Deserve to Exist in Free Markets?"[14] It was a hard question for a nation which, for two centuries, had been proselytizing the virtues of a "free market" and "free trade" globally, spreading the gospel of financial austerity and the bottom line. U.S. mainstream media, ever vigilant when dealing with Russia, albeit incompetently as always, heralded the OPEC+ breakdown at Vienna as the start of a Russia-Saudi oil war. *Time* magazine even called this war "A Battle Royal" and placed a Saudi intention to "flood the market" and "teach Russia a lesson" at the center of the purported dispute.[15] For such commentators, speaking on behalf of a nation whose benchmark price of oil was around $80, this was a rather reckless act. As it is always the case with the U.S. mainstream media, they got it all wrong. Most of them, anyway. Only the relatively fringe *Newsmax* was able to see the grim reality—for the United States—of the alleged Russia-Saudi dispute and did what any normal professional journalist would do under such circumstances: ask the Russians about how they viewed the whole situation. The Russians didn't see it as it was seen in the U.S. As Alexander Dynkin, one of Russia's most influential pundits, the President of the Institute of World Economy and International Relations in Moscow, a state-run think tank, stated: "The Kremlin has decided to sacrifice OPEC+ to stop U.S. shale producers and punish the U.S. for messing with Nord Stream 2. Of course, to upset Saudi Arabia could be a risky thing, but this is Russia's strategy at the moment—flexible geometry of interests."[16]

Events which followed completely validated this initial hypothesis and if someone was to be taught a lesson, it was the United States. The lesson was not just in theory but in the practical and successful application of geoeconomics and of sound geopolitical analysis. The Saudis' move on flooding the market with cheap oil was not against Russia, per se. Nor were the Russians necessarily intending to completely obliterate U.S. shale oil, having initially had as a main objective getting the United States to the negotiating table and turning OPEC+ into OPEC++. In the end, the Saudis themselves had scores to settle with U.S. shale oil. Russia could withstand any calamity on the global oil market, U.S. shale could not, especially against the background of the COVID-19 pandemic and the shutting down of the economies of the Western nations. U.S. shale oil drillers could draw on debt to survive for a little bit longer in the midst of falling oil prices, Russia could draw on the half-a-trillion U.S. dollar cushion she had prepared in advance. In fact, the Russians were on record regarding their ability to survive very low oil prices well before the Russian-Saudi frictions in Vienna. Speaking to CNCBC in October of 2019, Russia's Finance Minister, a rather pro-Western and liberal reformer, was pretty confident that even if the price of oil fell to "$30 or $20 per barrel, Russia would not suffer an economic shock and would be able to fulfil its budgetary obligations for three years, thanks to its vast gold reserves."[17]

In a classic case of arrogance, obstinacy, and incompetence, the U.S. media went on a speculation (and misreporting) spree about Russia's gold and currency reserves and even started exercising their favorite pastime of predicting Vladimir Putin's loss of power in Russia. Some Western reporters, as usual projecting their own incompetence and immaturity, a defining feature of journalist corps in the U.S., even started to explain in April of 2020, when oil prices hit below $30 per barrel and the slaughter of the U.S. shale oil industry started in earnest, that

Putin's (and Russia's) seeming inflexibility in a face of spiraling oil prices was a matter of Putin's pride.[18] Of course, there was no "challenge" to Putin's "power" as the articles suggested, and the Russians were very vocal in stating that they could live with the price of $25 per barrel for a duration of 10 years. The Russians also remained absolutely calm when the volume of U.S.-produced oil dropped, in an historically unprecedented move, into negative territory in late April of 2020. At some point the U.S. WTI (West Texas Intermediate) brand of oil was trading at -$40, a situation so out of the ordinary that it was becoming clear that there would be no return to oil prices in the $80 or even the $60 per barrel range in a very long time, if ever.[19]

It is a well-known truism that hindsight is 20/20, but anyone observing at this writing in the Autumn of 2020, the results of an alleged Russia-Saudi "price war," cannot ignore the main result of this price, which is the devastation it brought to the U.S. shale oil industry. Already in June 2020, after oil prices stabilized somewhat around $39 for U.S. *WTI* brand and started consistently hovering above $40 for Russia's main brand of *Urals*, CNBC, citing a Deloitte report, came out with a terrifying headline on June 22: "Shale industry will be rocked by $300 billion in losses and a wave of bankruptcies, Deloitte says."[20] If the signs of the U.S. shale oil's insolvency were visible already in the mid-2010s, as one oil industry observer headlined it, 2020 was a year of the "Great American Shale Oil and Gas Massacre."[21] It was an apt description of the catastrophic implosion of U.S. oil, the end result of which still saw the United States joining OPEC+ when it was discussing the cuts required for stabilization of the market as at exactly around the price of $40, which made Russia happy, Saudi Arabia unhappy and the U.S. shale oil industry effectively defunct. Russia initially wanted the United States at the OPEC+ negotiating table. Russia achieved that, including using Saudi Arabia as a third ball in Russian billiard, with two of the balls ending up in pockets.

The lesson for the United States was humiliating. It paraded, yet again, the cabal of U.S. purported Russia pundits and "experts" as a collection of ignorant ideologues who, far from knowing anything about Russia, or the oil industry for that matter, also knew very little about the United States and its main "ally" in the Middle East, Saudi Arabia. As one such self-proclaimed "expert" on Russia, George Friedman of STRATFOR fame, wrote in an incoherent, emotionally charged, delusional piece filled with all the customary U.S. propaganda tropes about Russia—ranging from Putin's pride, to Russia's dependence on oil, to oligarchs, to Russia's impending collapse—that Russia was the "world's biggest loser from oil crash."[22] The fact that such "experts" are still given a public tribune in the United States and are treated as experts is a powerful testimony to the decline of professional expertise in the United States, not just in fields inherently susceptible to fraud such as political science and political commentary but in fields which actually do require a good grasp of both reality "on the ground" and enough skills to have at least some understanding of the subject matter.

The oil crisis of 2020 did, indeed, teach lessons to anyone who wanted to learn. Even as one of the so called "supermajors" oil companies, British Petroleum, released a report which forecasted the end of the relentless growth of oil demand, the main lesson was not even the trajectory of the oil industry.[23] It was clear that shutting-down the Western economies due to an overreaction to the COVID-19 pandemic will change the structure of the demand. The main lesson was that Russia was absolutely impervious to U.S. pressures and was the only truly energy independent nation on earth, Russia's energy independence rested on a combination of military and economic power, which allowed Russia to press on with her main economic objectives, upscaling them in the process. Russia did it without any regard to opinion and threats from what seemed at that time as a collection of the most powerful oil market players, the United States and Saudi Arabia, among others. Some observers in the United States finally learned some lessons and as one concluded: "It was evident to anyone with even half a brain that the last Saudi-instigated oil price war would end in abject failure for the Saudis, just as the previous 2014-2016 effort did and for the very same reasons."[24] Simon Watkins, who so concluded at least had a right to trumpet such a conclusion; he had predicted Saudi failure as early as March of 2020, at the very start of the oil crisis.

Realistically, however, Watkins was one of very few who talked sense, but even such rare voices as his failed largely to identify the oil price war as primarily a Russian-American affair, with Saudi Arabia being merely Russia's proxy or, in keeping with American tradition of conspiracy—the global oil market Manchurian Candidate. Of course, the fact that Saudi Arabia, against the background of falling prices, had no other options but two—either to accept its fate and start living off its reserves while running a constantly ever-increasing budget deficit, or do something about it. Russia, by refusing production cuts in February, forced the Saudis, led by Mohammad Bin Salman, to unleash an armada of tankers filled with oil, which dropped the oil price to where it would initiate a complete collapse in the U.S. fracking industry. If there ever was a more consequential act of statesmanship in global economic affairs than that on the part of Kremlin, it must have been an event on the scale of OPEC's formation in 1960 and the oil embargo of 1973-74 by an Arab iteration of OPEC, OAPEC, which shook the foundation of America's economy and dramatically redefined the geopolitical landscape.

For American exceptionalists the whole notion that Russia could force the United States to do anything which benefited Russia, such as participating in oil output cuts and having an oil price which satisfied Russia, was unbearable. Adding insult to injury, however, was the fact that, while U.S. shale oil continues to undergo massive bankruptcies and radical downsizing, Russia has actually grown her gold and foreign exchange currency reserves to $600 billion.[25] Moreover, additional humiliation came in the form of China filling her oil storages with cheap oil, while simultaneously signing a massive strategic partnership deal with Iran, reportedly worth $400 billion, including the possibility of a military pact, which had massive geopolitical ramifications for the United States, which openly views both Iran and China as enemies.[26]

The scale of America's geoeconomic defeat, which couldn't be obscured by incessant propaganda by spin-doctors, illuminated one very important and fundamental truth—the oil industry, together with the hydrocarbon resources of a nation, was most effective in geoeconomic and geopolitical struggles only if under the direct control of a national government, such as was arranged in Russia's increasingly mixed economy. The other side of this defeat was the traditional American ignorance, if not altogether debilitating delusion, concerning Russia's economic matters and the role hydrocarbons played in Russia's economy. While Western pundits continued to exploit the myth of Russia depending solely on revenues from oil and natural gas sales, its reality was dramatically different.

As was noted in the Operative Report by Russia's Accounting Chamber in August 2020, Russia budget revenues in the first half of 2020 from hydrocarbons' sales accounted for less than one third (29.3%) of total budget revenues and had dropped by 13% compared to the same period of the year 2019.[27] Evidently Russia had, somehow for uneducated observers, 70.7% of revenues other than hydrocarbon revenues to keep her economy going. Russia has beaten, yet again, the expectations of Western pundits and "analysts," and instead of collapsing due to the deterioration of its domestic political and economic situation, has proceeded with accelerated industrial development. It was Obama's version of a Russian economy "left in tatters" all over again.

At this stage one is forced to question the competence of American elites whose record of utter failures to predict anything even within a "ball park" range correctly continues to grow exponentially, not only in matters of forecasting and understanding of foreign nations, of which modern U.S. elites have always known very little, if anything at all.[28] The question is increasingly whether those elites and decision makers have a grasp of their own nation. One could explain the lack of Russia's domestic reaction to the alleged worsening of the situation by "Putin's propaganda" only for so long before this "explanation" would become stale and tired, and therefore utterly ineffective. The issue is how the economy really works in Russia, or Iran, or China or elsewhere for that matter—a lesson American exceptionalists and evangelicals of a "free market" decidedly didn't want to learn for ideological and political reasons or, as the terrifying conclusion itself inevitably warrants, were and are simply incapable of learning. The oil crisis gave the answer—it was the latter rather than the former and it has massive geopolitical implications.

* * *

The COVID-19 pandemic and the grossly, and possibly deliberately, disproportionate response to it in the U.S. and Europe were the trigger for both economic collapse and, with it, for the most severe oil crisis in history. But both the global economy and, consequently, the demand for oil were shrinking well before the onset of pandemic. The issue was systemic and the collapse was inevitable with or without the pandemic. It is yet undetermined how much malicious intent was behind the decisions which were made, but in the larger scheme of things the crisis has proven that hydrocarbons in general and oil in particular are not going anywhere as the main driver of the global economy any time soon. The September 2020 report of the U.S. Energy Information Administration read like a verdict to adherents of the "green" energy utopia:

> Fossil fuels, or energy sources formed in the Earth's crust from decayed organic material, including petroleum, natural gas, and coal, continue to account for the largest share of energy production and consumption in the United States. In 2019, 80% of domestic energy production was from fossil fuels, and 80% of domestic energy consumption originated from fossil fuels.[29]

Needless to say, out of the 20% remaining related to non-fossil energy production and consumption, renewables constituted a slightly larger share than nuclear. Among those renewables traditional hydroelectric power and biomass exceeded the production of energy by the staples of environmentalists, solar and wind, by more than two times, thus reducing the share of politically important but economically and technologically questionable sources to slightly below 4% of the whole of America's energy output.[30] Energy trends were mercilessly oblivious of the "green" energy agenda and, realistically, left very few options for growing the United States Green movement, an ideological outgrowth supported primarily by the Democratic Party, if it were to have any realistic economic program based on actual, workable and economically viable technologies without destroying the foundation of the modern, completely energy-dependent civilization. For the United States, whose "romance" with the shale oil and status of net energy exporter was fairly short-lived in historic terms, the exhibit A of a complete economic madness induced by the ideology of the fight with climate change could have easily be found in Europe.

The issue of climate change stopped being a scientific issue long ago, turning into a moral crusade wrongly attributed in the United States to "the left," or more generally, to liberals. Of course, climate changes, but the core of the problem is the question of why it changes. A whole generation of people in the West have now grown up believing that climate change is anthropogenic, that is, caused by humans. This view dominates the Western climate change field and is serving as a new blanket diversion of a decades-old movement against the very real and, indeed, anthropogenic pollution of the environment. One of the most telling examples is this very shale oil industry into which the U.S. has plunged full throttle forward, which is extracted by the process of fracking, which leads to poisoning of the sources of drinking water, creates large underground cavities which threaten surface infrastructure and property with earthquakes and with damage to property. In the end, there are other health hazards associated with this, or even traditional, extraction methods. Yet, there is no a shred of viable evidence, except for ever unreliable models, that humanity's activity drives climate change.

Vladimir Putin, as a President of Russia, is certainly not a climate scientist, but he surely is advised by one of the best climate and environment scientists in the world and Putin is on record: climate change is not caused by humans.[31] But for the

West in general and the United States in particular where the views of largely uneducated celebrities, a semi-literate school girl from Sweden or of people with journalism background, a euphemism for a degree in language, constitute a viable pool of opinions, any truly scientific counter-argument is of no reason for contemplation for them. But the fate of Germany and her energy-suicide by laying down her once powerful industrial economy at the altar of ignorance and incompetence in pursuit of a green energy chimera should serve as a warning to everyone.

One of the most startling statistics for Germany is the fact that the German economy was in a state of paralysis or decline for years. Already by August 2019 the German economy had been, as one observer put it, stuttering for several months in a row as Germany's manufacturing levels fell to the lowest in six years.[32] By August of 2020, a year later, Germany's economy was in a free fall.[33] The connection between energy and Germany's economic decline may not be immediately evident for many but it is a direct connection, because Germany's goods are extremely energy dependent and energy, or rather its price, is the main contributor to costs, thus making Germany's goods, from cars to consumer products, less competitive to, as an example, Chinese goods which have both lower labor and, most importantly, lower energy costs. As *Forbes* reported in September of 2019:

> A new report by consulting giant McKinsey finds that Germany's *Energiewende,* or energy transition to renewables, poses a significant threat to the nation's economy and energy supply. One of Germany's largest newspapers, *Die Welt*, summarized the findings of the McKinsey report in a single word: "disastrous."...
> McKinsey issues its strongest warning when it comes to Germany's increasingly insecure energy supply due to its heavy reliance on intermittent solar and wind. For three days in June 2019, the electricity grid came close to blackouts.[34]

For anyone who has ever had layovers in Germany's airports, such as in Frankfurt-am-Main, during heat waves, which are not uncommon for Germany or Europe in summer months, the overriding feeling is utter discomfort from heat. Air conditioners simply are not allowed. The contrast between the instant transition between a cool and comfortable aircraft cabin and the airport itself in such weather can be shocking. Human comfort, and sometimes even health for those with heart and other conditions, takes a distant second place in Germany to "environmental concerns," since air conditioners allegedly harm the environment. This puts a better face on it than admitting to the factor of costs. In December of 2019 the cost of $0.38 per *kWh* (*kiloWatthour*) of electricity for an average German household was the second highest in the world, after Bermuda. For comparison, the same *kWh* in the United States cost $0.14, and in Russia—$0.06.[35] For businesses, Germany's price for kWh was $0.23—the highest among developed nations, with the United States at $0.11. Russia was at $0.08; China was at $0.10.[36] The conclusion thus is inevitable. Given that Germany has the highest energy costs in the world for a developed industrial economy the prospects for Germany's survival as a totally independent competitive advanced economy look increasingly slim, once one considers not only Germany's energy policy but that of the EU as a whole, which among competent industrial and energy professionals creates a sense of bewilderment.

But bewildered they must not be. Germany's approach, or rather madness, in its commitment to a false premise of "saving a planet" is rather simple:

> Ask almost any economist and she'll tell you the same thing: if you want to save the planet from runaway climate change, you have to make energy expensive. "Economics contains one fundamental truth about climate-change policy," wrote Yale University economist William Nordhaus in 2008, who won the 2018 Nobel Prize for his work. "For any policy to be effective in solving global warming, it must raise the market price of carbon, which will raise the market

prices of fossil fuels and the products of fossil fuels."
Various policies can be used to make electricity more
expensive. For example, you can tax carbon emissions
or put in place air pollution regulations. However,
the most popular way to make energy expensive is
to do what Germany has done and that's to subsidize
solar and wind energies through a surcharge (or tax)
on electricity. But such efforts beg the question: why,
if making energy expensive is required to reduce
emissions, does France generate less than one-tenth
the carbon emissions of Germany at nearly half the
cost?[37]

The answer to this question is rather simple, France produces
more than 72% of its electricity at nuclear power stations—an
absolute taboo in Germany, which by its own volition abandoned
its advanced nuclear energy industry in 2000s as a result of policies
promoted by Germany's vocal and influential "Greens" and after
public pressure mounted following the Fukushima nuclear plant
catastrophe. Today, the chickens have come home to roost, and
even France, which leads the world in a share of energy produced
at nuclear power plants, cannot shake the EU's utopian plans of
becoming "carbon-neutral" by 2050. These goals became law
in both Germany and France in 2019.[38] On paper the goals look
good and, moreover, nuclear energy holds a great promise as a
stepping stone towards new, non-hydrocarbon, sources of energy
but only under one condition—that these new sources are capable
of sustaining the cornerstone of modern advanced civilization—
the electric grid. Neither solar nor wind power—idolized by
generations of Greta Thunberg worshippers, most of whom
have never worked a day in the real productive economy—are
capable of maintaining the voltages and frequencies required for
the survival and stability of the electric grid. Nor is the issue of
storage of the energy required for maintaining a grid resolved.
   Yet this doesn't prevent the European and increasingly
radicalized American environmentalists from pushing an
agenda which undermines the very foundation of modern

human civilization, one which had overall improved the human condition—from transportation to abundance of food, to comfortable living—humanity's ability to extract resources and convert them into various types of energy. Remarkably in Europe, people who are behind the most radical environmentalist ideas are people who have absolutely no background in the energy industry or in any actual industry at all. In 2017 the French Ecology Ministry or, using its full title, the Ministry for Ecological Transition, or as it was known then, the Ministry of Ecological and Solidarity Transition, was headed by Nicolas Hulot. Hulot is a remarkable figure in the European environmental movement since all kinds of politically and ideologically attractive entries are in his resume, such as his being a journalist and an ecological activist, but there are no entries related to a natural or engineering science background, which might be regarded as required for running that ministry in such a nation as France, to be found.[39] Unsurprisingly, Hulot was for phasing out nuclear energy.

Hulot's personality and lack of any serious skills required for managing the extremely complex economic and technological issues in relation to ecology and its relationship to the technical needs of the infrastructure is instructive, but by no means unique for Europe. In her Address on the State of European Union, the President of European Commission, Ursula von der Leyen, went all in for ecology, placing it first in the address, and proposed even tighter restrictions on hydrocarbons' use.[40] Leyen, who is a gynecologist and a child care specialist by education and a political bureaucrat by calling, is known primarily by her disastrous tenure as Germany's Defense Minister.[41] In the Western world where professional and human qualities have been sacrificed at the altar of political correctness, media appearances and de facto corruption in the top political echelons, the survival and even thriving of the pseudo-scientific, economic laws and common-sense defying ideologies, such as radical environmentalism, are not only predictable, but inevitable. Things will get much worse in Europe and they may never get better.

The United States, however, is in no position to rejoice. The U.S. meritocracy is dead and most likely is never coming back, as the events of few last years have demonstrated so manifestly. Yet the United States, at least for now, has one crucial advantage over Europe, which will be eaten both from the inside and from the outside by the United States—if the U.S. survives as a unified nation. Contingent upon America's success in sabotaging the Nord Stream 2 gas pipeline from Russia to Germany, the United States may yet force Europe to abandon what amounts to the last straw in Europe's losing struggle against energy insufficiency and economic insolvency, grossly aggravated by its environmental fundamentalism. This may become the United States' largest geoeconomic triumph, even if short-lived, since it will enable the U.S. to kill two rabbits with one shot: forcing Europe to buy its much more expensive hydrocarbons, including Liquefied Natural Gas (LNG), thus simultaneously sinking the competitiveness of European goods, which are already barely afloat, and giving a boost to whatever other American-made products may be available for export to Europe, other than energy and weapons.

This is the name of the game today and the fate of Europe is of secondary, if not tertiary, concern to the United States which, quite naturally, will do all it can to survive. If that will be at European expense, so be it. All means of sabotaging European attempts at obtaining affordable energy are already being employed, from false-flag operations (e.g. Russia's "opposition" leader Alexey Navalny's "poisoning," with a possible involvement of British special services), to mounting campaigns of blackmail and subversion of those few remaining people in European politics who have not succumbed to an ideological brainwashing and addiction, to "two minute hate" sessions towards technological and economic sense, which diminishes in Europe with an astonishing speed.[42] Russians anticipated these developments. After Germany's transparently false statements on Navalny's "poisoning," Russia's Foreign Minister Sergei Lavrov, addressing the EU in general and Germany in particular in what for Russian diplomacy were unprecedentedly harsh terms, clarified Russia's intentions as:

In other words, to provide for ourselves for all possibilities, if the EU remains on its negative destructive positions, to be independent from its whims and that we can ensure our own autonomous development, as well as in partnership with those who are ready to cooperate on equal basis and mutual respect.[43]

Lavrov's statement amounted to a Kremlin ultimatum to Germany—to decide what Germany really wanted, reliable energy supply which would give her economy a fighting chance, or to finally completely succumb to American demands and irrevocably formalize her vassalage, which, in the end, would turn Germany into a third world nation with obsolete and insolvent industries which will fall victim to Chinese, American and even Russian competition. After all, it is not Russia's responsibility to sacrifice her interests for Germany. In the end, just a brief look at the EU's political power elite and its incompetence and cowardice leaves very little doubt that the days of EU are numbered. Some people in the United States understand that and work tirelessly towards this end, despite the fact that the incompetence and malfeasance of American elites sometimes exceeds all reasonable expectations.

Russia's message, however, contained one very serious and almost explicitly stated point. While the United States was going out of its way to sabotage Nord Stream 2, the geoeconomic and geopolitical reality remains unchanged. As one of the most respected and astute of Russia's geopolitical analysts, Rostislav Ishenko, noted: "For Russia the closing of Nord Stream 2 project is merely an unpleasantness, for Germany—it is a catastrophe."[44] Even Russia's proverbial patience has its limits, but Russia, unlike the EU and, in the end, also unlike the United States, has the luxury of energy and time, and a much larger number of degrees of freedom. Ironically, at the foundation of all that are Russia's enormous natural resources, especially energy, which have been used to pull Russia out of the rut of neoliberal economics and suicidal radical ideologies.

Endnotes

1 Mir Yusif Mir Babaev, "Azerbaijan's Oil History, A Chronology Leading up to the Soviet Era," *Azerbaijan International,* Summer 2002 (10-2), 34, https://www.azer.com/aiweb/categories/magazine/ai102_folder/102_articles/102_oil_chronology.html.

2 Ibid.

3 "Crude Oil Production," *Trading Economics,* https://tradingeconomics.com/country-list/crude-oil-production.

4 *Total energy production, 2019,* Global Energy Statistical Yearbook 2020, https://yearbook.enerdata.net/total-energy/world-energy-production.html.

5 "Electricity production, 2019," *Global Energy Statistical Yearbook 2020,* https://yearbook.enerdata.net/electricity/world-electricity-production-statistics.html.

6 Nayla Razzuk, Grant Smith , Natalia Kniazhevich , and Golnar Motevalli, "OPEC+ Talks Collapse, Blowing Hole in Russia-Saudi Alliance," *Bloomberg,* March 6, 2020, https://www.bloomberg.com/news/articles/2020-03-06/opec-fails-to-reach-deal-as-russia-refuses-deeper-oil-cuts.

7 Ibid.

8 US Energy Information Administration, "US Field Production of Crude Oil," August 31, 2020, https://www.eia.gov/dnav/pet/hist/LeafHandler.ashx?n=PET&s=MCRFPUS2&f=A.

9 "United States Crude Oil Production," *Trading Economics,* https://tradingeconomics.com/united-states/crude-oil-production.

10 Darius Rafieyan, "As Oil Prices Drop and Money Dries Up, Is the US Shale Boom Going Bust?" *NPR,* November 20, 2019, https://www.npr.org/2019/11/20/780879474/as-oil-prices-drop-and-money-dries-up-is-the-u-s-shale-boom-going-bust.

11 Jennifer Hiller, "Few US shale firms can withstand prolonged oil price war," *Reuters,* March 15, 2020,
https://www.reuters.com/article/us-global-oil-shale-costs-analysis-idUSKBN2130HL.

12 Andrew Hecht, "Breakeven Crude Oil Production Costs Around the World," *Yahoo Finance,* April 27, 2020, https://finance.yahoo.com/news/breakeven-crude-oil-production-costs-085329648.html.

13 Ibid.

14 Mitchel McGeorge, "Do US Shale Drillers Deserve to Exist in Free Markets?" *Yahoo Finance,* April 18, 2020, https://finance.yahoo.com/news/u-shale-drillers-deserve-exist-230000144.html.

15 Ian Bremmer, "Why Russia and Saudi Arabia Are In a Battle Royal Over Oil Prices," *Time,* March 19, 2020, https://time.com/5806218/russia-saudi-arabia-oil/.

16 Solange Reyner, "Oil Prices Collapse as Russia Targets Frackers, $20 Barrel Possible," *Newsmax,* March 8, 2020, https://www.newsmax.com/newsfront/russia-oilproduction-economy-oil/2020/03/08/id/957414/.

17 "Russia's Gold Reserves Will Cushion Oil Price Fall, Says Finance Minister," *Moscow Times,* October 21, 2019, https://www.themoscowtimes.com/2019/10/21/russias-gold-reserves-will-cushion-oil-price-fall-says-finance-minister-a67823.

18 Yale Global, "Oil Crisis Challenges Putin's Power," *Oilprice.com,* April 18, 2020, https://oilprice.com/Geopolitics/International/Oil-Crisis-Challenges-Putins-Power.html.

19 William Watts, "Why oil prices just crashed into negative territory—4 things investors need to know," *Market Watch,* 21 April, 2020, https://www.marketwatch.com/story/why-the-oil-market-just-crashed-below-0-a-barrel-4-things-investors-need-to-know-2020-04-20.

20 Pippa Stevens, "Shale industry will be rocked by $300 billion in losses and a wave of bankruptcies, Deloitte says," *CNBC,* June 22, 2020, https://www.cnbc.com/2020/06/22/shale-industry-will-be-rocked-by-300-billion-in-losses-and-a-wave-of-bankruptcies-deloitte-says.html.

21 Wolf Richter, "The Great American Shale Oil & Gas Massacre: Bankruptcies, Defaulted Debts, Worthless Shares, Collapsed Prices of Oil & Gas," *Wolf Street,* July 10, 2020, https://wolfstreet.com/2020/07/10/the-great-american-shale-oil-gas-massacre-bankruptcies-defaulted-debts-worthless-shares-collapsed-prices-of-oil-and-natural-gas/.

22 George Friedman, "Opinion: Russia is the world's biggest loser from oil's crash, and that's reason to worry," *Market Watch,* April 26, 2020, https://www.marketwatch.com/story/russia-is-the-worlds-biggest-loser-from-oils-crash-and-thats-reason-to-be-worried-2020-04-24.

23 Grant Smith, "OPEC Sees Weaker Outlook as Demand Falters, Shale Recovers," *World Oil,* September 14, 2020, https://www.worldoil.com/news/2020/9/14/opec-sees-weaker-outlook-as-demand-falters-shale-recovers.

24 Simon Watkins, "Saudi Aramco Is Now Suffering the Consequences of a Failed Oil Price War," *Oilprice.Com,* September 10, 2020, https://oilprice.com/Energy/Energy-General/Saudi-Aramco-Is-Now-Suffering-The-Consequences-Of-A-Failed-Oil-Price-War.html.

25 "$600 billion: Despite Covid-19 crisis & falling oil prices, Russia's gold & foreign exchange reserves reach all-time high," *RT.com,* 13 August, 2020, https://www.rt.com/russia/497956-russia-gold-exchange-high/.

26 Alam Saleh, Zakiyeh Yazdanshenas, "Iran's Pact with China Is Bad News for the West," *Foreign Policy,* August 9, 2020, https://foreignpolicy.com/2020/08/09/irans-pact-with-china-is-bad-news-for-the-west/.

27 "*В российском бюджете снизилась доля нефтегазовых доходов*" (The Share of oil-gas revenues in Russia's Budget has declined), *Ria.Ru,* 20 August 20, 2020, https://ria.ru/amp/20200820/1576013144.html.

28 Daniel Larison, "Why the US Fails to Understand Its Adversaries," *The American Conservative,* April 5, 2018.

29 US Energy Information Administration, "Fossil fuels account for the largest share of US energy production and consumption," September 14, 2020, https://www.eia.gov/todayinenergy/detail.php?id=45096.

30 US Energy Information Administration, Table 1.2 Primary Energy Production by Source, 2019, https://www.eia.gov/totalenergy/data/browser/index.php?tbl=T01.02#/?f=A&start=1949&end=2019&charted=1-2-3-4-6-13.

31 While 29% of the Russian economy is dependent on fossil fuels, Putin has no stake in promoting "climate denialism" because Russia leads the world in fast neutron nuclear reactors, and in the swiftly developing nuclear field, including MOX fuel. Moreover, Russia industry is driven by natural gas, which is clean, and by hydroelectric energy. Russian geophysics is more capable of assessing climate realities because it relies not only on top-notch mathematical modelling but on one of the best climate empirical data collecting machines. In the Arctic, nobody, I underscore it, nobody even approaches Russia's capabilities in terms of data collection. It is not even a theorem—it is an axiom. Western climate "science" is nothing more than white board-created math "models" operating on GIGO—Garbage In, Garbage Out, which is delivered in accordance to the current "ideological" trend. See, "Russian President Vladimir Putin says humans not responsible for climate change," *France 24,* March 31, 2017, https://www.france24.com/en/20170331-russian-president-vladimir-putin-says-humans-not-responsible-climate-change.

32 Yusuf Khan, "Germany's economy is flopping and the manufacturing sector just keeps declining — here's why recession could be around the corner," *Business Insider,* August 29, 2019, https://markets.businessinsider.com/news/stocks/german-economy-3-reasons-economy-is-flopping-headed-for-recession-2019-8-1028484056#.

33 "German economy contracts at record pace, recovery hinges on consumers," *CGTN,* August 25, 2020, https://news.cgtn.com/news/2020-08-25/German-economy-contracts-at-record-pace-recovery-hinges-on-consumers-Tfe0O3gQ00/index.html.

34 Michael Schellenberg, "Renewables Threaten German Economy & Energy Supply, McKinsey Warns in New Report," *Forbes,* September 5, 2019, https://www.forbes.com/sites/michaelshellenberger/2019/09/05/renewables-threaten-german-economy-energy-supply-mckinsey-warns-in-new-report/#4f4073be8e48.

35 *Electricity prices for households, December 2019*, Global Petrol Prices, https://www.globalpetrolprices.com/Germany/electricity_prices/.

36 Ibid.

37 Michael Schellenberg, "If Saving the Climate Requires Making Energy So Expensive, Why Is French Electricity So Cheap?" *Forbes,* February 5, 2019, https://www.forbes.com/sites/michaelshellenberger/2019/02/05/if-saving-the-climate-requires-making-energy-so-expensive-why-is-french-electricity-so-cheap/#274ff43d1bd9.

38 "Which countries have a net zero carbon goal?" *Climate Home News,* June 14, 2019, https://www.climatechangenews.com/2019/06/14/countries-net-zero-climate-goal/.

39 "Nicolas Hulot," Personnalite, *Le Point,* https://www.lepoint.fr/tags/nicolas-hulot#.

40 "ROUNDUP Von der Leyen: 'Machen wir Europa stark,'" *Cash,* September 16, 2020, https://www.cash.ch/news/politik/roundup-von-der-leyen-machen-wir-europa-stark-1619984.

41 Matthew Karnitschnig, "The inconvenient truth about Ursula von der Leyen," *Politico,* July 2, 2019, https://www.politico.eu/article/ursula-von-der-leyen-biography-career-inconvenient-truth/.

42 Poland works hard on US behalf to sabotage Nord Stream 2 as shown in one of many articles, such as this one from RT: "'Crazy' for Polish PM to suggest Nord Stream 2 pipeline is a 'threat' to European energy security," September 17, 2019, *RT,* https://www.rt.com/news/469024-nord-stream-threat-energy-security/].

43 *"Лавров: Мы убедились в ненадежности наших западных партнеров"* (Lavrov: We are now convinced of the unreliability of our western partners), *EDaily.Com,* September 13, 2020, https://eadaily.com/ru/news/2020/09/13/lavrov-my-ubedilis-v-nenadezhnosti-nashih-zapadnyh-partnerov.

44 Rostislav Ishenko, *"Ростислав Ищенко: Лавров предложил Меркель выбор между Россией и Навальным"* (Rostislav Ishenko: Lavrov offered Merkel a choice between Russia and Navalny), *Discred.ru,* September 11, 2020, https://www.discred.ru/2020/09/11/rostislav-ishhenko-lavrov-predlozhil-merkel-vybor-mezhdu-rossiej-i-navalnym/.

5. MAKING THINGS

How the Real Economy Works

Michael Hudson is not the only prominent Western economic thinker who is consistently on record warning about the travails and in the end, the inevitable grievous conclusion of finance capitalism. And not all American and Western elites are in complete denial of the fact that there is an inherent tendency at work that is much more profound and much more dangerous than capitalism's mere economic cycles, that is driving modern capitalism's unprecedented economic and political crises. Republican Senator from Florida Marco Rubio is one of the more unexpected if not corroborators, then at least not denialists of Hudson's view of the modern state of American economic affairs as analogous to a financial "parasite" killing its host. While Rubio, by his own admission, was an unabashed believer in American exceptionalism—precisely the very disease driving America's precipitous decline—he was forced to reassess his views after running his (unsuccessful) presidential campaign and learning that many Americans didn't share his "exceptionalist" views of their country.[1]

In the breaks between his traditional anti-China tropes and his exhibition of naivete about how manufacturing capacity and innovation are related, Rubio was surprisingly forthcoming when speaking about the state of the real—productive, that is—economy in the United States, and offered a glimpse of how some at the highest political level view and understand what the real economy and the foundation of national security are:

> American policymakers must pursue policies that
> make our economy more productive by identifying the
> critical value of specific, highly productive industrial

sectors and spurring investment in them. Industries like aerospace, rail, electronics, telecommunications, and agricultural machinery—in essence, the same industries China is trying to dominate via their Made in China 2025 initiative—will create opportunities for dignified work and be vital to national interest... Jobs in "physical economy" sectors like advanced manufacturing have historically been highly productive because they create tangible products...[2]

It was a rather startling statement, including Rubio's consternation concerning the role of the financial sector and Wall Street, coming from a member of a political party which is not just a synonym for the Wall Street presence in American politics but historically serving as an incubator for gestating and perpetuating policies which saw an historically unprecedented offshoring of American industries to China, thus greatly accelerating the emergence of America's economic, and ultimately geopolitical, rival. Republicans, ever confident in the virtues of free trade orthodoxy and neoliberal policies, played a direct role in China's economic miracle when they provided the bulk of the votes in favor of *House Resolution 4444 China Trade Bill* in May of 2000.[3] The GOP also didn't shy away from making the vote pass overwhelmingly in Senate on 19 September 2000.[4] While China's path to the World Trade Organization (WTO) was effectively, de facto, concluded on Democrat President Clinton's watch, its accession had already been formalized on December 11, 2001 during the George W. Bush presidency.

In one of the most profoundly mindless and ignorant statements of America's foreign and economic policy, Bill Clinton proclaimed that:

Today the House of Representatives has taken an historic step toward continued prosperity in America, reform in China and peace in the world. If the Senate votes as the House has just done, to extend permanent normal trade relations with China, it will open new

doors of trade for America and new hope for change
in China. Seven years ago, when I became president,
I charted a new course for a new economy—a course
of fiscal discipline, investment in our people and open
trade. I have always believed that by opening markets
abroad we open opportunities at home. We've worked
hard to advance that goal of more open and more
fair trade since 1993, all the way up to the landmark
legislation I signed just a few days ago to expand
trade with Africa and the Caribbean Basin.[5]

Cringeworthy in its sheer falsity and insufferable pathos—
the economic equivalent of Chamberlain's "Peace in Our Time"
1938 proclamation, after signing the Munich capitulation to
Hitler—Clinton's declaration rattled even those who otherwise
wouldn't even pay much attention to the economic affairs of the
United States. America's trade unions certainly were not amused
by his opening the door for American jobs to be shipped abroad.
Yet, as late as 2012, Bill Clinton still had two thirds of Americans
holding a favorable opinion of him, despite even the liberal
Huffington Post calling him an *outsourcerer-in-chief*.[6] China,
too, wasn't upset; why would it be? Both NAFTA and China's
accession to the WTO served as a massive vacuum cleaner
sucking the life from American industries and, to be sure, these
weren't banking or financial consulting "industries" which were
being shipped abroad. American manufacturing started to leave its
own shores. And even the Council on Foreign Relations, whose
many forecasts require a serious second opinion, summarized
rather accurately the extent to which China benefited from its
American-driven WTO accession. While the U.S. real economy
started its prolonged dive into oblivion, China's economy grew
8-fold since 2001, enabling China to lift an unprecedented 400
million of its citizens out of poverty.[7] While the Chinese success
was astonishing, the American benefits were very modest, and
that is speaking politely.
    The most remarkable aspect of the whole proceeding is the
fact that China realistically cannot be blamed for interfering with

America's committing economic suicide based on its abstract economic theories, which completely disregarded issues of real national power, the way this had emerged in the first half of the 20th century through the two world wars. China accepted what was offered; what was offered made China the de facto primary consumer goods manufacturing hub of the world. The offer was too good to be refused, and it made true a reference to the famous one-liner, misattributed to a variety of notable Marxists, from Lenin to Marx himself, that the capitalist will sell the very rope on which he will be hanged. Irrespective of the attribution of this one-liner, it described the entire accession of China to the WTO extremely well. The United States gave China the capacity to make things, the only capacity which matters in the real world, because it is in making things where real wealth and value are created. Marco Rubio, evidently, had that economic epiphany in 2020 when he concluded that: "…whether that's an in-orbit solar array, an electric vehicle, or a home… Their value isn't immediately diminished or reduced to zero after use, but instead endures and multiplies."[8]

This simple economic formula should have served from the inception as a Winston Smith reality measuring stick of sorts, that: "Freedom is the freedom to say that two plus two make four. If that is granted, all else follows."[9] But it didn't. The entire conceptualization of the role and place of manufacturing as such in the overall economy has been deconstructed, and that by America's political, financial, cultural and educational elites, most of whom have never worked a day on a manufacturing floor, and would qualify primarily for the title of office plankton. The attempts in the United States to praise men and women of productive industries have been few and far between, with even such cinematographic gems as John Wells' 2010 genuinely socially conscious movie *The Company Men* enjoying only a very moderate success, scoring a modest 6.7 at *IMDB* while the audience at *Rotten Tomatoes* gave this excellent film a dismal 55%. The consensus on the website reads: "It might be hard for most viewers to identify with *The Company Men*'s well-heeled protagonists, but writer/director John

Wells uses their plight to make universally resonant points—and gets the most out of his excellent cast."[10]

There is little doubt that few Americans can identify with the protagonist in the movie, played by Ben Affleck. After all, owning a new Porsche sports cars and memberships in elite golf clubs is beyond the reach of most Americans. But the point here is not the lack of identification with the characters of the Ben Affleck and Tommy Lee Jones corporate heavy-weights, it is about work in a productive capacity, about people engaged in productive labor with whom many Americans, as late as early 2000, could identify. But that time has passed. Instead, George Lopez' spoiled niece, Veronica, brilliantly played by the talented Aimee Garcia, is more in line with the contemporary audience perspective—Veronica, who cringes just from the mention of working for George Lopez' aircraft parts company, even though the job is in the office, not on the manufacturing floor.[11] Aimee Garcia's character in this show is easy for very many in modern America to identify with, including people who are adults. The fictitious Veronica does resonate with many, despite her being obnoxious and spoiled. In modern America the manufacturing professions are not held in high esteem, and the facts and numbers speak volumes. The 2018 Interagency report to Donald Trump identified the problem in no uncertain terms:

> Some of the most challenging aspects in the manufacturing sector are recruitment and retention. In a recent manufacturing skills gap study conducted by the Manufacturing Institute and Deloitte, only one third of respondents indicated they would encourage their children to pursue a career in manufacturing. Gen Y (ages 19-33 years) respondents ranked manufacturing as their least preferred career destination. Yet once a candidate is hired, the struggle continues. 79% of executives surveyed stated it is moderate to extremely challenging to find candidates to pass screening and/or the probationary period, leaving them with employees unable to perform

the work for which they were hired. While the total number of bachelor's degrees in the U.S. has increased steadily in the last two decades, the number of STEM degrees conferred in the U.S. still pales compared to China. In addition, the U.S. has seen an increase in students on temporary visas, many of whom would be unable to gain the security clearances needed to work in the defense ecosystem. Growth in advanced science and engineering degrees shows the U.S. graduating the largest number of doctorate recipients of any individual country, but 37% were earned by temporary visa holders with as many 25% of STEM graduates in the U.S. being Chinese nationals.[12]

For the U.S., having China as her main economic rival, the issue of its inadequate access to qualified scientific and engineering cadres is bad enough, but Russia, whose population is more than two times smaller than that of the United States, produced in 2017 almost exact number of STEM graduates as the United States: 561,000 versus 568,000.[13] That means that in per capita terms Russia produces more than two times more STEM graduates than the United States. Moreover, the majority of Russia's STEM graduates are Russians or Russian citizens, despite Russia having developed foreign students' programs in STEM. In other words, the majority of them stay in Russia. This is not the case in the U.S. where more than a third are not U.S. citizens. It is a telling statistic, which gives a glimpse of one of the most fundamental cultural factors in America's economic and industrial decline, because STEM degrees are, by far, not what many associate with this term—computer programming. Rather, these degrees provide highly qualified engineering cadres for modern industries ranging from food processing, to timber, to transportation, to energy, to aerospace, to shipbuilding, to construction. As Ciaran Hinds' character tells Frances McDormand's character in the light-hearted Hollywood flick *Miss Pettigrew Lives for A Day*: "There's a great deal of engineering in a gentlemen's sock, I'll have you know. In the stitching of the heel. By comparison, designing a brassiere is a piece of cake. Not that there aren't compensations."[14]

Somehow the message—that even simple things such as socks let alone more complex ones such as locomotives or cars require a constant flow of both engineering and manufacturing labor cadres in order to retain manufacturing expertise—has been lost in the contemporary United States. Studying for STEM is hard and the manufacturing floor can sometimes be physically demanding. It also requires a great deal of fundamental math and science skills and attention as well as following stringent workplace safety and quality management requirements. The manufacturing floor is certainly not a place for exercising "free thinking," or to be under the influence of drugs or alcohol. For very many modern American graduates of public schools where the issues of high school football, homecoming and proms, of self-expression, among many other natural problems dominating teenagers' minds, the transition to the rigorous manufacturing professional fields or STEM programs could be a cultural shock, exacerbated by the preceding permissive school environment, leading to America's educational standards in STEM nose-diving even as an oppressive political correctness indoctrination is being established as a main course in school and in many colleges and universities' studies.

In contemporary American culture dominated by poor taste and low quality ideological, agenda-driven art and entertainment, being a fashion designer or a disc jockey or a psychologist is by far a more attractive career goal, especially for America's urban and college population, than foreseeing oneself on the manufacturing floor working as a CNC operator or mechanic on the assembly line. Such occupations, ranging from electricians to laboratory technicians and many others, are not glamorous and they require discipline, focus and actual knowledge-based skills, which are not easily obtained. Making actual material things does require an ability to follow a lot of rules—a trait being discredited in the United States daily by the opposite, with breaking rules being extolled as a virtue. It would appear from coverage of the mainstream media that rebellion of any kind is viewed as moral and justified, and even praising murder is no longer shocking in the new America's political and cultural "normal"—as evidenced, surprisingly, in *a Law Enforcement Journal* article by Jenna Curren titled "Tough luck, don't be a Trump Supporter in Portland"—another sign of the United States spiraling toward the crude cultural and political behavior in third world nations.[15] Such an environment is not conducive to the emergence of social aspirations underpinning productive and creative labor. The times of *Rosie the Riveter* or of Uncle Sam putting his factory hat on in front of silhouettes of America's industrial plant are long gone—along with their high-paying jobs. America's massive deindustrialization in fact fostered its massive educational infantilization, and its political and cultural undoing followed.

Of course, one may write an entire treatise on how America's dominating cultural archetypes, granted they were pushed by propaganda, went from the remarkably resolute but still feminine Rosie the Riveter and Uncle Sam's masculine images to ones worthy of the decadent manifestations of the Weimar Republic, captured well in Bob Fosse's *Cabaret*. In the end, America's cultural and political decline are direct consequences of its precipitously diminishing ability to make—produce, that is—things which matter and that Americans need.

* * *

Anatol Lieven, in an article with the symptomatic title of *How the West Lost*, correctly assessed the West's dire economic predicament vis-à-vis China:

> One of the most malign effects of western victory in 1989-91 was to drown out or marginalize criticism of what was already a deeply flawed western social and economic model. In the competition with the USSR, it was above all the visible superiority of the western model that eventually destroyed Soviet communism from within. Today, the superiority of the western model to the Chinese model is not nearly

so evident to most of the world's population; and it is
on successful western domestic reform that victory in
the competition with China will depend."[16]

Despite his illustrious academic career in the West, Lieven
continues to exhibit a fragmented mentality when navigating from
larger abstracts and generalizations to particulars which, as the
saying goes, contain this very devil in the details that everyone
tries to avoid. It might be expected from a Ph.D. in political
science, but even while assessing things wrongly in terms of the
actual economy, Lieven does make this crucial observation that:

> Western triumph and western failure were deeply
> intertwined. The very completeness of the western
> victory both obscured its nature and legitimized all
> the western policies of the day, including ones that
> had nothing to do with the victory over the USSR,
> and some that proved utterly disastrous.[17]

Lieven is ultimately correct when trying to trace the pitiful
state today of the West in general and of the United States in
particular to the outcome of the Cold War. In fact, to understand
the present state of the affairs one has to look back even further,
to World War Two. The results and efforts of the allied powers
in defeating German Nazism and Japanese Imperialism have
been grossly misinterpreted in the West, which learned all the
wrong lessons, and which inevitably, in the words of Alexander
Zevin, after the end of the Cold War "turbocharged the neoliberal
dynamic at the *Economist*, and seemed to stamp it with an almost
providential seal."[18]

Neoliberalism and its free-market and deregulation orthodoxy inevitably led to financialization and the removal of
industries from the modern West, with the United States being
exhibit A of the bitter fruits of deindustrialization and the triumph
of the financial sector and the FIRE economy in general, at the
expense of a productive labor force that was already shrinking
due to technical innovation. One of the most startling testimonies

to the catastrophic hollowing out of the American economy by a financial "parasite," in Michael Hudson's parlance, is pointed out by Tyler Durden when discussing the Bank of America Research Investment Committee conclusions:

> As BofA notes, investors should be aware that traditional book value (assets minus liabilities) ignores many of the resources that are most important to companies today. This means that market leaders— such as enterprise software firms—generate cash flows in ways not easily recognized by conventional valuation metrics. At the same time, research & development performed by a company is recognized only as an expense, and investments in the skills of employees have conventionally only been recognized as administrative expenses. But, BofA asks, what's more intuitively valuable to a company like Google: the physical buildings and the network servers inside them, or the intangible algorithms running on those servers? In other words, whereas traditional book value makes sense in an economy composed of factories, farms, and shopping malls, it is increasingly irrelevant in an economy driven by intangibles like patents, licensing agreements, proprietary data, brand value, and network effects. And the punchline: from just 17% in 1975, the total value of corporate intangibles has risen to over $20 trillion, representing a record 84% of all S&P assets![19]

As has been already stated by a number of observers, the "valuation" of America's economy is generally a fraud. The post-industrial economy is a figment of the imagination of Wall Street financial "strategists" and is a cover for having removed productive industries, which are the main drivers of civilization, from their native countries, and then evaluating their own economy by GNP or GDP, a sum of the prices of all its products and services, many of them superficial, as a measure of economic power. The reality is, however, that the United States economy has not been the number one economy in the world for a long time and is hemorrhaging actual value. In other words, the size of American economy is nowhere near its declared "value," and against the background of a Covid-19-induced economic implosion is shrinking even more. As I wrote in 2019, when mathematically deconstructing U.S.-inspired models on the status of nations, China's influence is much greater than that of the U.S.

> This conclusion also follows from the fact that the actual American GDP is formed primarily by non-productive sectors such as finance and services known as the FIRE economy. That explains the consistent pattern of the ever-increasing overall trade deficit for the United States in the last few years. This means, in other words, that the actual size of the American economy is grossly inflated, which is done for a number of reasons primarily related to the status of the U.S. Dollar as reserve currency and the main engine for its proliferation, the Federal Reserve printing press in the U.S. which has long lived beyond its means and is facing a dramatic devaluation of its status, as dedollarization of world economy becomes a mainstream endeavor, in which Russia leads the way.[20]

The simple truth that the mutual shining of each other's boots by two close friends and then paying each other $10 for doing this does not produce $20 of value seems to escape most American economists, who still reside within an echo-chamber which continues to praise the U.S. economy as the "largest economy in the world" despite America's unfolding food insecurity for tens of millions of people and the wholesale collapse of many of America's remaining productive industries, such as a commercial aerospace. Even the news of the July 2020 U.S. trade deficit in goods reaching $80.9 billion, the highest on record, leaves this type of analyst unshaken in their convictions concerning the size of America's economy.[21] The fact that the United States continues to import an increasing amount of goods is also "supplemented" by an unfolding crisis in hunger. While noted in previous chapters, the food insecurity data in America is being compounded on a daily basis. New data draws a picture of a largely third world economy taking hold in the United States. As the *Financial Times* reports:

> Ms Babineaux-Fontenot forecasts a "meal gap" of 8bn meals over the next 12 months, unless more money is provided for people in need. Food prices at a 50-year high will make it even harder to fund those meals, she says. ... But her bigger worry is the long term: after the last financial crisis "it took us 10 years to return to pre-recession rates of food insecurity. So, it could take us 10 years to get out of this crisis." And she, of all people, knows the toll that can take on a generation of America's children.[22]

Apart from commercial aircraft, one of the hallmarks of America's global exports, the second most important indicator, was always America's motor vehicle production. The scale of lost American status vis-à-vis China is documented in 2019 statistics, with the U.S. producing around 10.8 million vehicles against China's 25.7 million—two and a half more vehicles produced than in the United States.[23] How the United States, which by 2015 was 90% dependent on China for its needs in laptops and videogames with TV, could claim the status of a number one economy in the world remains a complete mystery.[24] But American economic valuations, the same as America's election polling starting from 2016, are as reliable as the boy who cried wolf. Raw economic data is damning for the United States. Despite the Trump Administration's attempts to decouple from China, by 2019 China still dominated America's key imports ranging from cellphones and computers to toys.[25] In turn, in 2019 the United States' main exports by far were crude, processed petroleum oils and petroleum gasses. Crude exports alone surpassed the U.S. export of cars, the largest of U.S. finished goods exports, by a hefty $10 billion margin.[26]

Obviously, the United States still retains a significant industrial and agricultural capacity and still produces a variety of finished goods but the size of the manufacturing sector in the United States in January of 2020 was approximately $2.158 trillion, which in itself, when expressed in U.S. Dollars does not provide the full picture.[27] For the same period, the "value" of U.S. GDP provided in services reached an astonishing $13.1 trillion.[28] That is six times more than the manufacturing sector. Even when, the value of the agricultural sector, productive by definition, is added to this calculation, it still cannot change this dramatic third-world economic ratio.

By July 2020, against the background of a massive 31%, drop in GDP, the United States was exhibiting all the traits of an economy which was in a death spiral. No doubt, the stock market continued to grow but the comparisons with China, whose manufacturing plus agriculture ratio to services was roughly 1 to 1.51 in favor of services, could not be made less disturbing for the United States—even when factoring in an additional roughly $600 billion for construction, the ratio was still overwhelmingly in favor of services. Already by 2017, out of all the developed economic entities globally, the United States occupied a position of dubious distinction, having the lowest share of its economy in productive sectors while service at 80% was overwhelmingly dominating the American economic landscape.[29] Even the declining EU had a smaller share of services in its GDP; when compared to Russia or China's ratios, the U.S. was increasingly looking like a nation of slackers capable of producing mostly white collar workers, people who would to a large degree identify with Veronica in the George Lopez sitcom mentioned above, who sought to pursue their future anywhere but on the production floor of the dwindling number of American factories.

As *Industry Week* noted in 2019:

Three years after Donald Trump campaigned for president pledging a factory renaissance, the opposite appears to be happening. Manufacturing made up 11% of gross domestic product in the second quarter, the smallest share in data going back to 1947 and down from 11.1% in the prior period.[30]

This was reported before the Covid-19 closures, which marked the slaughter of the remnants of America's physical economy in which a majority of its real wealth, intellect and expertise had resided for so many years. It was one thing to see a downturn as a result of Covid-19, which introduced grossly overdone, baneful measures but the American economy had been sputtering long before the world heard anything about Covid-19.

* * *

If anything came to embody America's loss of world-class industrial capability it was the story of America's crown jewel and global status commercial aerospace industry, headed by *Boeing*, committing suicide.

The ruthless competition between the aerospace giants Boeing and Airbus is a classic example of geoeconomics. One of the most shining examples of "war by other means" is the scandal related to the air tankers replacement program for the United States Air Force, which initially was won by Airbus' parent, the aerospace concern EADS. Initially EADS won the bid with its tanker based on its A-330 airframe. But after political arm twisting the $35 billion contract went to Boeing in 2011, which won the contract by offering a better price on the tankers based on a B-767 design. The reasons for such a stunning development, as reported by the *Seattle Times,* were:

> Advocates for Boeing had spent months carping that European government subsidies to EADS would give that company an insurmountable price advantage. EADS' allies, mostly from the states around its planned tanker-assembly plant in Mobile, Ala., countered that their plane was a better value.

According to OpenSecrets.org, a website that tracks the influence of money on U.S. politics, Boeing spent more than $17.8 million on all its lobbying expenditures in 2010, more than any other military-aerospace company. In the same year, EADS spent $3.2 million. Boeing also outspent EADS in political campaign contributions to supporters in Congress.[31]

It seemed that the quality of the product was of secondary import when played out against the background of not only the naturally developing economic nationalism sentiment in the United States—after all, it was U.S. Air Force which needed the tankers—but also of political lobbying, a euphemism for bribery. Boeing "won" the contract in 2011 and since then Boeing's *KC-46 Pegasus* tanker's main feature was, and remains, the huge number of technical problems which have plagued this aircraft from its inception. In fact, the never-ending embarrassing technical problems for Boeing's tanker seem only to pile up, with the latest one in 2020—excessive fuel leaks—adding Category 1 issues, the category covering significant impacts on safety and operations, to the issues plaguing the hapless *KC-46 Pegasus*. As a result, 16 aircraft have been grounded to fix, with "utmost urgency" in Boeing's words, yet another embarrassing problem.[32] As expected, those problems have been addressed on Boeing's dime. This also added to a whiff of long-time circulating rumors of Boeing's growing incompetence and dubious design and manufacturing practices until it all came to a head with two deadly crashes of Boeing's B-737 Max commercial aircraft, which took 346 lives.

In 2019 the main reason the B-737 Max killed hundreds of people was reported as follows:

New evidence indicates that Boeing pilots knew about "egregious" problems with the 737 Max airplane three years ago, but federal regulators were not told about them. Investigators say the plane's new flight control system, called MCAS, is at least partially to blame for 737 Max crashes in Indonesia in 2018 and Ethiopia this year that killed 346 people. Acting on data from a single, faulty angle-of-attack sensor, MCAS repeatedly forced both planes into nosedives as the pilots struggled, but failed to regain control.[33]

The faulty MCAS was not just due to incompetent programming, outsourced primarily to India—the bottom line needs to be followed after all.[34] Nor was it just the result of an obsolete, low clearance Boeing-737 constantly updated design, which traces its history back to the 1960s. It was a result of the wholesale loss of American technological and industrial expertise compared to that of Boeing's main rival, Airbus, which was offering a much newer design, conceived in the 1980s, with its first A-320 taking to the skies in 1987, exactly 20 years after Boeing-737's flying for the first time. The A-320 was and is simply a newer and much more flexible aircraft when compared to the venerable Boeing-737, whose low clearance led to a major design flaw in marrying the latest jet engines to an insufficiently high wing in such a manner that it led to the B-737 Max trying to lift its nose uncontrollably, necessitating a forced leveling in the flight performed by the MCAS. Once the system malfunctioned, people died. As one internal e-mail from Boeing's engineers revealed, some viewed the B-737 Max as a plane "designed by clowns who in turn are supervised by monkeys."[35]

Every great industrial nation which produces complex technology tends to have its own share of faulty designs and engineering catastrophes. This is inevitable in the many cases of technological trailblazing; such was the case with the British *de Haviland Comet*, which was the first commercial jet airliner in history, which sustained a number of mid-air disintegrations due to metal fatigue issues not fully understood at the time. But these air catastrophes, as was the case with the Soviet *Tupolev Tu-104*, the world's second commercial jet, known in USSR as a *flying coffin*, were the inevitable teething problems for a new age of commercial aviation. Eventually adjustments and redesigns were implemented both for the *Comet* and the *Tu-104* and they both continued in service into the 1980s.

But by 2018 and 2019, when the B-737 Max crashes occurred, the B-737 basic design had been flying for 50 years. Boeing's attempts to compete with the enormously successful A-320 led to a disastrous attempt to adapt the old design of its main cash earner, the B-737, to modern requirements, an impossible task without the design of a modern, entirely new, aircraft. The crashes of the Indonesian Lion Air Boeing-737 Max on 20 October 2018 and the Ethiopian Airline crash on 10 March 2019 meant more than the crash of a reputation of a particular model of Boeing's aircraft—it was a deadly blow to the reputation of Boeing as a whole. A crown jewel of American industry, a top American industrial brand globally, an embodiment of America's global aerospace and engineering prowess, was exposed as a company with backward design and manufacturing procedures, corruption and caring only for its bottom line.

It may have been unjust for Boeing to have been viewed this way, since it still continued to produce a magnificent and safe wide-body B-777, beloved all over the world for its design. But the B-777 was not Boeing's main cash cow, that was the B-737 in its various iterations. By mid-March 2019 all of the B-737 Max fleet globally was grounded. This was a PR and financial disaster for Boeing. It was especially pronounced compared to the stories of all passengers surviving during the Miracle on the Hudson of U.S. Airways Flight 1549 on 15 January 2009, due to the extraordinary and heroic actions of the crew of Captain Sullenberger, and then in 2019 of Ural Airlines Flight 178 on 15 August 2019, with all passengers surviving due to the skills and heroism of the crew of Captain Yusupov. In both cases the reason for aircraft crash-landings were bird strikes which disabled their engines leading to the aircraft losing power. In both cases the aircraft landed without disintegrating, one on the water and the other in a corn field,. In both cases the pilots and crews were hailed as heroes around the world. In both these cases of miraculous escapes, the aircraft which performed those miracles happened to be the Airbus-320 and Airbus-321. No aircraft manufacturer in the world could even dream about better publicity than that for their aircraft. Reliable, sturdy Airbus-manufactured aircraft which helped their crews to save lives, played out well against the background of the main Airbus competitor destroying lives by allowing aircraft with a deeply flawed design to fly passengers, without even issuing warnings to airlines about serious problems with the B-737 Max. The comparison between Airbus and Boeing was not just warranted, it was irresistible.

Things didn't blow over as was hoped at Boeing. The B-737 Max disasters opened a Pandora's box of trouble for beleaguered Boeing. Things went from bad to worse. Next it was Boeing's cutting-edge B-787 Dreamliner, which was exposed as a plane that didn't meet several of Boeing's own benchmarks. As the *Wall Street Journal* reported:

> The review by the federal regulators extends back to almost a decade and pertains to non-adherence to the aerospace company's own design and manufacturing benchmarks, according to an internal FAA memo seen by the *Journal*. The Dreamliner's rear fuselage reportedly fell short of engineering standards and the FAA is mulling mandatory inspections that could span 900 out of the 1,000 such planes rolled out since 2011. Recently discovered additional lapses in production led to the grounding in August of eight Dreamliners, which are currently being repaired...[36]

While the global commercial aerospace industry was facing a dramatic downturn due to Covid-19 shutting down air travel, it was becoming clear that Boeing's problems were piling up for completely different reasons; events connected to the B-737 Max crashes were unfolding long before the Covid-19 pandemic. At issue was the larger problem of America's dramatically diminishing competence, especially in producing complex, very high-end engineering products. While America was good at making money out of thin air, it was getting increasingly bad at making tangible things. Airbus and its new line of aircraft ranging from A-320NEO to wide-body A-350 looked extremely attractive. Airbus continued to solidify its de facto win over Boeing with November 2019 net orders reaching 719 aircraft, Boeing was at negative 95. There was another factor in Boeing's long-term survival.[37] While the United States continued to shed its manufacturing and with it, the technical expertise required for producing goods from washing machines to commercial aircraft, Boeing was getting some bad news from Russia.

Out of many whiteboard examples of practical geoeconomics, U.S.-Russian economic relations are of a particular interest since historic Russia, first as the Soviet Union and now as the Russian Federation, has been under U.S.-driven international economic sanctions pretty much non-stop since the end of the World War Two. But it was on Barack Obama's watch that it was declared that Russia's economy "was left in tatters," after Russia returned Crimea back home.[38] Obama's statement is a peculiar example of the economic views of America's top political echelon, which are, again, the views of people with primarily social sciences education and experience, ranging from law to political science, most of whom could grasp finance as seen by Wall Street, but have been detached from all aspects that concerned national manufacturing capability all their lives. Popular at that time with regard to anti-Russian sanctions was the argument that, once denied access to "Western technology" due to imposed sanctions, Russia would be incapable of developing her hydrocarbons extraction and processing. Of course, such declarations were ultimately proved false. It's almost impossible to explain to the primarily Ivy League graduates with MBAs or degrees in journalism, political science or sociology, that for a country that builds space stations and taxies American astronauts into orbit there, developing complex industrial technology is a routine process. Not only has Russia successfully proceeded with her own import substitution program, she has counter-sanctioned the West, gone on to win the oil price war, developed her own cutting-edge extraction and processing technologies and, adding insult to injury, gone on to dominate the global wheat market.[39] As the *Financial Times* admitted in the title of its 2020 analysis of Russia's economy: "Russia: adapting to sanctions leaves economy in robust health. Analysts say Moscow now has more to fear from a removal of restrictions than additional ones."[40]

These were hardly the signs of a country with an economy "in tatters," but what was of a particular concern for ailing Boeing was Russia's return to her traditionally rich roots in commercial aviation. Russia's massive global impact in combat aviation can no longer be hidden or obfuscated; no amount of spin can hide a simple fact that not only is Russia a direct and successful competitor to the U.S. combat aviation industry, but that, other than the United States, Russia is the only nation in the world which possesses a complete enclosed technological cycle for her aircraft, meaning a full capability to design, conduct R&D and manufacture completely indigenous, state-of-the-art combat aircraft, a process that involves all stages of design and manufacturing the indigenous airframe, avionics, systems, weapons and engines. The performance and capabilities of Russia's modern combat aircraft, ranging from the multi-purpose SU-30, to the state-of-the-art SU-35, and the fifth generation SU-57 is so above and beyond anything flying today, that for any person who is even remotely acquainted with engineering and complex manufacturing practices, there never was a doubt that Russia would come up with modern and extremely competitive commercial aircraft in the most popular and in demand category—a single aisle medium range airliner. As indeed, Russia did.

As the old aviators' saying goes: "if we are catching flack, we must be over the target." Russia's own medium-range MC-21 aircraft is the most sanctioned aircraft in history. As the media reported:

> MC-21 is a modern, improved mid-range plane, which is set to compete on the market with Airbus 320 and Boeing 737," said Oleg Panteleyev, an aviation analyst who heads industry website Aviaport.ru. An MC-21 prototype made its maiden flight in 2017 but serial manufacturing has been delayed, in part due to U.S. sanctions affecting the production of its carbon composite wings.[41]

In fact, the MC-21 performance is either superior or vastly superior to performance by Boeing, which recognized the obsolescence of its performance assumptions as it related to all modern iterations of the B-737, especially range-wise.[42] The MC-21 is also the only aircraft in its class in the world with composite wing. But if that wasn't bad enough, the MC-21 has what no other non-Western commercial aircraft, such as Chinese COMAC-919, or Brazilian Embraer has—a state-of-the-art high bypass engine, the 100% Russian designed and built PD-14.

The ramifications primarily for Boeing are strategic in nature. Apart from Boeing's woes due to the B-737 Max crashes, the embarrassing revelations about B-787 and a number of totally expected damaging law suits, at the minimum it means the loss of the voluminous Russian market, which by 2020 was saturated with Boeing's aircraft. If Russia's main carrier *Aeroflot* cancelling $5.2 billion worth of 22 B-787s in 2019 wasn't bad enough, the future of Boeing in this most popular segment looks even grimmer.[43] Boeing and its aircraft are omnipresent on the Russian market. Some Russian carriers such as *Azur Airlines* operate with only Boeing aircraft; the fleet of another carrier, *Pobeda*, has 34 aircraft, all of them B-737 800s. Even *Aeroflot*, which prefers the Airbus middle-range A-320/321 still maintains its fleet of 47 B-737s of different modifications.[44] The appearance of an indigenous Russian aircraft superior to the B-737 or A-320 on the Russian market means only one thing in the context of serious geopolitics—the eventual replacement of the Western aircraft by the MC-21. And that was the minimum but the writing is on the wall.

The American reaction was predictable. The U.S. blocked deliveries of carbon-fiber composites to Russia. Vladimir Putin was explicit when calling such practices boorish and underscored the well-known fact that this is the way the West in general, and the U.S. in particular, "compete."[45] The further Russian reaction was also predictable: Russia unveiled her own fast-growing composite materials industry and proceeded to certify the MC-21 with Russian-made composite parts.

The events of Covid-19 and a dramatic downturn in air travel make Boeing's prospects in Russia not very bright. Nor is it looking good for Airbus which now faces stiff competition from the upcoming MC-21 and the regional (much maligned in the West) *Sukhoi Super Jet-100 (SSJ-100)* which serves many routes previously served by middle-range aircraft. Aeroflot alone has a fleet of 54 *SSJ-100s* and the aircraft not only flies actively, it has received very many positive reviews from pilots and passengers The Boeing story in relation to Russia has a lot of hidden irony in it, since for years Boeing's largest engineering office abroad has been located in Moscow. Russian engineers and designers played a major role in developing such aircraft as the B-787, as well as in developing the airframe, interior, and systems design for the 747-400 BCF, 777-200LR and 777-300ER models, as well as the design of the 747 LCF (Large Cargo Freighter).[46]

* * *

What can be said of the coming and inevitable restructuring of the global air travel market applies to any markets which are related to both resources, energy and finished goods, especially complex machinery, where the future portends an increasing competition in the most advanced industrial fields between the declining West, re-emerging Russia and emerging China. This is not just the trivial political scientist catch-phrase of a "return of great power competition," which never went away to start with. It is primarily competition—or if one is willing to operate within a framework of geoeconomics, war by other means—in which the ability to produce needed tangible things of the required quantity and quality becomes crucial for the survival and prospering of any nation that aspires to the stature of a great one.

Today, when one observes America's steadily declining manufacturing capacity, a decline which may be past the point of no return, and when no efforts to reindustrialize may succeed or even be possible, one is tempted to foresee an explosive industrial development in Eurasia, especially in China and Russia. This development ranges from shipbuilding, to aerospace, to cutting edge scientific research to producing a majority of finished goods for the global economy. Of course, even today the United States remains a significant industrial power, but her key industries, with the exception of commercial aircraft, are constantly being overshadowed by "competitors." Even Russia's commercial shipbuilding dwarfs that of the United States, while China's simply makes it irrelevant.

China has its own program, granted fairly conventional and laborious at its birth, of a medium-range commercial aircraft COMAC-919. It is yet to really start fulfilling its certification flight program, but what is significant here is that this attempt is doing exactly the opposite to what the United States did with regard to its own manufacturing by shipping it abroad—China is producing it locally. As Herbert Spencer, one of the fathers of Western liberalism and ideologues of early globalism, noted:

> With the spread of industrialism, therefore, the tendency is toward the breaking down of the divisions between nationalities and running through them of a common organization, if not under a single government, then under the federation of government.[47]

As life has manifestly demonstrated, Spencer was and is wrong—a truth beyond the comprehension of the Wall Street types and political operatives who were brought up on the myth that America cannot be challenged economically, or militarily, and that time will stay still—demonstrably disproved by today's American Rust Belt, her declining cities, disintegrating political system and armies of jobless.

Making things requires more than just a set of technologies, know-how and a skilled labor force, however important these are. It requires a vision and a national self-awareness—a concern for the overall wellbeing of the nation itself—traits which are anathema to modern globalist-oriented American elites who have long been residing in their own delusional bubble, completely detached from reality and the passage of time, which is as ruthless as it is irreversible. In one of the most important observations of the last 50 years, which should be emblazoned at the entrance to any U.S. university claiming to be an alma mater for America's elites, the truth of the matter and the lesson for the future is summarized by the great Corelli Barnett:

> ... swift decline in British vigor at home and the failure to exploit the empire were not owing to some inevitable senescent process of history. That cause was a political doctrine.... The doctrine was liberalism, which criticized and finally demolished the traditional conception of the nation-state as a collective organism, a community, and asserted instead the primacy of the individual. According to liberal thinking a nation was no more than so many human atoms who happened to live under the same set of laws.... It was Adam Smith who formulated the doctrine of Free Trade, the keystone of liberalism, which was to exercise a long-lived and baneful effect on British power.... Adam Smith attacked the traditional "mercantilist" belief that a nation should be generally self-supporting...[48]

The future students of America's greatness should even try to memorize it, or save the image of this ultimate geopolitical and geoeconomic truth emblazoned on their iPhones, all of which, of course, are made in China.

Endnotes

1 "Common Good Capitalism: An Interview with Marco Rubio," *American Affairs,* Vol. IV, No. 1, Spring 2020, 3.

2 Ibid., 10-11.

3 *H.R, 4444 (106th): China Trade bill, In the House,* Govtrack, https://www.govtrack.us/congress/votes/106-2000/h228.

4 *H.R, 4444 (106th): China Trade bill, In the Senate,* Govtrack, https://www.govtrack.us/congress/votes/106-2000/s251.

5 The Associated Press, "President Clinton's Remarks on the Passage of the China Trade Bill," *NYT Archives,* May 25, 2020, https://archive.nytimes.com/www.nytimes.com/library/world/asia/052500clinton-trade-text.html.

6 Jane White, "Bill Clinton's True Legacy: Outsourcer-in-Chief," *Huffington Post,* September 4, 2012, https://www.huffpost.com/entry/bill-clintons-true-legacy_b_1852887.

7 "What Happened When China Joined the WTO?" *World101, CFR,* https://world101.cfr.org/global-era-issues/trade/what-happened-when-china-joined-wto.

8 "Common Good Capitalism," op cit.,11.

9 George Orwell,*1984* (Planet eBook.Com), 103, https://www.planetebook.com/free-ebooks/1984.pdf.

10 "The Company Men," *Rotten Tomatoes,* https://www.rottentomatoes.com/m/the-company-men.

11 George Lopez, "George Gets Caught in a Powers Play," *George Lopez,* Season 5, Episode 16, ABC, originally aired February 22, 2006.

12 Interagency Task Force, *Assessing and Strengthening the Manufacturing and Defense Industrial Base and Supply Chain Resiliency of the United States,* Report to President Donald J, Trump in Fulfillment of Executive Order 13806 (September, 2018), 44.

13 Niall McCarthy, "The Countries with The Most STEM Graduates" [infographic], *Forbes,* February 2, 2017, https://www.forbes.com/sites/niallmccarthy/2017/02/02/the-countries-with-the-most-stem-graduates-infographic/#25a12c13268a.

14 *"Miss Pettigrew Lives for A Day* (2008)," Quotes, *IMDB,* https://www.imdb.com/title/tt0970468/quotes/?tab=qt&ref_=tt_trv_qu.

15 Jenna Curren, "Women on murder of conservative man: 'Tough luck, don't be a Trump supporter in Portland,'" *Law Enforcement Today,* September 19, 2020, https://www.lawenforcementtoday.com/women-on-murder-tough-luck-dont-be-a-trump-supporter-in-portland/.

16 Anatol Lieven, "How the West Lost," *Prospect,* August 31, 2020, https://www.prospectmagazine.co.uk/magazine/how-the-west-lost-victory-communism-moral-defeat.

17 Ibid.

18 Ibid.

19 Tyler Durden, "A Staggering 84% Of All S&P500 Assets Are Now Intangible," *ZeroHedge,* September 15, 2020, https://www.zerohedge.com/markets/staggering-84-all-sp500-assets-are-now-intangible.

20 Andrei Martyanov, *The (Real) Revolution in Military Affairs* (Atlanta: Clarity Press, Inc., 2019), 42.

21 US Census Bureau, "Foreign Trade," *Press Highlights,* July 2020, https://www.census.gov/foreign-trade/statistics/highlights/PressHighlights.pdf.

22 Patti Waldmeir, "A new era of hunger has hit the US," *Financial Times,* September 21, 2020, https://www.ft.com/content/14324641-7be1-4efa-b544-09395429c0e7.

23 OICA, *2019 Production Statistics,* http://www.oica.net/category/production-statistics/2019-statistics/.

24 Caroline Freund, "How Dependent Are US Consumers on Imports from China?" *Peterson Institute for International Economics,* June 7, 2016,

https://www.piie.com/blogs/trade-investment-policy-watch/how-dependent-are-us-consumers-imports-china.

25 Ken Roberts, "After Trump's' 'Order to Look' Tweet, A Look at Top 10 U.S. Chinese Imports, Percent Market Share," *Forbes,* August 23, 2019, https://www.forbes.com/sites/kenroberts/2019/08/23/after-trumps-order-to-look-tweet-a-look-at-top-10-u-s-chinese-imports-percent-market-share/#5b411f16a928.

26 Daniel Workman, "*United States Top 10 Exports,*" *World Top Exports,* August 22, 2020, http://www.worldstopexports.com/united-states-top-10-exports/.

27 "United States GDP From Manufacturing, 2005-2020 Data," *Trading Economics,* https://tradingeconomics.com/united-states/gdp-from-manufacturing.

28 "United States GDP From Private Services Producing Industries," *Trading Economics,* https://tradingeconomics.com/united-states/gdp-from-services.

29 "GDP—composition, by sector of origin," *The World Factbook,* CIA, https://www.cia.gov/the-world-factbook/field/gdp-composition-by-sector-of-origin.

30 Bloomberg, "Manufacturing Is Now Smallest Share of US Economy in 72 Years," *Industry Week,* October 29, 2019, https://www.industryweek.com/the-economy/article/22028495/manufacturing-is-now-smallest-share-of-us-economy-in-72-years.

31 Dominic Gates, "*Tanker shocker: Boeing 'clear winner,'*" *The Seattle Times,* February 25, 2011, https://www.seattletimes.com/business/boeing-aerospace/tanker-shocker-boeing-clear-winner/.

32 Valerie Insinna, "*The Air Force's KC-46 tanker has another serious technical deficiency, and Boeing is stuck paying for it,*" *Defense News,* March 30, 2020, https://www.defensenews.com/air/2020/03/31/the-air-forces-kc-46-tanker-has-another-serious-technical-deficiency-and-boeing-is-stuck-paying-for-it/.

33 David Schaper, "*Boeing Pilots Detected 737 Max Flight Control Glitch 2 Years Before Deadly Crash,*" *NPR,* October 18, 2019, https://www.npr.org/2019/10/18/771451904/boeing-pilots-detected-737-max-flight-control-glitch-two-years-before-deadly-cra.

34 Peter Robison, "Boeing engineers blame cheap Indian software for 737 Max problems," *The Print,* July 2, 2019, https://theprint.in/world/boeing-engineers-blame-cheap-indian-software-for-737-max-problems/256999/.

35 David Shepardson, "'Designed by clowns': Boeing employees ridicule 737 MAX, regulators in internal messages," *Reuters,* January 9, 2020, https://www.reuters.com/article/us-boeing-737max-idUSKBN1Z902N.

36 Shivdeep Dhaliwal, "Boeing Faces Wider Federal Probe Over Dreamliner Jets Failing to Meet Company's Own Benchmarks," *Yahoo Finance,* September 7, 2020, https://finance.yahoo.com/news/boeing-faces-wider-federal-probe-015820812.html.

37 Daniel McCoy, "Airbus cruising to order and delivery wins over Boeing," *Wichita Business Journal,* December 9, 2019, https://www.bizjournals.com/wichita/news/2019/12/09/airbus-cruising-to-order-and-delivery-wins-over.html.

38 "Obama Says Western Sanctions Have Left Russia's Economy 'In Tatters,'" *Moscow Times,* January 21, 2015, https://www.themoscowtimes.com/2015/01/21/obama-says-western-sanctions-have-left-russias-economy-in-tatters-a43069.

39 Anatoly Medetsky and Megan Durisin, "Russia's Dominance of the Wheat World Keeps Growing," *Bloomberg,* September 23, 2020, https://www.yahoo.com/finance/news/russia-dominance-wheat-world-keeps-230100145.html.

40 Henry Foy, "Russia: adapting to sanctions leaves economy in robust health," *Financial Times,* January 29, 2020, https://www.ft.com/content/a9b982e6-169a-11ea-b869-0971bffac109.

41 Andrea Palasciano, "Russia aims high with new passenger plane," AFP, *Yahoo! News,* August 27, 2019, https://news.yahoo.com/russia-aims-high-passenger-plane-030903330.html.

42 Stephen Trimble, "Boeing revises 'obsolete' performance assumptions," *Flight Global,* August 2, 2015, https://www.flightglobal.com/boeing-revises-obsolete-performance-assumptions/117817.article.

43 Eric M. Johnson and Tim Hepher, "Boeing's 787 under pressure as Russia's Aeroflot cancels order," *Reuters,* October 9, 2019, https://www.reuters.com/article/us-boeing-787-orders-idUSKBN1WO2N8.

44 *Перечень эксплуатантов, имеющих сертификат эксплуатанта для осуществления коммерческих воздушных перевозок (выборка из ФГИС "Реестр эксплуатантов и воздушных судов" для сайта Росавиации на 02.09.2020),* [The list of companies with the certificate of a user granted the conduct of commercial flight operations (the excerpt from Federal Government Informational Service "List of users of air ships" for the site of RosAviation 2 September, 2020)], https://favt.ru/dejatelnost-aviakompanii-reestr-komercheskie-perevozki/.

45 *"Путин назвал хамством прекращение поставок деталей для МС-21"* (Putin calls the stoppage of supply of parts for MC-21 a boorishness), *Ria. Ru,* September 24, 2020.

46 Ksenia Zubacheva, "How Boeing and Airbus use Russia's expertise to develop their airplanes," *Russia Beyond,* August 24, 2017, https://www.rbth.com/business/2017/08/24/how-boeing-and-airbus-use-russias-expertise-to-develop-their-airplanes_827604.

47 Herbert Spencer, "The Military and the Industrial Society," *War: Studies From Psychology, Sociology, and Anthropology* (Basic Books, Inc, Publishers, 1964), 306.

48 Corelli Barnett, *The Collapse of British Power* (New York: William Morrow & Company, Inc., 1972), 91.

6. WESTERN ELITES

Incompetent Bunglers at the Helm

Speaking on the Senate's floor on 23 March 2020, Senator John Neely Kennedy of Louisiana encapsulated America's political conundrum in the most definitive terms which, as the history so vividly demonstrated, were not entirely untrue. Addressing the obvious pork barreling of the economic Stimulus Bill by the Democratic Party, a method equally employed by GOP, he reiterated his earlier 2018 point that "Our country was founded by geniuses, but it's being run by idiots."[1] Similarly Stephen Walt went on record in *Foreign Policy* to address American decline, and concluded that one of the pillars of American power which can now be regarded as dead due to its lamentable response to the Covid-19 pandemic was America's competence. Walt didn't mince words:

A third pillar, however, is broad confidence in U.S. competence. When other countries recognize the United States' strength, support its aims and believe U.S. officials know what they are doing, they are more likely to follow the United States' lead. If they doubt its power, its wisdom, or its ability to act effectively, U.S. global influence inevitably erodes. This reaction is entirely understandable: If the United States' leaders reveal themselves to be incompetent bunglers, why should foreign powers listen to their advice? Having a reputation for competence, in short, can be a critical force multiplier.[2]

There is one problem here. Both Senator Kennedy and Stephen Walt were too late in stating the obvious, which many people were beginning to notice long before the Covid-19 pandemic, the financial crisis of 2008 or for that matter, Bill Clinton's presidency.

America's 42nd President, *outsourcer-in-chief*, William Jefferson Clinton, was still admired by large segments of American society in 2015 and that is all one needs to know about the present state of the American politics and how American elites are judged.[3] As one psychological assessment of Bill Clinton concludes:

One of the most important questions here is how a president defines accomplishment. How much is "good"? How much is "enough"? What functions does accomplishment serve in the president's overall psychology? The combination of intense ambition, high self-confidence, and strong self-regard leads Clinton to be very directed toward achievement, but it is achievement of *a particular type*. Modest successes are not sufficient; they are not what he has in mind. His achievement is self-defined at extremely high—even grandiose—levels of attempted accomplishment. Nor is the passage of *some* major policy initiatives enough. Some, even many, can be too few, given Clinton's definition of success.[4]

This psychological portrait of Bill Clinton may be a curious trivial detail in an overall assessment of America's decline—but it reveals a crucial fact helping to complete the picture of America's deadly political dysfunction, because Bill Clinton can serve as an Exhibit A symptom of an ailment which has afflicted America's ruling class as a whole: grandiosity. Clinton's presidency also marks the starting point of America's overstretching itself into the friable self-proclaimed global hegemon, which today, far from being able to control its empire, is going through an historically unprecedented dissolution of the governance of its own country. Bill Clinton's 11-foot brass statue and a namesake boulevard in the city of Pristina, the capital of a Serbian province turned, with the decisive help of the United States and NATO, into the initially self-proclaimed nation of Kosovo are good reminders, together with the massive U.S. Army base Camp Bondsteel in this very same Kosovo, of the American political class's inability not only to formulate modest and realistic objectives but its reflection of Bill Clinton's traits of extreme ambition and self-regard—now a defining trait of most in the American elites. It is legitimate to state that the majority of American elites suffer from Bill Clinton's syndrome—a grandiose misjudgment of their own capabilities when pursuing America's many utopias, a process which has finally resulted in what can broadly be defined as a national catastrophe.

America is a country steeped in the extremes, intense ambitions and grandiosity. Everything American must be the largest, the fastest, the most efficient or, in general, simply the best. Since the times of the famous Alexis de Tocqueville observation on the "garrulous" American patriotism in 1837 little has changed.[5] Sometimes this grandiosity is pardonable—some of America's claims to greatness are definitely valid—but even when it is explicitly not the best, its propensity for grandiosity still overtakes discourse despite all facts negating such a state of affairs. This trait manifests itself most profoundly at the levels of what can broadly be defined as America's intellectual class, sometimes called *intelligentsia,* and its political and business leaders. The majority of regular Americans are generally very nice folks, who do not necessarily bother themselves with matters of the global balance of power or international relations, and instead just go about their everyday business, trying to earn a living. Most only get more or less excited about politics around presidential election time. They are generally patriotic and very many have common sense and a good sense of humor. That said, the average American representative of what passes in the U.S. for its political and intellectual elite is, to reapply Leo Tolstoy's observation about the English, "self-assured, as being a citizen of the best-organized state in the world, and therefore always knows what he should do and knows that all he does… is undoubtedly correct."[6]

Here is a conundrum. Tolstoy's description of the sense of assurance remains correct, but the reality of the U.S. being the best-organized state, of course, no longer is. If the United States could lay claim, as Great Britain did at some point in time, to having the best state organization, in the 21st century, this is no longer the case. Nor is it so in the modern United Kingdom, or for that matter, in most Western states, which are bogged down in corrupt politics and substitute statesmanship with a fig leaf of demagoguery and populist pathos designed to cover their catastrophic failures in the economy, culture and demographics, to name just a few features of these nations' current malaise.

Today's United States, moreover, is increasingly exposed as being ruled by an oligarchy, or rather by two ruling clans, and de facto is neither a democracy nor a republic. For most international observers who specialize in understanding the realities of U.S. politics and policies, this hasn't been a secret for a while now, and has been especially reinforced after four years of the political debacle of Russiagate, which completely dispelled any doubts about the corrupt and malicious nature of the present American statehood. As Scott Ritter observed after the first presidential debates between Donald Trump and Joe Biden:

> America long ago ceased functioning as a beacon of democratic values to which the world could look for guidance and support. But the Trump-Biden debate exposed our true dysfunction. We are now little more than the laughingstock of the world, armed with nuclear weapons. And if that does not scare you, nothing will.[7]

Yours truly has been scared of that for a long time, first when I opened my own blog dedicated to geopolitical matters in 2014 where I went on record more widely, after noting this in 2017:

> The very phenomenon which was responsible for the United States emergence as a superpower—war, WWII in particular—was never a factor which had a real impact on the nation and created no real inhibitors in the political elites to their often ignorant, boastful

and aggressive rhetoric nor created a necessity to study the subject, which was foundational to American prosperity and success after WWII. This still hasn't been done. The outcomes, in full accordance with Clausewitz' dictum that "it is legitimate to judge an event by its outcome for it is the soundest criterion," have accumulated today into a body of overwhelming empirical evidence of a serious and dangerous dysfunction within America's decision-making process. From the debacle in Iraq, to the lost war in Afghanistan, to inspiring a slaughterhouse in Syria, to unleashing, with the help of its NATO Allies, a conflict in Libya, to finally fomenting a coup and a war in Ukraine—all of that is a disastrous record of geopolitical, diplomatic, military and intelligence incompetence, and speaks to the failure of American political, military, intelligence, and academic institutions.[8]

American elites today, apart from being a clear and present danger globally, are one of the major reasons for American statehood being destroyed from within primarily because of their inherent inability to formulate America's real crucial national interests—not just because these may run contrary to their own personal and particular interests, and not just because most in those elites cannot define American nationhood due to ideological malice, but rather due to their total inability to study and accept reality. Like Bill Clinton, those at the helm have a grandiose opinion of themselves while having rather mediocre skills when it comes to true statesmanship and average, at best, intellectual capabilities. If one ever needed any proof of a grandiose American intellectual failure, American geopolitical thought of the last 30 years stands as a most outstanding example. As Lieven notes:

> Throughout, the U.S. establishment discourse (Democrat as much as Republican) has sought to legitimize American global hegemony by

invoking the promotion of liberal democracy. At
the same time, the supposedly intrinsic connection
between economic change, democracy and peace
was rationalized by cheerleaders such as the *New
York Times*'s indefatigable Thomas Friedman,
who advanced the (always absurd, and now flatly
and repeatedly falsified) "Golden Arches theory
of Conflict Prevention." This vulgarized version
of Democratic Peace Theory pointed out that two
countries with McDonald's franchises had never been
to war. The humble and greasy American burger was
turned into a world-historical symbol of the buoyant
modern middle classes with too much to lose to
countenance war."[9]

Following the collapse of the Soviet Union and America's
self-proclaimed "victory in the Cold War," America's academia
unleashed onto an unsuspecting world an avalanche of
academically second-rate at best, pathos-ridden. triumphalist
fodder which, like Friedman's preposterous 1996 Big Mac-
based geopolitics, completely lost any touch with reality. While
Friedman was building his "theory" on the fast food foundation,
both Fukuyama's *The End of History* and Huntington's *The Clash
of Civilizations*, despite some interesting insights in the latter,
demonstrated clearly the severe limitations of American political
science as a valid study, and of American intellectuals' views of
the surrounding world. Within ten or so years of those works being
published, in 1992 and 1996 respectively, both were proven false
in their main points in the most dramatic fashion, and by the 2010s,
the ideas expressed in those much-touted tours de force of American
intellect looked decidedly far-fetched, if not altogether silly.

One of America's main "specialists" in geopolitics, the
late Zbigniew Brzezinski, was forced to defend his policy of
supporting jihadi forces in Afghanistan as it was working out
in 1998, in an interview which started to look very peculiar
after the tragedy of 9/11.[10] His 1997 magnum opus *The Grand
Chessboard*, for which he was praised as expected by the same

actors of America's geopolitical study echo-chamber, had become irrelevant by 2007, as evidenced by Vladimir Putin's Munich Speech rejecting the U.S. supranational hegemonic endeavor, stating that "it is inadmissible that one country, the United States, extends its jurisdiction beyond its national borders,"[11] and marking the beginning of Russian resistance. Brzezinski's treatise was nothing more than a collection of clichés, wishful thinking and geopolitics catch phrases, as is most of what comes out of the deep recesses of the American geopolitical scholarship and think-tanks that nonetheless achieves widespread acceptance throughout it.

Even when arriving at correct conclusions, as did Samuel Huntington on the West's decline, Huntington's caveat was that this decline was only relative.[12] The idea that the West as a whole, along with the U.S. as its de facto leader, could implode didn't even enter the imagination of numerous American scholars, whose ideas were being sold as the pinnacle of American geopolitical and governance insight, without paying much attention being paid to the complete breakdown of the relation between cause and effect in most of them. Historical causality was never a strong point of American geopolitical thought, which was good at producing primarily self-serving narratives or agendas rather than real studies, with many containing little knowledge of formative geopolitical factors such as the real economy, real national power and real knowledge of their subjects, be they Russia, China or larger phenomena such as warfare or culture. This is not to say that attempts to correct or revisit those narratives which have passed for ideas have not been made. That would be grossly unfair to some American thinkers, such as Daniel Larison, who have tried to question the grossly false narrative of the current American preeminence in international affairs as something if not permanent, then at least very durable, and even if declining, only doing so at a slow pace in a controlled fashion.

Henry Kissinger, one of the most respected of America's diplomatic elders in the United States and in the West, enjoyed a long spell of reverence by America's political elite. But Kissinger's constant geopolitical platitudes could not hide the simple fact that he was, as Thomas Meany noted, "a far less remarkable figure than his supporters, his critics—and he himself—believed."[13] The myth of Henry Kissinger's acumen typified American PR going into overdrive to promote analysts who forwarded an approved agenda but were singularly lacking as outstanding minds, as actual extraordinary figures, capable of grandiose achievements. This has shaped American foreign policy since its Vietnam War disaster. In the end, Kissinger is just another American exceptionalist, mislabeled a "realist," despite the fact that even this term has become absolutely meaningless, among a myriad other labels complicating matters, most likely with a view to multiplying academic sinecures in the American political science and international relations field. As Meany contends:

> Since leaving office, too, Kissinger has rarely challenged consensus, let alone offered the kind of inconvenient assessments that characterized the later career of George Kennan, who warned President Clinton against *NATO* expansion after the Soviet Union's collapse. It is instructive to measure Kissinger's instincts against those of a true realist, such as the University of Chicago political scientist John Mearsheimer. As the Cold War ended, Mearsheimer was so committed to the "balance of power" principle that he made the striking suggestion of allowing nuclear proliferation in a unified Germany and throughout Eastern Europe. Kissinger, unable to see beyond the horizon of the Cold War, could not imagine any other purpose for American power than the pursuit of global supremacy.[14]

In general, American foreign policy, or rather diplomatic failures, leading to the war in Vietnam and then to the debacles of Yugoslavia, Iraq and Syria, among many others, is a collection of anomalies which have been created by many people with Ph.Ds and impressive resumes, and is very American in nature. There never was a war Kissinger wouldn't endorse, and Daniel Larison, comparing achievements and qualities of Henry Kissinger and George F. Kennan, postulated:

> Kissinger insisted on just the opposite: that the cynical and stubborn pursuit of extravagant and unpromising objectives was necessary to prove American resolve. Kissinger couldn't have been more wrong, as subsequent events showed beyond any doubt, but his profound wrongness had little or no effect on his standing in the U.S. It is no accident that Kissinger has repeatedly endorsed pursuing such objectives up to and including the invasion of Iraq. The blunders that Kennan warned against and correctly foresaw would be costly and wasteful are the same ones that Kissinger approved and defended. Our government usually listens to and employs the Kissingers to make our foreign policy, and it ignores and marginalizes the Kennans once they start saying inconvenient things. Kissinger had great success in advancing himself, and he has continued to be a fixture in the foreign policy establishment almost fifty years after he last served in government, because he knows how to provide arguments that lend legitimacy to dubious and aggressive policies. He made bogus claims about "credibility" in the '60s that helped to perpetuate one war, and later generations of hawks have used the same claims to justify involvement in new ones. Despite all the evidence that his "credibility" arguments were nonsense, Kissinger's reputation has bizarrely continued to improve over time.[15]

But there is absolutely nothing bizarre, from Washington D.C.'s point of view, in Kissinger and his followers' type of "statesmanship" being popular and in demand in the top power echelons of the U.S. Practically the entire "intellectual apparatus" dealing with foreign relations, and geopolitics in general in the United States, is ignorant of the main drivers behind an actual formation of a power balance. Primarily staffed with "thinkers," even those who nominally wouldn't qualify as being hawks, they remain America's one trick ponies, since they operate on the assumption of America's omnipotence. This myth is unquestioned due to the simple fact that most, albeit not all, cadres of the U.S. foreign policy establishment lack the understanding that America's agency is not absolute, that it never was, and that any kind of a political act, in words of Bismarck, "is the art of the possible, the attainable—the art of the next best."[16] American elites, many of whom are infected with the Clinton and all-American syndrome of grandiosity, are not conditioned to think multi-dimensionally and to assess the costs and benefits, as well as consequences, of their decisions. Considering the questionable grasp by most in the U.S. top political echelon of the power-balance factors required for developing and implementing truly realist foreign as well as domestic policies, it is not surprising that America's foreign policy of the last almost thirty years, including the intellectual assumptions behind it, is a litany of continuous unmitigated disasters.

If one had wanted to see the actual intellectual level of modern American political discourse, it would have been sufficient to tune in on September 29, 2020 to the first presidential debate between incumbent Donald Trump and contender former vice-president Joe Biden to know all one needs to know about the contemporary state of U.S. politics and political thought. Apart from being a national disgrace and perceived as an embarrassment around the globe—a shouting match between two genuinely geriatric debaters, which could make Leonid Brezhnev in his early 70s look like an intellectual and a man of dignity—the debate exposed the same old American ailment by continuing to frame America's future as that of a global leader or hegemon. All this was proclaimed even as the American, and other Western economies were imploding and the United States was being purged from Eurasia proper by both Russia and China. The very structure of the Liberal World Order was crumbling before the very eyes of the whole world. It wasn't just the scaffolding anymore; the whole edifice was going down in flames and smoke. Its substantiating theory—American exceptionalism—had turned out to be entirely wrong.

Vladimir Putin's famous speech in 2007 at Munich's Conference on Security Policy started the countdown to a new world. In it, the Russian President declared the unipolar moment, a euphemism for American hegemony, dead:

> I consider that the unipolar model is not only unacceptable but also impossible in today's world. And this is not only because if there was individual leadership in today's—and precisely in today's— world, then the military, political and economic resources would not suffice. What is even more important is that the model itself is flawed because at its basis there is and can be no moral foundations for modern civilization. Along with this, what is happening in today's world—and we just started to discuss this—is a tentative to introduce precisely this concept into international affairs, the concept of a unipolar world.[17]

The speech made the news around the world but was met with sarcastic smiles from many powerful players in the U.S. establishment. Nothing could shake, it seemed, the confidence of the self-proclaimed hegemon. The reaction from the White House was pretty expected: the "accusations" were called "wrong" and, bar some worrying in the primarily right-wing fringe American media, few would take it too seriously.[18] Needless to say, the old tune of America's foreign policy establishment and its court "analysts" and "scholars" about Russia being a second-rate power with a GDP smaller than that of Texas, Italy, South Korea or whatever was the flavor of the month, was put on repeated playback.

All Western forecasts and assessments went out the window when the Russian Armed Forces disposed of the Georgian Armed Forces, which professed to be NATO-trained and partially equipped, within a time span of a mere 5 days during Russian-

Georgian War of August 2008, and hit home a month later, when the financial crisis erupted with the bankruptcy of Lehman Brothers in September of 2008. Events in Iraq and Afghanistan also gave ample reasons to doubt America's power but that didn't preclude a host of U.S. geopolitical academics and politicians feeding off it to praise America, reiterating their preposterous claims of the U.S. Armed Forces being the "finest fighting force in history."[19] That was a red flag—even if those claims of American supremacy were being made only for the consumption of a gullible American public, highly unsophisticated in international affairs.

Confirmation Bias

But there was more to it. The horrifying truth lay in the fact that many—very many—at America's political and intellectual pinnacles really believed it with all their hearts. This was a level of ideological fervor and detachment from reality that could make the most dedicated Maoists blush. What followed next—the United States and European Union fomenting trouble in Ukraine, resulting in a civil war and Crimea leaving for Russia after a referendum—demonstrated the utter incompetence of the American political, intelligence, academic and economic institutions which had unleashed the process—which indeed was and remains extraordinary in its scale and consequences. The fact that the U.S. elites did not recognize what they were doing and what was soon coming as a result signaled their complete intellectual collapse and a severe case of epistemic closure across the board. These were first signs of a profound existential crisis within the entirety of American society and its institutions, especially its military-political ones, which I had predicted in 2014, while observers such as Dmitry Orlov had seen the writing on the wall as early as 2011. Andrei Raevsky, known in the international blogosphere as The Saker, was on it even earlier. Only a few establishment American thinkers truly reacted rationally to what was coming.

But if Vladimir Putin's Munich speech was met with sarcastic smiles by many in 2007, nobody was smiling after the Russian president, in his June 2019 interview to *The Financial Times*, "eviscerated" Western liberalism. As *FT* put it:

Vladimir Putin has trumpeted the growth of national populist movements in Europe and America, crowing that liberalism is spent as an ideological force. In an *FT* interview in the Kremlin on the eve of the G20 summit in Osaka, Japan, the Russian president said "the liberal idea" had "outlived its purpose" as the public turned against immigration, open borders and multiculturalism... "The liberal idea has become obsolete. It has come into conflict with the interests of the overwhelming majority of the population."[20]

That meant that globalism, a sublimation of America's aspirations for actual grandiosity, was dead too.

For many American scholars and the politicians who depended on and continue to depend on these scholars, and nurture themselves on their narratives, many of which were ultimately untrue, even the idea that America's greatness came not just as the fruit of America's undeniable genius and power, but was largely due to a set of a providential circumstances which preserved America from destruction in the course of the worst war in human history, can be a severe test of their personal and even academic convictions. For people who put their faith in the ideas espoused by the court minds of Brzezinski, Fukuyama, Huntington or even the relatively independent Mearsheimer, to say nothing of an army of American and Western military porn purveyors ranging from cadre officers to even comic artists, facing a world in which America is regarded as a big mouth bully that nobody is afraid of, and which economically is primarily smoke and mirrors, is a life changing experience. A very unpleasant one, and understandably so, especially given the peculiar fact that most of the American intelligentsia, across the whole spectrum of political views, failed to see what has been obvious for many for years, if not decades.

It is next to impossible to explain to an American-educated political scientist or to a lawyer turned politician, that while the past does dictate the future, truly coming to grips with it requires a bit more finesse than provided by advanced graduate or post-graduate degrees from leading American universities.

The fact that much of the truth is not really relative and that it is knowable—a premise which many in the American academia refuse to acknowledge—could come as a cultural shock for such scholars. Richard Haas, who is the President of the Council on Foreign Relations, a rather grossly overrated collection of America's statesmen and stateswomen if viewed in the context of their utterly catastrophic "achievements," may bloviate on the issue of Donald Trump's foreign policy, saying whatever he wants, as he did in *Foreign Affairs* in October 2020. He may even look back at America's history, lauding a list of America's "creations," such as the International Monetary Fund, the World Bank, "and that it constructed a modern foreign policy and defense apparatus, including the National Security Council, the CIA and the Department of Defense,"[21] obviously unable to even grasp the dark irony of listing the main drivers behind America's demise and the world's refusal to live by American rules.

The humor of situation is that Haas, being a former consummate American military-diplomatic bureaucrat, still cannot recognize that the problems with the United States and the West in general are not just institutional—they are systemic. As former CIA officer Philip Giraldi, describing the present state of the Central Intelligence Agency, noted:

> …there was considerable concern that the agency had to some extent lost its ability to perform traditional tradecraft. While it would be a gross exaggeration to suggest that the agency had abandoned the spy business, by some accounts it has largely given up on unilateral operations and has instead become heavily dependent on often unreliable information shared by friendly intelligence liaison services.[22]

Earlier, the same Philip Giraldi, describing an appalling level of incompetence in the CIA's "spying craft," which is represented by the National Clandestine Service, which prides itself on being an elite, stressed that:

This strong group identity has led to an acceptance of extraordinary levels of mediocrity or even incompetence within the ranks. As the alcoholic and utterly inept Aldrich Ames learned, it is very hard to get hired but even harder to get fired. ...Senior officers, in denial over their own lack of language and cultural skills, frequently maintain that "an op is an op," implying that recruiting and running spies is the same everywhere—an obvious absurdity. The Agency's shambolic overseas assignment process means that officers often receive only minimal language training and are expected to learn the local idiom after arriving at a post, presumably through osmosis. Most fail to do so."[23]

But if America's premier intelligence service appears to have experienced such an obvious intellectual and cultural decline in the 21st century, the former CIA chief historian, Benjamin B. Fischer, confirms that this is not just a recent phenomenon. During the Cold War the Soviet, East German and Cuban intelligence services literally staffed the CIA with double agents, which Fischer terms a massive intelligence failure, which "wreaked havoc" on the CIA.[24] That failure was overlooked, which clearly demonstrates a pattern for what serves by definition as America's best intelligence and intellectual service. If the CIA struggles both in its intelligence activity and its cadre recruitment policy, one would expect people such as Haas or people like him, who depend on CIA data in their analyses, to experience intelligence inadequacies similar to those the CIA experiences even today.

In the end, the main task of any intelligence service in the world is collection of information and this is where America's human intelligence and analysis processes break down. Haas uses the term "a distorted lens," when trying to describe Donald Trump's worldview.[25] But neither Haas nor most of his colleagues in the Council on Foreign Relations are in any position to criticize Trump, since their own view of the world and history is no less distorted than his. Claims that the American institutions that Haas tries to defend have allegedly prevented great powers wars for almost 75 years, or were responsible for the 90-fold growth of the U.S. economy, among other now traditional tropes about the "spread of democracy," are not only bogus and ahistorical, they show the intellectual dishonesty and extreme mental feebleness of America's allegedly top intellectuals.[26]

Richard Haas is not alone in his delusions concerning history and geopolitics, delusions which do not pass any factual or scientific scrutiny. Haas is but one of many influential intellectuals in America who are in the business of creating narratives. There is nothing new, or presumptuous, in creating or framing narratives. In the end, it is a default task of what usually passes for the intellectual elite in any nation. The main issue as it concerns narrative-creation is whether those who create or order the narratives *actually know the real state of affairs*. This where the trouble with the American establishment or mainstream intellectuals lies—most of them truly believe their own narratives. If the CIA fails to properly collect and juxtaposition facts to produce a reliable and realistic assessment of the outside world, while specializing in activities which are grossly detrimental to U.S. national security, such as Russiagate, it is highly unreasonable to expect a cabal of American geopolitical analysts and scholars to get anything right. The track record of their ultimate failures is out there for everyone to see. Those failures are inevitable in the almost hermetic echo-chamber of American thinktankdom and punditry which is unable to separate the narrative of an omnipotent America viewing the rest of the world with ignorant contempt from its reality.

An Analytical Echo Chamber

The American Russian Studies field provides a classic example of an American analytical echo-chamber. As I have been writing for years—it is a wasteland of Solzhenitsified pseudo-history, rumor-mills and narratives delivered by people, both of Russian and foreign origins, who cannot be described as objective observers by a long shot. The situation gets even grimmer with the passage of time, leading to today's Russian Studies being little more than a propaganda machine that doesn't even bother actually studying Russia and its culture, as represented by the majority of Russia's peoples of different ethnicities. What passes for "studying Russia" in the U.S. is the same old tired routine of imagining that Russia is still the Soviet Union and then trying to defeat it, not noticing that the times have changed dramatically.

But even the spectacular failure of a major, and utterly false, geopolitical stratagem introduced by Zbigniew Brzezinski, which served as one of the pillars of United States' strategy toward, or rather against, Russia went almost unnoticed by U.S. establishment intellectuals—despite the fact that not only was the stratagem wrong but it also was one of the major drivers behind America's precipitous decline across the board. For decades, Brzezinski, who passed in the United States as one of the main experts on the USSR/Russia, which he was not by a long shot, had promoted the idea that Ukraine was a primary battlefield that the United States must dominate in order to remain the sole superpower and prevent Russia from reconstituting itself as a Eurasian empire.[27] Remarkably yet expectedly, this delusional drivel received wholesale praise from all quarters of the American and Western intelligentsia engaged in foreign policy issues. The delusion was best encapsulated in the *New York Times* praise for the Brzezinski's magnum opus *The Grand Chessboard: American Primacy and Its Geostrategic Imperative.*

> Brzezinski has now provided another scholarly blueprint for what he believes the United States should do in coming years to further America's interests, maintain the hegemony it commands, and prevent global anarchy. For Brzezinski this is a strategic game, not unlike chess to outwit potential rivals...[28]

It's no secret that many in Russia, from its political peak down to the average Ivan, were happy to see the entire Brzezinski worldview collapse on itself, especially considering his position as President Obama's foreign policy advisor. Not only was Russia disinterested in the Ukraine as a battlefield, but after Crimea returned to Russia in 2014, the Russians didn't want to have anything to do with Ukraine. In the short six years since the violent bloody Maidan coup, they have decoupled themselves economically from the increasingly dysfunctional regime in Kiev, even redirecting two pipelines to Europe so as to avoid their passing through Ukraine, thus simultaneously sentencing it to a slow economic death.

Brzezinski didn't outwit anybody but himself, and the followers of his radically Russophobic views, because the Ukraine affair resulted in consequences reflecting a tectonic albeit unacknowledged geopolitical defeat for the West. It also released Russia from the debilitating burden of providing economic welfare for Ukraine, allowing Russia to redirect the released resources for its own development, thus ensuring Russia's return as a pivotal Eurasian and global power. Brzezinski might have been playing geopolitical games, but he was a white board theoretician with a Harvard doctoral thesis focusing on the Soviet Union and, even despite his tenure as a National Security Advisor to President Carter, was absolutely disoriented in the real modern world of extremely technologically complex economic and military power in the period of a real revolution in military affairs. Praised as one of the best American minds, Brzezinski epitomizes even today the utter ignorance and incompetence of the American political and intellectual class in regard to the only country in the world which can wipe the United States off the map.

In the end, Brzezinski's incessant promotion of Poland-centric policies with a view to weakening Russia achieved the absolutely opposite result and ensured that massive, possibly irreparable, damage to Russian /American relations took place on Obama's watch—relations which were then and remain crucial for achieving both American and global security. By so doing, Brzezinski damaged the United States real interests in the larger scheme of things even more than did America's own pro-Israel neoconservatives, with whom Brzezinski was in disagreement more often than not. But as practice shows, given the dramatic damage to America's statesperson-producing machine, ranging from its Ivy League educational institutions to its media—the United States simply has no good options left to provide it with high quality political and intellectual analysis. The standard is very low and continues to fall. This process is irreversible under current circumstances. The intellect of American policymakers varies inversely with its hegemonic ambitions, as forwarding this agenda has been the only modus operandi acceptable to America's elites for the last three quarters of a century.

Epistemic Closure

In addition to the Russian Studies field, the punditry which provides its main opinionmakers offers a further demonstration of the decline of American cognitive faculties and critical thinking. One of the major voices on Russia in the U.S. media is *The New Yorker's* very own Masha Gessen, whose writings on Russia and especially on President Putin are seriously regarded as expert analysis by many in the U.S.—and also serve as an indication of the degree to which the U.S. media has become increasingly unhinged and resorts not only to outright lies, which is by now expected of them, but more alarmingly exhibits symptoms of a deep personal animus. Gessen wrote in March of 2020, at the onset of the Covid-19 panic, a startling piece in which she drew parallels between the actions of President Putin during the *Kursk* submarine disaster and Trump's response to Covid-19 pandemic. One has to seriously struggle to make even a remote connection between the *Kursk* tragedy and the virus, but Gessen had no qualms about doing so. Assessing her "nemesis" Putin, she writes:

> But there is more. The most striking aspect of Putin's failure to accept responsibility for the Kursk disaster was his retreat into bureaucratese. It was a preview of the twenty years since (and possibly the next twenty). Putin's use of bureaucratic language is a means of misleading the public and deflecting responsibility, but it also offers an insight into his understanding of government. He saw himself as a figurehead who might get in the way of people doing their work, and seemed unaware that his job was to lead the effort. Perhaps as a result, the Russian Navy

and government were overcautious, rejected foreign help, and didn't even respond to the S.O.S. signals from the submarine.[29]

It seems germane to mention that Gessen, a dropout from architectural school and touted as a journalist insofar as having been published by *The New Yorker*, not only has no idea how today's Russian government operates but also fails to realize that what she describes are the actions of a president, who indeed, governed wisely by allowing professionals to do the job. The fact that many of those professionals turned out to be inadequate for a job was not, then, the fault of the absolutely new Russian president but reflects the mess he inherited from his predecessor. In an act unprecedented in Russia's politics Vladimir Putin personally met with the relatives of the deceased crew of the *Kursk* and took it upon himself not only to change the lives of people there but also to raise the *Kursk* from the bottom of the Barentz Sea. On both accounts he delivered.

Gessen's hatred of Russia in general, and Putin in particular, similar to that of another Russian Jewish immigrant and pundit, Julia Ioffe, can be explained by both their longstanding personal grudges and Putin's radically anti-global policies, including his promotion of true conservative values, not least through reaffirming the traditional family as a fundamental building block of society, while Gessen, a notable LGBT rights advocate, views it as inimical and to be destroyed—the aim of very many in U.S. political and media.

But psychosis about Russia or Putin in the U.S. is not merely an issue of policies, it is also the issue of a process that can be only described as the *infantilization* of America—discussed here simply to demonstrate the level on which it is taking place. In 2015, a lawyer and the editor in chief of Lawfare blog and a Senior Fellow in Governance Studies at the Brookings Institution, Benjamin Wittes, posted an eyebrow raising and embarrassing offer for President Putin to... fight him. Wittes, who professes to be a martial artist, wrote:

> What do former world chess champion Garry
> Kasparov, former State Department policy planning
> chief Anne-Marie Slaughter, former U.S. ambassador
> to Russia Michael McFaul, and big-name journalists
> Charles Lane, Jonathan Rauch, and Jeffery Goldberg
> all have in common? All of them think Russian
> President Vladimir Putin needs to man up and meet
> me in single combat in a location where he can't have
> me arrested.[30]

And in a stroke, Wittes has placed all those purported supporters on a similarly puerile level to his own, reflecting a culture based on personal one-uppance and ad hominem attack as substitutes for substantive discussion, Wittes provides an excellent illustration of the level of immaturity rife among rank and file American intellectuals.

It is also a great indicator of the lack of intellectual nourishment in American culture as a whole due to a combination of factors, among which epistemic closure is the most important. The American belief system as it exists today is *incapable of accepting empirical evidence because it destroys American exceptionalism's extreme confirmation bias and most modern American intellectuals on both the nominal left and the nominal right cannot deal with it.* They cannot deal with it not only because it is personally extremely painful and difficult, but also because they simply are not professionally equipped to deal with it. In the modern world filled with the extremely fast and complex interactions and in permanent systemic economic and cultural crises, skills and degrees in law, history, even an MBA, let alone journalism, are drastically insufficient to produce even a semi-rational explanation of the gigantic changes the modern world is going through.

The lack of these skills, inevitably, results in all kinds of severe cognitive dissonances, and results in all kinds of psychoses, especially in a country which was convinced that everything must go in accordance with the plans and beliefs of Washington, D.C. Today's means of communications and global access to information and competing perspectives blew the myth of American exceptionalism out the door. Modern American intellectuals not only were not ready to explain the new reality to their own people; in a folly of a historic proportions, they turned out to be as similarly confused and incapable of orienting themselves toward the new reality and in doing so they proved that they are, in the world of Senator Kennedy, those very idiots who today run the country into the ground.

* * *

Vladimir Lenin left an astonishingly accurate definition of what he perceived as a bourgeois culture: "One cannot live in society and be free from society. The freedom of the bourgeois writer, artist or actress is simply masked (or hypocritically masked) dependence on the money-bag, on corruption, on prostitution."[31] Of course, it was a blanket statement, forgivable for its broad stroke in 1905, when first published, but its general principle was correct. In 2011, 106 years later, a Pakistani Muslim apostate, Ibn Warraq, noted in his treatise *Why the West Is Best*, extolling the virtues of liberal democracy as the main reason he left Islam: "The excess of Western popular culture—a price we pay for our freedom—can make a person cringe and render the defense of Western civilization more difficult."[32]

There is very little doubt for any even rudimentarily educated person that the world we all live in today was shaped primarily by the combined West, and Warraq doesn't hold back when it comes to praising Western rational thought, the promotion of the rule of law, philosophy, scientific achievements and art, which had and continue to have a global impact. But Warraq's argument, in his enthusiasm for the West, can only be accepted with some serious caveats, and that makes his case for the West circa 2020 extremely weak. The combined West of the contemporary period is no longer the West of Aristotle, Plato, or of rational thought or free scientific inquiry. Rather, it is increasingly an Orwellian world in the process of suppressing or getting rid of all of those values which had made the West what it was known for over the last few centuries, due to the Age of Enlightenment.

Even Henry Kissinger, in his meandering assessment of the Covid-19 pandemic, called on "world democracies to defend and sustain their Enlightenment values."[33] But the defense of those values reminds one of a rear-guard effort by a retreating force which in actuality has no alternative strategy to its continuous retreat. What drives this retreat is precisely the above-mentioned *excesses of Western popular culture* which infested the American rank and file at the behest of West European political and cultural elites who, within the lifespan of a single generation, substituted remaining Western norms of human existence with the most radical cultural views of the counterculture of 1960s. The imagery of peaceful hippies trying to remake the world in the image of a Brady Bunch had very little in common with reality on the ground for masses of young Americans, which was driven primarily by fear of being sent to Vietnam and a hatred towards those institutions which were, in the view of 1960s radicals, responsible for such state of the affairs. Indeed, the Vietnam War was an abhorrent affair from any point of view, as was segregation and, in general, what later became known as a practice of abuse of human rights, primarily against blacks, which became a banner of what would be resurrected to form a driving force for radical change.

But the original antiwar animus and half-baked revolutionary efforts could not survive beyond their historically brief moment. With the proponents soon disillusioned by organizational difficulties and divisions on the ground, exacerbated by governmental infiltration, cooptation, redirection and sabotage, a post-modernist popular culture swiftly emerged, still combative but deeply cynical. Times changed from the Rolling Stones' song "Street Fighting Man" to the Beatles' counterpoint, "Revolution," with its "I don't want to change the world" refrain, giving way in 1978 to David Bowie, who with typical self-irony, quipped, when asked on his contribution to rock: "I'm responsible for starting a whole new school of pretension."[34] Bowie didn't have to claim anything, being an artist of a true talent, but his self-deprecating description might have as well been applied to a whole new social and political order and simmering irreconcilable contradictions which evolved from the counterculture of the 1960s and the reaction to it which came with the Reagan Presidency.

It was all about pretension, across the board. If 1960s radicals dabbled into an eclectic mix of radical social and political ideas, thus sowing the seeds of America's modern age dysfunction, the so called "conservative" reaction proved to be no less destructive than its allegedly left-wing counterpart. In the end, what came to be known as the American "left" was not really left as such had been understood for over a century, it was just angry and anarchic, while what came to be known as American conservatism, had very little to do with conservatism, but reflected an equally angry reaction and defense of a status quo that was unsustainable. The school of pretensions, to be sure, is there, but the principles that form the philosophic planks of analysis—not so much. But that is expected from a generation of lawyers, journalists, art and literary critics, who today constitute the bulk of the American cultural elite which is postmodernist in its very foundation once the whole concept of nonpartisan truth had become meaningless on both flanks of America's political spectrum.

The late Christopher Hitchens noted in 2002 that: "In the last three decades of the twentieth century, Anglo-Saxondom was itself extensively colonized by the school of post-modernism and 'deconstruction' of texts by the ideas of *nouveau roman* and by those who regarded 'objectivity' as an ideology."[35] Remarkably, Hitchens, himself a product of both a nominal Western "left" and a literary educational background, was exhibit A demonstrating a complete confusion as to the reality of the post-Soviet world and the very common transition of Western "left" radicals, primarily Jewish, towards what would become known as neoconservatism— which also hid itself under the moniker of liberal interventionism, and a variety of other delusional foreign and economic policies and concepts, all of which were possible due to the radical illiteracy of Anglo-Saxondom in the real history of the twentieth century. Ironically, for a man who helped drive an aggression against the Serbs and sat on the Committee for the Invasion of Iraq based on utterly false narratives, Hitchens should have addressed his remark about "objectivity" to himself first.[36] Objectivity, after all, derives from natural and precise sciences, and cannot operate on the basis of narratives as opposed to empirical evidence.

Hitchens may have decried the post-truth post-modernists in the Anglo-Saxon academe but he was far from the only one who sensed the massive tectonic shift, together with the accelerating self-immolation of Western "intellectualism." Ilana Mercer dedicated an entire lengthy chapter titled "Why Do WASP Societies Whither?" in her treatise on the fate of South Africa's white population and concluded: "The Afrikaners illustrate perfectly what has happened to the Protestant-Calvinist world; it has sunk into a paralyzing paroxysm of guilt, for which there seems to be no cure."[37] There is no cure, because the cure runs contrary to the verities of the modern West and especially Anglo-Saxondom.

Lenin, certainly, was correct when stating that "one cannot live in society and be free from society." Today this self-evident truth transcends the borders of political ideologies and is not defined by Marxist, Libertarian or Liberal labels; it is an axiom—a statement that requires no proof—and that resonates with Corelli Barnett's views of liberalism as a main driver behind what Mercer defines as the withering of WASP societies." The United States, no matter what the juxtapositioning of historic facts—which passes in the Anglo-Saxon world and Anglo world in general for scholarship—is the epitome of liberalism, no matter which party affiliations. No amount of mislabeling the manifestations of a complex modern social and economic dynamic, ranging from cultural Marxism to totalitarianism, can continue to hide the simple fact that the Anglo-Saxon political and economic model, which also is being marketed under different confusing labels, has simply run its course and is nothing more than the crumbling edifice of the Western financial oligarchy, which can no longer handle the global centrifugal forces of which it has little understanding—a result of shoddy scholarship that is completely oblivious to the factors forming the actual global power balance. This was inevitable in an "intellectual" environment over-saturated with people with minimal serious life experiences, most of them in so-called "elite" educational establishments with shaky academic backgrounds—

some of which provide only an extremely shallow set of skills and a body of random, allegedly scientific, facts which cannot constitute, in principle, a crucial block of systemic knowledge under any circumstances. The only viable skills those people can operationalize are partisanship and rejection.

The media-generated Covid-19 hysteria and foregrounding of Greta Thunberg overshadowed any concern with the fate and livelihood of average American Joes or Janes, as it sought to determine how political power would be distributed between the two wings of a single-minded American political establishment, which, in order to preserve the veil of democratic legitimacy, is still represented as a contest between two opposing political forces, which are nonetheless united in their attempt to squeeze the last remaining drops of financial juice from the neoliberal economic model, which long ago stopped producing any value.

In the post-modernist world of sheer emoting and of the alleged validity of all and any narrative, the whole notion of right and wrong, and the whole notion of truth which is knowable become irrelevant. The epistemological closure comes by the way of informational noise where everything is true and valid—and is not, at the same time. It is truly a contemporary iteration reminiscent of the Orwellian world of double-speak or even of an earlier version of that, the world of Humpty-Dumpty in which words mean "just what I choose it to mean—neither more nor less."[38] By now the puzzle of who is the real master in choosing the meaning of words, thus determining what is real, has been solved—a financial oligarchy and a self-proclaimed intellectual class from both "left" and "right" which finally failed to predict just about anything, since objectivity is not only impossible but irrelevant, and therefore, as Hitchens noted, whatever is put forward as truth is necessarily "ideology."

The U.S. State Department

The first sign of a real intellectual is his or her understanding of the limits of their own expertise and of the validity of the forecasts they produce. It is not just the sign of a good intellect but of morality and culture to be aware of the limited weight of one's own input. This is not the case with the American "intellectual" class, which prostituted itself long ago to a highest seasonal bidder and which proved itself to be decidedly unteachable. This, in the end, puts a serious question mark over America's scholarship as such. The fecund American geopolitical and geoeconomic thought of the last thirty years has produced an astonishing record of failure when measured against practical results. Yet, the same people who produced, one after another, such pseudo-scholarly demagoguery continue to have a say in American policy formation, thus providing a living demonstration of Einstein's definition of insanity. In fact, in some quarters, failures are celebrated as achievements! American military thought and the way it emerges in both doctrines and practical matters ranging from the arms industry to war fighting is a perfect example of both an exercise in futility and a complete lack of situational awareness, despite proclaiming this awareness to be a pivot of the America's war fighting, as I have demonstrated extensively in my previous books, *Losing Military Supremacy* and *The (Real) Revolution in Military Affairs*.

It is normal in America to have lawyers or even artists passing judgements on military matters, despite none of them having an iota of real military expertise which requires a set of skills and knowledge which is decidedly not taught in the colleges from which they graduate.

In one of the indictments of America's lack of competence, never mind malignant intentions, Dana Frank, describing her experience with U.S. foreign policy elites, made a grim discovery:

> I was disturbed to learn that much of the foreign policy of the United States Congress is developed by twenty-six-year-olds who, however well-trained or well-meaning, are each responsible for U.S. relations with the entire world (although in the Senate they might only have half the world)—with the exception of committee staffers, who are more specialized and who just have entire regions. Those aides answered, in turn, to Legislative Directors and Chiefs of Staff...[39]

Frank may be too generous here. The extremely low professional level of U.S. "twenty-six-year-olds" in relation to the outside world is well documented. America's colleges and universities rank traditionally high in all kinds of "rankings," but not as high as claimed. While a *Forbes* listing, among many other U.S. listings, might rank U.S. universities as topping the world list,[40] a 2017 Pew Research Center report states U.S. students' academic achievement still lags that of their peers in many other countries, and stands in the middle as it concerns science, mathematics and reading.[41] There is no scale that measures the ranking of statesmen; there we must rely on such practical measures as results—*et voila.*

In matters specifically concerned with foreign policy and national security, they produce people whose ideological convictions, which in many cases might be said to reflect a process of brainwashing, produce outstandingly ignorant people who are utterly unqualified to pass judgement on pretty much any affair, which have as much relation to reality as Wall Street financial machinations do to the real economy.

In 2016 Philip Giraldi, when describing the mayhem the United States helped to unleash in both Syria and Libya, singled out "The White House inclination to respond to claims of genocide" being perpetrated by the leadership of the targeted countries as "the principal driver" of U.S. war-mongering, which even the Pentagon couldn't stomach, as it realized attacking Syria was not truly in U.S. interest.[42] Ironically, it was on Nobel Peace Prize winner Obama's watch that his main foreign policy body, the U.S. Department of State, buried whatever was left of its professional reputation by appealing to Obama "to go big" in Syria in 2016. In a letter signed by fifty-one mid- to high-level diplomats, the rationale for military intervention presented was a prime example of Humpty-Dumpty post-modernist narrative-mongering.

> The moral rationale for taking steps to end the deaths and suffering in Syria, after five years of brutal war, is evident and unquestionable.... The status quo in Syria will continue to present increasingly dire, if not

disastrous, humanitarian, diplomatic and terrorism-related challenges.[43]

This was a pretense of moralism from employees of a department which was one of the main driving forces behind the deaths of millions and the humanitarian catastrophes in Syria, Iraq, Libya, Afghanistan, and the 1999 bombing of the Federal Republic of Yugoslavia, which originated the ironic use of the term Humanitarian Bombing.[44] Apart from the gaping lack of grasp of the events on the ground in Syria, the letter was also a prime example of the utter incompetence of American elites. These were those "twenty-six-year-olds," and some older than that, who, in the words of Frank, were not just developing U.S. foreign policy, they were doing this not exactly by the book. As Frank notes:

> Some aides actually worked for the State Department itself, in a clear violation of the constitutional separation of powers. The State Department offers year-long "fellows" as free labor to key Senate and sometimes House offices. These staffers return to careers at State once the fellowship is over.[45]

The entire concept of Humanitarian Intervention operationalized by the now notorious R2P (Right to Protect) project as realized by the United States in the 20th and 21st centuries—all bore hallmarks of sheer classic imperialism covered, granted, with the traditional fig leaf of American moralism. But there were certainly indications of a counter-cultural rejectionism and passions, if not outright zealotry, primarily hatred, which were decidedly American and fit perfectly into the U.S. foreign policy establishment's version of Bowie's "school of pretension." Diplomacy is traditionally associated around the world with intelligence, highly developed intellect and refinement. Judging by the last 30 years, however, American diplomacy, or whatever passes for it today in the United States, loses all these universally accepted and admired traits with an alarming speed, producing people who not only can barely satisfy even the lowest of diplomatic standards, but who in general do not fit the profile of intellectuals, let alone serious thinkers, not to speak of rising to the level of true statesmanship, which ought to be available in a country such as the United States. Sadly, this is not the case. It is also largely not the case for European diplomacy and its degenerating foreign policy establishment.

The infamous Letter of 51 State Department officials critiquing Obama for failing to conduct air strikes against the Syrian government and arguing a "moral rationale" to prevent suffering[46] is exhibit A of a serious problem with an American worldview. Obama's three main advisers on foreign policy were Susan Rice, Valery Jarret and Samantha Power. Despite their education in elite Western universities, none of those people had any life-forming and highly focused formal education *in the diplomatic field*, akin to the graduates of the prestigious Moscow Institute of International Relations (MGIMO), and certainly none of them, including Susan Rice, who had tenure in National Security Council, had even a rudimentary education in matters crucial for understanding the dynamics of a global power balance formation. This failure of what passes in the United States as diplomacy today was noted not for once by a number of U.S. foreign policy professionals themselves, such as Ambassador Burns, who noted not only U.S. diplomacy failure but pointed out its militarization.[47] Obama's policy in Syria may have been viewed as "cautious," insofar as the United States didn't commit to outright massive military intervention in Syria, but for those fifty-one signatories it was obviously beyond their grasp that at the time of their risible letter—classified since then—that the United States had neither the resources nor the actual military wherewithal to remove Bashar Assad. American "diplomats" wanted bombs, not negotiations. Moreover, the Pentagon, which is responsible for the tools of power politics, didn't want to do it to start with, citing reasonable fears of chaos as one of the main arguments against such an intervention.[48]

The overwhelming majority of American elites today are neither educated nor have even rudimentary tools for assessing the most important driver of global politics—*the balance of power*—nor are they equipped to predict, even on the most general level, the consequences of the military actions they are promoting. While many in the U.S. Department of State or in the educational institutions largely responsible for the formation of the U.S. elites and bureaucracy know catch-phrases such as "no-fly-zone," "pin-point strikes" and "operation," practically nobody understands the multitude of ramifications which flow from any actual policy deployment cossetted behind those catchy phrases. Graduate or post-graduate degrees in philosophy, political science, international relations or law may have been a good foundation for getting into serious global politics fifty or sixty years ago—today it is radically not enough, especially for decision making circles. But this is precisely the dominating educational background of America's policymakers and intellectuals.

This is not the way to run the country, let alone a nuclear armed country such as the United States, the only other country in the world besides Russia capable of obliterating all life on earth. Yet, the non-ending stream of lawyers, journalists or political scientists into the upper echelons of political power and America's intellectual Parnassus continues unabated, a venue where the opinion of some barely literate Hollywood celebrity may carry more weight than professional opinions. This is particularly evident in climate change discussions, in which celebrities, such as director James Cameron and his wife, are very active. Oscar winner Morgan Freeman added his voice to the mainstream media message in 2017 that Moscow is conducting an attack on U.S. "democracy," as if he were competent to discern that.[49] Three years ago, General Latiff, Ph.D. in physics and a man with 20 years long service in DARPA, effectively repeated a warning I issued in 2017 when writing my first book:

> U.S. elites have simply stopped producing any truly competent people; the U.S. stopped producing real statesmen, not just politicians, even earlier. When experts fail, as they failed America, not least due to many of them not being real experts at all, actors,

comedians, sportsmen, conspiracy theorists and demagogues from the mass-media take their place... Now threatening this very "democratic society," or whatever is left of it, is a powerful neocon and liberal interventionist establishment which has a virtual veto power and is working hard, both consciously and not, to end this very republican government. In general, the current American elites and their so-called expert enablers have betrayed American vital interests both at home and especially abroad. What has specifically and greatly contributed to their miserable failure is an almost complete lack of understanding of the nature of military power, of war and its consequences. It couldn't have been otherwise in the country whose military history is, to a very large degree, a triumphalist myth.[50]

Latiff's warning, apart from concluding that most of what U.S. elites know about warfare originates in the entertainment industry, is additionally disturbing when he states that American political leaders "act based on emotion and political expedience rather than on facts."[51] U.S. emoting in both domestic and foreign policy in the last 20 years is an obverse side of the American loss of rational thinking and its impotence, due to incompetence, when it comes to influencing events outside the U.S. borders and even controlling events inside them. This is an absolutely organic trait for political discourse which in the United States long ago turned into a show, or to be more precise—into the circus. Some observers use other terms when describing it: "It's nuts. It's bonkers. It's an insane soap opera."[52] It is a third world country, a banana republic's self-demolition derby, or an iteration of the prolonged explosion scene from Antonioni's counterculture cult movie, *Zabriskie Point,* in which destruction becomes the only avenue for those who regard themselves an belonging to an American intellectual elite. Nor is there anything intellectual in discussions on the merits of their "advanced" economic concepts or geopolitical or geoeconomics doctrines when none of them work and never did. Apart from producing an opaque stream of far-fetched and radically unscholarly theories in subjects ranging from geopolitics, to the economy, to warfare, such intellectuals—Western in general, and American in particular—are now parading themselves as proponents of Critical Race and Queer theories on one end (with suspect reasons why this was promoted and further questions on the modus operandi that enabled it to become accepted), while on the other leaving unquestioned and in place the laissez faire economic atrocity with its financial and corporate beneficiaries parading themselves as people of no principles or morality, where the phenomenon of truth occurs only when appropriate dividends are ensured.

Moral Degeneration

What began in the 1960s with innocence and good intentions morphed into moral degeneration and pretense. The real pedophilia of the Western upper-class is now a well-established phenomenon, demonstrated dramatically by the Jeffrey Epstein saga, which proved that the tradition of Western intellectuals and the powerful's striving for underaged coitus never went away. French intellectuals' 1977 Age of Consent Letter in *Le Monde* marked one of the first attempts to change the view of pedophilia by assuming that the sex between a minor (13-year-old) and an adult was permissible as long as the 13-year-old has consented to it. Needless to say, the inclusion among intellectual signatories and supporters of such sexual relations of many persons such as Jacques Derrida, one of the fathers of post-modernism, should no longer surprise anyone. As *The Guardian* wrote about the French 1968 "Revolution" in 2001 when a trove of documents pertaining to 1968 "sexual practices" with children surfaced in France:

> *Libération*, the left-leaning French newspaper that emerged from the barricades of 68, devoted four pages to the issue yesterday. It pointed out that in the '70s, French leftists held "a very serious debate about whether parents should leave their bedroom door open when they were having sex." May 68 did not

invent pedophilia, said *Libération's* editor Serge July. "The existing moral order was the enemy," he said. "The cultural revolution that followed May 68 was a social triumph in many, many ways. But its discourse on the sexuality of children has served to legitimize practices that are, at times, criminal."[53]

The fact that the counterculture of the 1960s had a serious pedophilic element in it is usually left out of the spotlight whenever modern Western power and its intellectual elite is discussed, but this is expected from modern Europe, drowning in sodomy and making slow progress towards the eventual legitimization of pedophilia. The American leg of Epstein's business was finally uncovered, and in the end, Epstein was arrested on American soil. Yet, after Epstein was suicided, the full scale of his operation and the depth and breadth of its penetration into the American establishment may never be known. As Paul Brian of *The American Conservative* noted:

> Jeffrey Epstein was the talented Mr. Ripley of shadowy sexual predators. With a mind-numbing contact list, from Henry Kissinger and Bill Clinton to Prince Andrew and Mohammad bin Salman, the leering billionaire financier and alleged eugenics enthusiast evaded real punishment for almost his entire life.... The media and Hollywood—despite Ricky Gervais' recent remarks at the Golden Globes—remain largely uninterested in this massive story. Epstein's Hollywood connections are numerous, including disgraced actor Kevin Spacey, who flew on Epstein's jet to his pedophile island various times, and Harvey Weinstein, who's currently on trial for his alleged sexual abuses.[54]

Explicit sexuality or the lack of restraint on what today would be termed as pornography, has been with humanity for millennia, be that via the Kama Sutra or the explicit sexual scenes paraded, together with phallic symbols as a claim to good fortune and vitality, in ancient Pompeii. So much so, that some explicit frescoes from the walls of houses of wealthy Pompeiians remain removed from public display in the museums which own them, even today. The modern growth of pornography, including some of the most perverted forms, however, is unprecedented due to the development of modern media. The news of vast pedophile rings being busted all around world is a regular occurrence. But one has only to look at the prominence of Nabokov's *Lolita* theme among the "artistically-gifted" and powerful in the West to recognize that pedophilia, served up as art, is an extremely exciting topic, both for Hollywood and the artsy types, who profess themselves to be intellectuals, and for the political elite which, through funding support, buys them to serve it. Both in the U.S. and in Europe. And among the privileged, as James Pinkerton defines them:

> As for the Epstein case, so wounding to our collective conscience, we can start our reform effort with a thoroughgoing inquiry into what went wrong—not just at the Metropolitan Correctional Center on August 10, but also at the larger societal level. ...If we fail to pierce this regnant impunity of privilege, we know what will happen: more conspiracy theorizing, more angry distrust, and perhaps, down the road, some worse national breakdown.[55]

It would be highly unjust to paint all of the so called privileged of the modern West with a broad brush of sexual perversity or outright pedophilia. But it is worth noting that many people who consider themselves authorized to speak on behalf of America—the American mainstream news outlets—have no reservation not only about what they must know as lying, as the prolonged failed Russiagate narrative demonstrated so vividly, but also support proven and convicted pedophiles such as Yuri Dmitriev—a man with no academic training, whom they label as a "historian"—as a victim of Putin's "repressions."[56] Pinkerton may exercise illusions about "piercing this regnant impunity" but in modern day America, which bids adieu to the illusion of a free press and scientific inquiry, and which drowns in the cesspool of its own conspiracy theories and bouts of mass hysteria, piercing the "impunity of privilege" is not a realistic proposition. From trivial and contrived geopolitical theories, to degenerate art and culture, to a nouveau PC "science," the whole contemporary cultural and intellectual milieu of the West is akin to a Warhol can of Campbell's Soup, which is nothing more than a "school of pretense" whose fifteen minutes of fame, measured on history's time scale, are up.

The Western elite's moral and intellectual degeneration is not accidental, it is systemic, in the same way as the crisis of liberalism is systemic. "Piercing" impunity is not going to help, it is too late, and the "national breakdown" of which Pinkerton writes with dread is no longer down the road, it has arrived. One can always use a Marxist argument of nascent historical forces shaping our reality, and this argument is true in many important respects, but it is not the whole truth. Out of all the traits defining human nature, the American and in general the West's, power and self-proclaimed intellectual classes, preferenced the most despicable and revolting ones. In doing so, they rejected the whole notion of truth and betrayed the majority of people they were supposed to serve. They prostituted themselves to the highest bidder, a globalist oligarchy, which dominates the corridors of power in Washington D.C., and in doing so, they not only arrested their own development, they lowered themselves to a full-blown treason against majority of American people, on whose labor and aspirations a once proud Republic rested. No longer. Moreover now, as facilitated by modern global communications, American intellectuals came across as feeble and unconvincing, if not laughably incompetent and trite, when measured against the best minds from Russia, China, Iran or many other regions of the globe. Moreover, they have paraded themselves as pretentious and no amount of piercing will help.

For the United States to survive as a unified country, a completely new narrative, grounded in reality, is required and the current American policy elites, be they purportedly left radicals and those forces which support them or the nominally conservative, no less grossly indoctrinated forces on the right, are utterly incapable of formulating the real American national interests, or of creating a new narrative, because the United States is in the process of the fragmentation of what used to be an American proto-nation, but ultimately never fully turned into the real thing. Political creeds, or abstract, often utterly wrong ideas are simply not enough to inspire and, most importantly, to sustain the growth of a nation. The modern American elites and their European followers have proved that beyond a shadow of a doubt, and as such should leave the historic stage as those who believed, that contrary to Lenin's dictum, they could be free from society, especially from the one they betrayed.

This is no longer an issue of just Marxism, Liberalism, Conservatism or any other Isms Western intellectuals so love to produce—it is an issue of the physical survival of the West, which is in a state of clinical extremity.

Endnotes

1 Cathy Burke, "Louisiana Sen. Kennedy: America Is 'Being Run by Idiots,'" *Newsmax,* January 19, 2018, https://www.newsmax.com/politics/john-kennedy-america-nation-politics/2018/01/19/id/838311/.

2 Stephen M. Walt, "The Death of American Competence," *Foreign Policy,* March 23, 2020, https://foreignpolicy.com/2020/03/23/death-american-competence-reputation-coronavirus/.

3 Chris Cillizza, "Bill Clinton is incredibly popular, How much will that help Hillary's 2016 campaign?" *Washington Post,* March 13, 2020, https://www.washingtonpost.com/news/the-fix/wp/2015/03/13/bill-clinton-is-incredibly-popular-how-much-will-that-help-hillarys-2016-campaign/.

4 Jerrold M, Post, ed., *The Psychological Assessment of Political Leaders: With Profiles of Saddam Hussein and Bill Clinton* (The University of Michigan Press, 2003), Electronic version, 313.

5 Alexis de Tocqueville, translated by Henry Reeve, *Democracy in America* (The University of Adelaide), Chapter 16.

"*All free nations are vainglorious, but national pride is not displayed by all in the same manner. The Americans in their intercourse with strangers appear impatient of the smallest censure and insatiable of praise. The most slender eulogium is acceptable to them; the most exalted seldom contents them; they*

unceasingly harass you to extort praise, and if you resist their entreaties they fall
to praising themselves. It would seem as if, doubting their own merit, they wished
to have it constantly exhibited before their eyes. Their vanity is not only greedy,
but restless and jealous; it will grant nothing, whilst it demands everything, but
is ready to beg and to quarrel at the same time. If I say to an American that
the country he lives in is a fine one, 'Ay,' he replies, 'There is not its fellow in
the world.' If I applaud the freedom which its inhabitants enjoy, he answers,
'Freedom is a fine thing, but few nations are worthy to enjoy it.' If I remark the
purity of morals which distinguishes the United States, 'I can imagine,' says
he, 'that a stranger, who has been struck by the corruption of all other nations,
is astonished at the difference.' At length I leave him to the contemplation of
himself; but he returns to the charge, and does not desist till he has got me to
repeat all I had just been saying. It is impossible to conceive a more troublesome
or more garrulous patriotism; it wearies even those who are disposed to respect
it.*"

6 Leo Tolstoy, *War and Peace,* Chapter X, Book IX, Online Literature, http://www.online-literature.com/tolstoy/war_and_peace/177/.

7 Scott Ritter, "Trump-Biden debate put US democracy on display – we're now little more than the world's laughing stock armed with nukes," *RT,* https://www.rt.com/op-ed/502155-trump-biden-debate-democracy/.

8 Andrei Martyanov, *Losing Military Supremacy: The Myopia of American Strategic Planning* (Atlanta: Clarity Press, Inc., 2018), 13.

9 Anatol Lieven, "How the west lost," *Prospect,* August 31, 2020, https://www.prospectmagazine.co.uk/magazine/how-the-west-lost-victory-communism-moral-defeat.

10 *The Brzezinski Interview with* Le Nouvel Observateur (1998), University of Arizona Archives, https://dgibbs.faculty.arizona.edu/brzezinski_interview.

11 "Many leaders now share Munich speech ideas, despite being angered at the time — Putin," *TASS Russian News Agency,* March 10, 2020, https://tass.com/politics/1128657.

12 Samuel Huntington, *The Clash of Civilizations and the Remaking of World Order* (New York: Simon & Schuster Paperbacks, 2003 edition; originally published 1996), 29.

13 Thomas Meany, "The Myth of Henry Kissinger," *The New Yorker,* May 11, 2020, https://www.newyorker.com/magazine/2020/05/18/the-myth-of-henry-kissinger.

14 Ibid.

15 Daniel Larison, "No One Should Be Missing Kissinger," *The American Conservative,* May 11, 2020, https://www.theamericanconservative.com/larison/no-one-should-be-missing-kissinger/.

16 "Otto von Bismarck Quotes," *All Author,* https://allauthor.com/quotes/160685/.

17 Transcript: "President of Russia, Speech and the Following Discussion at the Munich Conference on Security Policy," *Kremlin.ru,* February 10, 2007, http://en.kremlin.ru/events/president/transcripts/24034.

18 Louis Charbonneau, "Putin says U.S. wants to dominate world," *Reuters,* February 10, 2007.

19 Transcript: "President Obama Iraq speech," *BBC News,* December 15, 2011, http://www.bbc.com/news/world-us-canada-16191394.

20 Alex Barker, Lionel Barber, Henry Foy, "Vladimir Putin says liberalism has 'become obsolete,'" *The Financial Times,* June 27, 2019, https://www.ft.com/content/670039ec-98f3-11e9-9573-ee5cbb98ed36

21 Richard Haas, "Present at the Disruption: How Trump Unmade U.S. Foreign Policy," *Foreign Affairs,* September/October 2020, 24.

22 Philip Giraldi, "CIA Gets Back to Spying," *Unz Review,* April 26, 2016, https://www.unz.com/pgiraldi/cia-gets-back-to-spying/?highlight=CIA+gerts+back+to+spying.

23 Philip Giraldi, "Counter Intelligence," *Unz Review,* February 23, 2009, https://www.unz.com/pgiraldi/counter-intelligence/?highlight=do+not+know+how+to+spy.

24 Bill Gertz, "CIA Fooled by Massive Cold War Double-Agent Failure," *The Washington Free Beacon,* December 28, 2015, https://freebeacon.com/national-security/cia-fooled-by-massive-cold-war-double-agent-failure/.

25 Richard Haas, "Present at the Disruption: How Trump Unmade U.S. Foreign Policy," *Foreign Affairs,* September/October 2020), 26.

26 Ibid.

27 Chris Ernesto, "Brzezinski Mapped Out the Battle for Ukraine in 1997," *AntiWar.com,* March 15, 2014, https://original.antiwar.com/chris_ernesto/2014/03/14/brzezinski-mapped-out-the-battle-for-ukraine-in-1997/.

28 Bernard Gwertzman, "Endgame," *New York Times,* October 26, 1997, https://archive.nytimes.com/www.nytimes.com/books/97/10/26/reviews/971026.26gwertzt.html.

29 Masha Gessen, "The Coronavirus and the Kursk Submarine Disaster," *New Yorker,* March 18, 2020, https://www.newyorker.com/news/our-columnists/the-coronavirus-and-the-kursk-submarine-disaster.

30 Benjamin Wittes, "I'll Fight Putin Any Time, Any Place He Can't Have Me Arrested," *Lawfare,* October 21, 2015, https://www.lawfareblog.com/ill-fight-putin-any-time-any-place-he-cant-have-me-arrested.

31 V.I. Lenin, *Партийная организация и партийная литература* (Party Organization and Party Literature), *Novaya Zhizn* #12, November 13, 1905.

32 Ibn Warraq, *Why the West Is Best: A Muslim Apostate's Defense of Liberal Democracy* (New York, London: Encounter Books, 2011), 87.

33 Henry A. Kissinger, "The Coronavirus Pandemic Will Forever Alter the World Order," *The Wall Street Journal,* April 3, 2020, https://www.henryakissinger.com/articles/the-coronavirus-pandemic-will-forever-alter-the-world-order/.

34 David Bowie speaks on musical influences, 'Ziggy Stardust' era and getting older in final in-depth interview with the Daily News. Jim Farber. New York Daily News. 9 June, 2002, https://www.nydailynews.com/entertainment/music/david-bowie-final-in-depth-interview-daily-news-article-1.2492396.

35 Christopher Hitchens, *Why Orwell Matters* (New York: Basic Books, 2002), 193.

36 Richard Seymor, "Christopher Hitchens: From socialist to neocon," *The Guardian,* 18 January 18, 2013, https://www.theguardian.com/books/2013/jan/18/christopher-hitchens-socialist-neocon.

37 Ilana Mercer, *Into the Cannibal's Pot: Lessons for America from Post-Apartheid South Africa* (Stairway Press, 2011), 213.

38 Lewis Carroll (Charles L. Dodgson), *Through the Looking Glass* (New York: Macmillan, 1934; first published in 1872), Chapter 6, 205.

39 Dana Frank, *The Long Honduran Night* (Haymarket Books, 2018 eBook), 163.

40 Michael T, Nietzel, "U.S. News Ranks The World's Best Universities For 2021, U.S. Institutions Again Top The List," *Forbes,* October 20, 2020, https://www.forbes.com/sites/michaeltnietzel/2020/10/20/us-news-ranks-the-worlds-best-universities-for-2021-us-institutions-again-top-the-list/?sh=4aad0a706eb8.

41 Drew Silver, "U.S. students' academic achievement still lags that of their peers in many other countries," *Pew Research,* February 15, 2017, https://www.pewresearch.org/fact-tank/2017/02/15/u-s-students-internationally-math-science/.

42 Philip Giraldi, "The Pentagon Fights Back," *Unz Review,* February 9, 2016, https://www.unz.com/pgiraldi/the-pentagon-fights-back/?highlight=Giraldi+Vietnam.

43 Krishnadev Kalamour, "The Letter Urging a U.S. Rethink on Syria," *The Atlantic,* June 17, 2016.

44 "Humanitarian bombing," *Military, wikia.org,* https://military.wikia.org/wiki/Humanitarian_bombing.

45 Dana Frank, op cit., 163.

46 Krishnadev Calamar, "The Letter Urging a U.S. Rethink on Syria: Fifty-one State Department officials are urging the Obama administration to conduct airstrikes against the Assad regime," *The Atlantic,* June 17, 2016, https://www.theatlantic.com/news/archive/2016/06/state-department-syria-letter/487511/.

47 Jeremy Suri, "The Long Rise and Sudden Fall of American Diplomacy," *Foreign Policy,* April 17, 2019, https://foreignpolicy.com/2019/04/17/the-long-rise-and-sudden-fall-of-american-diplomacy/.

48 Seymour M. Hersh. "Military to Military: Seymour M. Hersh on US intelligence sharing in the Syrian war," *London Review of Books,* Vol. 38, No. 1, January 2016, https://www.lrb.co.uk/the-paper/v38/n01/seymour-m.-hersh/military-to-military.

49 Al Jazeera English, "US actor Morgan Freeman's cameo against Russia draws criticism," *Youtube,* September 21, 2017, https://youtu.be/zB9FDl1siS4.

50 Andrei Martyanov, *Losing Military Supremacy, The Myopia of American Strategic Planning* (Atlanta: Clarity Press, Inc, 2018), 202.

51 Robert H. Latiff, Future War, *Preparing for the New Global Battlefield* (New York: Alfred A. Knopf, 2017), 124, 131.

52 Charlie Stone, "Let's face it, US politics is just a showy soap opera laced with enough nepotism and corruption to make a banana republic blush," *RT,* October 11, 2020, https://www.rt.com/op-ed/502812-us-politics-banana-republic/.

53 Jon Henley, "Calls for legal child sex rebound on luminaries of May 68," *The Guardian,* 23 February, 2001, https://www.theguardian.com/world/2001/feb/24/jonhenley.

54 Paul Brian, "The Talented Mr. Epstein," *The American Conservative,* January 29, 2020, https://www.theamericanconservative.com/articles/the-talented-mr-epstein/.

55 James Pinkerton, "After Epstein, Our Elites Must Reform or Face the Fire," *The American Conservative,* August 14, 2019, https://www.theamericanconservative.com/articles/after-epstein-our-elites-must-reform-or-face-the-fire/.

56 Olivier Rolin, "Yuri Dmitriev: Historian of Stalin's Gulag, Victim of Putin's Repression," *NYR Daily,* October 7, 2020, https://www.nybooks.com/daily/2020/10/07/yuri-dmitriev-historian-of-stalins-gulag-victim-of-putins-repression/.

7. LOSING THE ARMS RACE

*"The gunboats don't appear in your economics textbooks.
I bet your price theory didn't have gunboats in them, or the
crime sector. And probably they didn't have debt in it either."*
—Michael Hudson[1]

Geoeconomics as Doctrine-mongering

Edward Luttwak and other geoeconomic theorists may have defined geoeconomics as "a warfare by other means," but in doing so they literally suppressed considerations of the actual role of warfare, real, kinetic ones. The range of views of the majority of Western economists and political "scientists" when speaking of modern global economy is limited to monetarism, Wall Street indices, and some "techy" fads, mostly in "green" energy and electro mobiles, and oil. For practically any American mainstream economist the fact that hegemony of U.S. dollar rests primarily on real and perceived American military power, not on some mythical competitive and productive traits of U.S. economy, which allegedly is the largest in the world, may come as a cultural shock. America's military supremacy is either accepted as a given or ignored altogether.

But there are critical lacunae in this position. First, the U.S. economy is much smaller and much less advanced than many of them believe. Secondly, the main American export today is inflation and in order to export inflation and maintain the dollar's status as the world's reserve currency, the U.S. doesn't need many competitive products. In fact, it doesn't need pretty much any products as long as it maintains the myth of its military omnipotence, the key factor which sustains the dollar printing press. In fact, remove the myth of American military omnipotence and the U.S. economy will pretty much collapse.

This is exactly the process which is ongoing right now.

While of course, economists, political scientists and politicians are aware of the role of U.S. military power, this awareness is skin deep and, in the opinion of General Latiff and other professionals, is shaped primarily by the entertainment industry, ranging from Hollywood movies to the mainstream media.[2] As Professor Roger Thompson noted, when speaking of late Tom Clancy's military fiction and even non-fiction, which helped to enforce the myth of American military omnipotence:

> Americans have placed too much stock in Clancy's writings, and that is perhaps especially damaging since Clancy moved from novels to nonfiction. The result ... is that millions and millions of people have gotten most of what they know about warfare and the U.S. military from an ex-insurance agent who never served a day on active duty.[3]

The U.S. dollar's primacy is the obverse side of the U.S. Navy's Carrier battle Group augmented by U.S. Air Force, and vice-versa. In fact, both are connected and sustained by an umbilical cord that cannot be cut without killing both—a symbiotic relationship developed and evolved from the times of classic imperialism and gunboat diplomacy. One cannot exist without another; these guns helped and continue to benefit the metropole.

The fallacy of regarding geoeconomics as the transfiguration of a military conflict into an economic one was apparent by the beginning of the "Tanker War" in the Persian Gulf in 1984-1988, about a couple of years before Luttwak's attempt to divorce modern geopolitics from geoeconomics. Geopolitics by the 1990s, however, had stopped merely having its original "geographic" focus and had evolved into an interdisciplinary study covering pretty much most aspects of national security in a broader sense, or what Michael Lind described as: "Debates about national security and the global economy... merging into a single debate about relative national power."[4] A sensible debate about the economy, culture and security outside of the framework of national power, which is built on the foundation of military power, is simply not possible. And that is where the Tanker War comes into the picture.

The Tanker War was a sideshow of the bloody Iraq-Iran War in which both the Soviet and the U.S. navies were forced to conduct escort operations in an attempt to defend oil tankers' marine traffic from attacks by both Iran and Iraq. As one American naval observer put it:

> Fueled by bitter religious and political acrimony, the Iran-Iraq War, one of the longest interstate conflicts of the 20th century, spread into the Persian Gulf in 1987. Forced to protect vital petroleum tankers, NATO and Soviet naval forces in the Gulf faced new and old challenges from a variety of Iranian and Iraqi threats.[5]

Hence, their deployment of escort operations—military operations which involve significant naval assets including, in case of the Tanker War, a wide use of air defense means against a variety of threats, among which aircraft and anti-shipping cruise missiles emerged as preeminent. In fact, far from being a mundane escort deterrent operation, the whole affair saw some very real casualties on both sides, not least that of the Iraqi anti-shipping missiles' attack on the *USS Stark*, an Oliver Hazard Perry-class frigate, on 17 May, 1988—in one of the worst cases of target misidentification. Twenty-nine U.S. servicemen died. Heightened tensions inevitably led to the even larger tragedy of the *USS Vincennes*, a Ticonderoga-class cruiser, shooting down the Iran Air Flight 655 passenger jet liner, killing all 290 people on board. These were only some of the episodes of the very real war which was taking place in the Persian Gulf. By any measure the whole war was a classic example, per Luttwak's definition, of a geoeconomic affair. Of course, by default it was a geopolitical one too.

The major rationale for the United States involvement in this conflict was twofold: while Caspar Weinberger, then Secretary of Defense, saw U.S. involvement as largely a geopolitical issue of enforcement of "freedom and security of the seas"' and the "minimization of Soviet influence in the area," the other part was purely geoeconomic.[6] As Admiral William J. Crow, Jr., the chairman of the Joint Chiefs of Staff expressed it, when commenting on Kuwait's request to reflag her tankers, thus making them formally a U.S. asset and offsetting Kuwait's earlier lease of three Soviet tankers:

> It seems to me that reflagging would go a long way toward mending our fences in the region.... My conclusion, then, was that we should go into the Persian Gulf, not because of freedom of the seas, and not because we didn't want the Soviets there, but because it was the best chance we had to repair our Arab policy and to make some significant headway in an area where it was absolutely crucial for us to forge the strongest ties we could manage—despite the congressional undermining.[7]

If ever there was a "geoeconomic" warfare rationale in both a formal sense and a classic not "by other means" one, it was Crowe's clear understanding of the economic interests and benefits of the United States as it concerned the Persian Gulf. Yet at that time, Weinberger's group, which favored reflagging, recognized that geopolitics and combat capability were inseparable. Speaking before the Senate Foreign Relations Committee in 1987, Under Secretary Michael Armacost spoke in the rather recognizable lingo of classical geopolitics and power balance, which, in the end revolved around good old vital economic interests, with combat capability being ready to defend those:

> There is plenty of evidence that the Soviets are eager to exploit the opportunity created by the Iran-Iraq war to insert themselves into the gulf—a region in which their presence has traditionally been quite limited. The strategic importance of this region, which is essential to the economic health of the Western world and Japan, is as clear to the Soviets as it is to us. Most

governments in the gulf states regard the U.S.S.R. and its policies with deep suspicion and have traditionally denied it any significant role in the region. However, the continuation and escalation of the war have created opportunities for the Soviets to play on the anxieties of the GCC [Gulf Cooperation Council] countries and to press for increased diplomatic, commercial, and military relations. They were prepared to take on much larger responsibilities for protecting the Kuwait oil trade than they were ultimately offered; we must assume that they would readily step in to our place if we were to withdraw.[8]

If it was warfare, then it was certainly a traditional one which depended not on "displacing military methods" but on exactly the opposite—enforcing them. At the height of *Earnest Will*, the title of the operation of escorting Kuwaiti oil tankers by the U.S. Navy, the U.S. naval force in the Persian Gulf reached 30 combat ships, with as many additionally contributed by other Western nations.[9]

Fast forward 25 years. The short-lived illusion of geoeconomics as a stand-alone warfare by other means has evaporated and the well-known great power competition across a whole spectrum of nation-states' activities has returned and this is a full blown conflict now raging across a spectrum of fields—economic, psychological, cultural and military—including a set of very hot and very real kinetic military conflicts the United States either directly or through proxies has unleashed on the world. So what was "geoeconomics" but a trendy and historically obtuse term coined by America's brass to try to burnish a traditional set of instruments of conflict used since the dawn of humanity—which includes both regular and irregular means, ranging from massive military operations to economic sabotage and psychological warfare, just to name a few.

The propensity of America's theorists to complicate matters and multiply substances beyond any reason or necessity is well-known. The chief editor of Russia's popular military-analytical bi-monthly, *Arsenal of Fatherland (Arsenal Otechestva)*, former cadre Russian Air Force officer Alexey Leonkov, is explicit when stating that Americans are global leaders in a number of developed strategies, but there is only one problem with all of them—they are not survivable when faced with reality.[10]

Yours truly has been on record for years stating that the ailment of doctrine-mongering among the U.S. top brass and self-proclaimed intellectual class is one of the major factors denying the already feeble American elites from facing a strategic reality which is increasingly becoming dire for the United States. Geoeconomics may be an attention-grabbing vantage point or angle from which to look at great powers' competition or rivalry, but it is absolutely irrelevant in the matters which define the global dynamics in the 21st century. These dynamics have everything to do with what means of destruction the United States, China or Russia place on the negotiating table when trying to decide if the rapidly changing world survives at all, and if it does—what it will look like after the global storm and turbulence hopefully passes. This debate, which happens both at the actual negotiating table and on the various battlefields, depends on who has more power and resolve. This power is not measured by Wall Street indices or by the size of a military expenditure—it depends on the probability of each of the contenders being able to assure not only its own survival but the defeat of the others in a conventional, non-nuclear that is, warfare.

The Role of Weapons and Kinetic Power

The real revolution in military affairs—as I wrote in an earlier book by that name, as opposed to the array of hypotheses which have so often been proposed as such—has ensured that the very foundation of American post-WW II hegemony has been destroyed—the faith in America's ability to punish those who doubted America's military omnipotence or had alternative visions of the financial and economic future of the world, in which the U.S. dollar was no longer the only measure of the value of humanity's labor. The bottom line of the present-day American crisis—and there are very few who deny the existence of such a crisis—is the fact that the American globalist agenda is crumbling because the United States cannot win wars. That is not to say that the United States doesn't try, it surely does, and does so with every tool at its disposal from economic sanctions, lawfare and sabotage to bombing and even invasion. But the success record of these operations is rather timid. To be sure this "hybrid" warfare creates a lot of misery around the world, from effectively starving people to killing them outright—an example being the U.S. economic sanctions imposed on Iran for a variety of reasons, ranging from the campaign by the pro-Israel lobby to a general Iran obsession by U.S. power elites who still cannot come to terms with their inability to subdue Iran. As the World Bank reported on the effect of U.S. economic sanctions on Iran in 2019:

> Inflation has been especially high for food items (e.g., 116 percent, YOY, for meat products in April) and disproportionately affected the rural population (e.g., in August 2019, 46 percent, YOY, in rural areas vs. 41 percent, YOY, in urban areas).[11]

Starving nations, assassinating political and military leaders such as General Soleimani, conducting bloody overthrows of legitimate governments—these are all tools from America's arsenal of "spreading democracy" and upholding the "rules-based order." Those tools have zero relation to any pseudo-intellectual constructs such as geoeconomics and have everything to do with raw powerplays designed to achieve the main Clausewitzian object of war—"to compel our enemy to do our will."[12] For America, most of the world is the enemy. The more independent and powerful any nation is, the more it is viewed by the American elites as hostile. Purely economic considerations, such as those independent nations being economic competitors on global markets, are but one of the many constituent instances of intolerable affronts to modern America, affronts which only are so due to its self-delusion of being most powerful nation in history. If a few million people will be killed, starved to death and displaced in order to satisfy the U.S. elites' desire to feel themselves at the top of the world, so be it for U.S. elites, not average Americans who consistently vote for the restrained foreign policy, which is promised to them every election cycle and never delivered. As Daniel Larison put it, describing the inhumanity of the U.S. favorite "Maximum Pressure" tool in relation to Venezuela:

> Sweeping sanctions typically hurt the most vulnerable, weaken the political opposition, and strengthen the government's grip on power. This has happened several times before, and it will keep happening wherever these inhumane tactics are employed. The reasons for this are not hard to understand, but policymakers seem determined not to understand them.[13]

This ignorance and inability to learn are foundational to and the main driver of America's modus operandi after World War II. Utterly wrong lessons have been learned and applied, resulting in a dramatic decline of American society under the most favorable conditions in what is, on a historic time scale, a very short period of between 70-75 years-long—the life span of a single generation.

Not only is the United States increasingly uncompetitive in the real economy sector globally, especially in such a seemingly mundane field as consumer goods, but it has lost both its competitive edge and its competences in some crucial fields such as building complex machines, commercial aerospace, and shipbuilding. And the United States was placed back into the position of energy net-importer as a result of the 2020 oil-war, ostensibly between Saudi Arabia and Russia. Under these circumstances, the only tool which remains at the disposal of the United States, with the exception of its traditional direct blackmailing and twisting the hands of U.S. "partners," is its military power.

Of course, this is where the main problem for the United States lies today—it has lost the arms race. Not in a traditional way as might be discerned by the public—when one country simply outproduces and outperforms another on a battlefield and the issue is settled, such as when the Soviets not only outproduced Nazi Germany in the World War II but also beat the Wehrmacht and

Germany's allies on the battlefield, ending the war by hoisting a red flag over the Reichstag. This was a visible and highly tangible demonstration of victory. In the nuclear age, however, the arms race is a totally different affair altogether, because modern battlefield weapons are of dual use—both conventional and nuclear, if need be. And hopefully will never be used.

The American-made Tomahawk Land Attack Missile (*TLAM*) is a dual ordnance weapon; it can carry conventional and nuclear warheads. The Russian-made *3M14 Kalibr* land-attack missile can do the same. Both missiles have seen a lot of actual combat use with conventional ordnance. The American TLAM, however, has an issue with its main nuclear ordnance. The *W-80* nuclear warhead has been retired and the missile itself became not so much a nuclear threat as an item for target practice by more-or-less working and moderately well-trained air-defense systems, as happened in Syria on 14 April 2018, when 70% of TLAMs were shot down by the Syrians.[14] It was an event destined to be largely unnoticed by the American public, whose attention was immediately diverted by a massive propaganda spin campaign designed to forestall a stream of rather embarrassing news from Syria on the vulnerability of America's premiere stand-off weapon.

Indeed, this fact was an indicator of a much more profound event:[15] the decline and subsequent bankruptcy of the entire American approach to warfare, and with it, a dramatic shift in the balance of power globally. In general, the year of 2018 was not good in the both short and a long run for the American power.

The fact that much in the American view of warfare was not really applicable to peer competition had been pointed out on many occasions for at least a couple of decades. But the second go at Saddam Hussein's grossly unprepared, demoralized and bribed army in Iraq in 2003, while not as effective in providing Americans with an emotional high and sense of ultimate confidence as had the outcome of *Desert Storm* in 1991, still played an important, albeit deceptive, role in impeding the recognition of the fast-changing technological and operational warfare paradigm which had now rendered many American war-fighting concepts obsolete. Even before the landmark address by Russian President Vladimir Putin

to the Federal Assembly in early March 2018 and his revelation
of Russia's new arsenal—ranging from hypersonic anti-shipping
missiles to strategic weapons with unlimited range, such as the
nuclear-powered cruise missile *Burevestnik (Petrel)*—it was
becoming absolutely clear that the age of "The American Way of
War" was pretty much over for anyone who bothered to follow
the technological development of warfare over the last 50 years.

This exposition in 2011 by Lieutenant Colonel of U.S. Army
Reserve, Rose Lopez Keravuori typifies the historically ongoing
pattern of similar conclusions such as that by Ricard Pipes in 1978
concerning what is known among military professionals elsewhere
around the world since Vietnam War as the American way of war:

> From a strategic standpoint, the American way
> of war seeks swift military victory, independent
> of strategic policy success; the desired political
> and military outcomes do not always align. When
> analyzed, this style of warfare reveals the American
> under-appreciation for historical lessons and cultural
> differences often leads to a disconnect between the
> peace and the military activity that preceded it. The
> strategic way of war also includes alternative national
> strategies such as deterrence and a war of limited
> aims. Given this model, it appears that there is not a
> singular American way of war. Rather, the American
> way of war is twofold: one is a tactical "way of
> battle" involving a style of warfare where distinct
> American attributes define the use of force; the other
> is a strategic "way of war," attuned to the whims of
> a four year political system, a process not always
> conducive to turning tactical victories into strategic
> success.[16]

The fact that America doesn't know what war with a peer
nation-state is and what its consequences are, is somehow always
absent from a critique of America's war-making considerations—

an organic and natural trait for a country which saw its last real war in the1860s. As the late Richard Pipes correctly noted:

> The United States wants to win its wars quickly and with the smallest losses in American lives... Extreme reliance on a technological superiority, characteristic of U.S. warfare, is the obverse side of America's extreme sensitivity to its own casualties; so is indifference to the casualties inflicted on the enemy.[17]

Keravuori is generous when she speaks about the U.S. "under-appreciation for historic lessons and cultural differences." In fact, when speaking of the American way of war one is inevitably led to the conclusion that this is precisely what the American way of war is—together with ignoring technological, tactical, operational and strategic reality. American technological superiority was assured for the last 50 years at least, due to the Soviet collapse, primarily due to internal dynamics and problems of the country not related to the issues of the Cold War. This relieved America from facing a grim military-technological reality in the 1990s and postponed a reckoning.

But this reality came back with a vengeance in 2010s. Given 20 years of a free reign, the United States squandered its political capital and demonstrated the severe limitations of its military and technological power. This was a strategic mistake, because a superpower must roughly match its declared potential (or military might) with commensurate outcomes. As Patrick Armstrong, a long-time analyst with Canadian Department of National Defense noted: "Most American opponents have been small fry."[18] Armstrong went further and introduced a succinct and sarcastic definition of the American way of war as articulated by Vietnam War veteran Fred Reed: "The American military's normal procedure is to overestimate American power, underestimate the enemy, and misunderstand the kind of war it is getting into."[19]

Military theory is good only insofar as it is able to provide a path to practical outcomes which accumulate towards winning the war or, in a more professional lingo—achieving this war's political objectives. This hasn't been the case with the United States since World War II. In 2015, while discussing what was then an acute issue of a practical platform for the U.S. Navy, and in particular the role of aircraft carriers—a foundation of the American naval might—retired Commander Jim Griffin quoted the opinion of a Retired Captain Robert C. Rubel about aircraft carriers: "[They] are large and imposing... they provide excellent visuals."[20] While there is no denial that modern aircraft carriers are magnificent and imposing ships, one is forced to question both validity, if not sanity, of an argument in favor of spending astronomical sums of money on visuals, when already by 1980s those ships could not survive even a real, conventional war with the Soviet Union. Today they are incapable of surviving in the modern battlefield due to the real revolution in military affairs.

No number of expensive escorts with even the most up to date anti-air and anti-missile defenses can prevent a whole Carrier Battle Group from becoming a set of prestigious targets. By 2019, Rubel, who used to teach in U.S. Naval War College, still exhibited a soft spot, understandable from an emotional point of view, for the carrier and continued to push for retaining these ships for other reasons than their combat effectiveness:

> In peacetime and in cases of limited warfare, they have proven to be highly useful, which is why the demand for them by Geographic Combatant Commanders is so extensive. They can be moved around the globe like queens on a chessboard, responding to disasters, minor aggressions, and showing the flag either in threat or in support. They are big, impressive, and prestigious, which is why, despite their expense and presumed vulnerability, countries that can are either building or buying them. In the global presence arena, the issue of justification revolves around expense versus political effect. Carriers can retain high end warfighting utility also.[21]

The retention of a high-end warfare for "political effect," is at best a dubious reason, when one considers the revolutionary improvement of defensive capabilities of the so-called green water navies. These navies operate and will continue to operate under the screen of their air forces and air defenses, which will reduce the effectiveness of modern American carriers in power projection and sea-control operations, i.e. their political effect.

When it comes to engaging near-peer or peers, the picture changes dramatically. The U.S. aircraft carrier today is a gateway weapon system—a gateway towards escalation possibly to the nuclear threshold because in a conventional war they would be detected, tracked and destroyed before providing any serious impact on operations against such nations as Russia or China. One can only speculate on the scale of the domestic crisis in the U.S. upon their receiving the news of a destruction of a whole CBG.

This is not a new issue. Former Chief of Naval Operations Admiral Elmo Zumwalt was already contemplating this horrifying scenario in the early 1970s. Even Rubel, himself a former naval pilot, had to begrudgingly admit that:

> More and more, missiles are becoming the principal strike weapon of all the world's armed forces. Navy fleet design should pivot on that assumption, especially when hypersonics begin to proliferate. Once freed of the onus of being the Navy's "main battery," aircraft carriers could be put to more innovative uses and the actual number and type needed would be based on a different set of criteria, leading to different numbers. This, in turn, would allow the Navy to adopt a fleet design more compatible with projected technological, geopolitical, and budgetary conditions. In the final estimate, it should also obviate the futile controversy over whether aircraft carriers are vulnerable or not.[22]

The American super-carrier died as a viable weapon system designed for modern war with the arrival of long-range supersonic anti-shipping missiles. As I have contended on record for years, the arrival of hypersonic missiles has changed warfare forever and made the 100,000-ton displacement mastodons of the U.S. Navy obsolete and very expensive sacrificial lambs in any real war. Modern Russian hypersonic weapons such as the Mach=9 capable aero-ballistic *Kinzhal* have a range of 2000 kilometers and are not interceptable by existing U.S. anti-missile systems. Even basic calculations provide an insight into the daunting task any combination of defensive weapons will have trying to intercept even a single missile of such a class. Intercepting a salvo of 4 to 6 such weapons is practically impossible, even with the use of a whole spectrum, from hard to soft kill, of defensive means of a whole carrier battle group.[23] The *Kinzhal*, a terrifying weapon in itself, was deployed back in late 2017.

The now assured coming of the *3M22 Zircon,* one of whose test-launches was made public for the first time on October 7, 2020, and the variety of platforms from which this missile could be launched, changes the calculus of both naval and ground warfare completely. In the case of most Russian anti-shipping missiles, some of which have a land-attack mode, the ranges of the launch of these weapons exceed—either significantly or dramatically—the ranges of carrier aviation, including their airborne early warning aircraft, such as the *E-2C/D Hawkeyes*. If one theoretically can theorize intercepts of some of the older anti-shipping missiles with the use of Cooperative Engagement Capability (CEC) which allows, as an example, for new AN/APY-9 radar installed on *Hawkeyes*, to guide anti-air missiles such as the SM-6 beyond the range of the platform (such as a Destroyer) launching them, with hypersonic systems it makes no difference whatsoever, since M=3.5 SM-6 missile is simply not designed to intercept targets with velocities almost three times higher that are maneuvering throughout their entire flight, including at the terminal approach. It's doubtful that radar will even see or be able to track such hypersonic weapons, let alone provide reliable targeting.

Russia's Defense Minister Sergei Shoigu was explicit when he defined the role of aircraft carriers: "We don't need aircraft carriers, we need weapons to sink them with."[24] This foreshadows the removal of the U.S. Navy's Carrier Battle Groups from the littorals and remote sea zones of states which will be or already are recipients of advanced air-defense systems, combat aircraft and long-range anti-shipping missiles. For now, the range of anti-shipping missiles is limited to 300 kilometers due to *Missile Technology Control Regime (MTCR)*, an informal political understanding among states that seeks to limit the proliferation of missiles and missile technology.[25] Yet, this arrangement in many respects has been grossly undermined by the actions of the United States and NATO since the mid-1990s and pushed the issue of the proliferation of missile technologies to the fore of the larger global security agenda, because many countries who view the United States as a threat to their national security are seeking weapons which provide for what in the United States was christened A2/AD (Anti-Access/Area Denial). Captain Rubel is correct he when assumes that hypersonic weapons will eventually proliferate. Supersonic anti-shipping missiles, such as the Russian-made *P-800 Oniks*, are already a hot item on the international weapons market and demand will only grow. Syria reportedly bought 72 *Yakhont* missiles (a 300-km range export version of *Oniks*) from Russia in 2009, and in 2016 some of those missiles were used on ISIS land targets.[26]

Even these systems, when properly deployed, can completely shift the balance of power in such crucial geographic locations as the Persian Gulf and render traditional American tools of power projection—a euphemism for bombing defenseless enemies into the stone age—extremely vulnerable.

Yet Iran, as an example, is not a defenseless nation, but rather exhibited a forbidding posture even while under the most severe economic and other sanctions, as NATO forces learned firsthand after the mindless U.S. assassination of Iranian General Soleimani, leading to an Iranian response attacking U.S. and NATO bases in the region. The effect of finding themselves under fire from such a serious weapons system as intermediate-range ballistic missiles was so devastating that NATO contingents, such as the Danish one in Iraq, at which the retaliatory strikes were aimed, have been removed to the safety of Kuwait after the attacks.[27]

Iran's retaliation was instructive on many levels, since it clearly demonstrated the impotence of U.S. anti-missile technology which failed to intercept a single Iranian ballistic missile. Earlier, on September 14, 2019, there had been the embarrassing failure of the American (and Saudi) Air Defense to prevent Houthi drones attacks on Aramco refineries, which sustained extensive damage. But if the low level of military proficiency of the Saudis is well-known, the fact remains that during the attack, there were American AD crews present, adding insult to injury. As the *Washington Post* was forced to observe:

> For years, Saudi Arabia has been a major buyer of U.S.-made weapons. That relationship intensified after President Trump took office, with the American leader pushing oil-rich Riyadh to buy more weapons and Saudi Arabia pledging a purchase of $110 billion in U.S. arms just months after his inauguration. After this weekend, when a devastating attack on Saudi oil facilities blindsided the kingdom, some observers were left wondering what protection Riyadh's outreach to the United States has bought it.[28]

The comparison between U.S. and Russian air-defense systems thus became not only warranted, it became irresistible. Throughout almost 5 years of operating her military base at Khmeimim in Syria, Russian air-defense systems, both missile complexes and Electronic Warfare measures, have proved outstandingly efficient against incessant attacks on the base over a duration of five years, having shot down the overwhelming majority of drones, rockets and missiles aimed at it. As the same article in the *Washington Post* noted:

> Russian President Vladimir Putin responded to Saturday's attack with mockery. At an event Monday in Turkey, Putin suggested that Saudi Arabia buy the Russian-made S-300 or S-400 missile defense system, as Iran and Turkey had done. "They will reliably

protect all infrastructure objects of Saudi Arabia,"
Putin said. Iranian President Hassan Rouhani, also
in attendance at the event, was seen grinning at the
remarks. The S-400 system is untested in real-life
situations, but it costs less than the Patriot system and
has technical features that are, on paper at least, an
improvement on the U.S. system, including a longer
range and the ability to operate in any direction.[29]

Military illiteracy and sour grapes were on a full display here,
since an awareness that air-defense can be layered with a variety
of air-defense systems covering different ranges and elevations
seems to evade the author, who is equally mistaken in contending
that the S-400 are "untested in real-life situations" with Soviet/
Russian AD complexes' combat usage which dwarfs anything
the United States ever experienced in this respect. A dramatic
difference between the two technological and operational concepts
was on full display in Saudi Arabia and the comparison was not
in favor of the American approach to air-defense, or to warfare as
a whole. Remarkably, one of the major Arab monarchies of the
United Arab Emirates had no problems with buying around 50
Pantsir S-1 air-defense systems from Russia early in the 2000s
and having them updated recently.[30] Saudi Arabia, being a main
ground for recycling U.S. dollars and a main dumping ground for
U.S. military technology, has no such freedom in choosing any
supplier other than the United States, or in the best case scenario,
the United Kingdom or France.

In general, the U.S. lag behind Russia in air-defense systems
is massive, and both qualitative and quantitative—Russia produces
an unrivaled variety of air-defense weapon systems which form an
integrated air-defense system designed to fight every single possible
aerial target. The record of the U.S. weapon systems, in general,
and air-defense ones in particular, however, raises many legitimate
questions as to their effectiveness, especially so against a nation
which, like Syria, may become a beneficiary of the "proliferation"
of modern missile technology. Although Iran did claim that her
latest ballistic missiles are capable of striking not only stationary

but also moving targets such as aircraft carriers, it remains to be seen if those claims are true. At this stage it is difficult to confirm, or otherwise, their veracity. What is undeniable, however, is the fact that Iran has enough modern ballistic wherewithal to incur massive casualties and destruction on U.S. and NATO assets in the region and most of those missiles will not be intercepted and will hit the target. The appearance of the *Bastion* (a coastal system using P-800 Oniks) complex, together with modern air-defense complexes such as the S-400, in addition to modern combat aircraft such as SU-30SM(2) or SU-35 changes the balance of power in the region completely and makes any American attempts to employ its fleet near Iranian shores, both in the Persian Gulf and Indian Ocean, an extremely dangerous affair.

Iran's acquiring such systems is no longer a matter of speculation since the international arms embargo on Iran expired 18 October 2020. A feverish activity on Saudi and American sides followed, with U.S. Secretary of State Mike Pompeo issuing blanket threats to any who dared to resume military cooperation with Iran. But even the *Washington Times* had to admit:

> ...Washington's influence over the global community's approach to Iran is waning, raising questions about whether other countries will heed the administration's warnings. U.S. efforts earlier this year to extend the arms embargo failed at the U.N. A subsequent American push to reinstate all international economic sanctions on Iran also was brushed off by the rest of the world. Those sanctions that had been lifted as part of a landmark 2015 agreement that offered economic relief in exchange for Iran giving up key aspects of its nuclear weapons program."[31]

This doesn't mean automatically that Russia, or India, which operates a P-800 Oniks clone known as Brahmos, or China will necessarily rush into re-arming Iran. Despite Russia and Iran being de facto military allies on the ground in Syria and Iran having a massive $400 billion investment agreement with China, the issue of national interests and policies is not going away. Yet it is clear that both Russia and China were and are looking at Iran as not only a friendly nation but also as a market. Moreover, Iran wants Russia's weapons. While Iran denied going on a weapons' buying spree, there are many reasons to believe that Iran has continued talks with Russia precisely about the details of such a spree.[32] Already in November 2019 the Pentagon warned about Iran looking at advanced Russian weapon systems, which it would be able to purchase once the embargo expires.[33] It is totally logical and expected, then, to see Russia and China offering credit lines to Iran for weapon systems capable to effectively neutralize any attempts on part of the United States to attack Iran, enabling it to shut down the Persian Gulf and Hormuz Strait completely, and possibly even entrap one of the U.S. Navy's Carrier Battle Groups there, if the United States should decide to commit national suicide by attacking Iran—a long-time aim of the most corrupt and ignorant neocon warmongers and Israel-firsters in the top echelons of power in Washington D.C.

The day after the expiration of the embargo, Iran's Minister of Defense Amir Hatami confirmed that Iran and Russia and China already have an agreement on military cooperation after the expiration of the embargo and in fact, a "very important" agreement exists between Moscow and Tehran on the "development of an Iranian Air Force."[34] For any military specialist this means that the appearance of SU-35 or SU-30SM(2), against the background of Tehran's limited resources, is more likely to precede the appearance of S-400s, which were also a focus of Hatami's attention during his visit to the exhibition "Army-2020" in Moscow.[35] This is the worst case scenario for the Pentagon, Israel and Saudi Arabia, because both aircraft are capable of controlling the airspace of the whole region and apart from being net-centric capable, also carry a variety of anti-shipping missiles, including latest versions of the high supersonic, M=3.5, anti-radiation and anti-shipping missile X-31.

Whatever the outcome will be in terms of particular military technology Iran wants to buy or the method of payments financing the already settled deal, one fact cannot be denied anymore: the window of opportunities to attack the last country where the United States could theoretically "restore" its image of an omnipotent military power without sustaining the kind of catastrophic losses the U.S. would otherwise incur trying to attack China, let alone Russia, is closing really fast. With it, the chance to preserve the fast disappearing impression of a power capable to dictate its will to anyone is becoming slimmer and slimmer for the United States.

But if that is not bad enough for an overstretched "superpower," the real insult to injury is the fact that the United States can sustain its clients for its most important export—weapons—only through blackmail, arms twisting and those proverbial visuals produced by America's military-propaganda machine whose efficiency drops precipitously with each passing month—because even propaganda has to be based on some reality, where weapons perform as advertised, where military victories, even against manifestly weak enemies, translate into favorable and honorable political settlements, those proverbial political objectives of any war, and where the Clausewitz' dictum "it is legitimate to judge an event by its outcome for it is the soundest criterion" rules supreme.[36]

The United States even today continues to produce some state-of-the-art weapons such as submarines, satellites, computers and some other systems which it uses to dominate the battlefield against third-rate opponents. This concept, the Ledeen Doctrine—picking up "some small crappy little country" and throwing it "against the wall, just to show the world we mean business"—doesn't work anymore.[37] In fact, it never worked to start with—the United States lost all of its wars of the 21st century, which is not even a point of contention, it is a hard cold fact. Those "small crappy little countries" didn't want to be "thrown against the wall" to the benefit of America's "business" posture. They fought back.

Today, when one looks at the state of America's military and its numerous failures both technologically and operationally, one inevitably arrives at the conclusion that there is no way out of this conundrum, because the United States simply lacks the resources to even uphold its grossly embellished, if not falsified, image of "the finest fighting force in history." The Russians, Germans and

French, at least, will have issues with such a claim stretching back over history, while the Vietnamese may demand a mention here, too. Not to mention the Italians as direct heirs to the Romans, which, in its turn will lead to Greeks pointing out their glorious antiquity.

Constant declarations about its own military greatness reveals a long and deeply hidden U.S. inferiority complex when it comes to warfare. It is normal, of course, for the propaganda machine of any nation, be it Russia, China or France, among many, to be in the business of self-praise while belittling the others; this is pretty much what propaganda is all about. But the reactions in the United States, sometimes reaching a level of uncontrolled hysteria, to any demonstration of Russia's military might since Crimea's return home, not to mention its successful operation in Syria and, of course, Vladimir Putin's historic address to the Federal Assembly in March 2018, has made very many Russians question the rationality, if not the sanity, of the American military-political leadership. After Putin's March 2018 speech which in effect announced the arrival of a new world order, and not the one as conceived in Davos or Washington D.C., the reaction in the U.S. to it was so bizarre and infantile, following at times the stages of the Kubler-Ross Grief Model, that as late as October 2020, Dmitri Simes was forced to elaborate on this issue. Speaking to Russia's main news channel *News at First Channel*, the publisher of *The National Interest* magazine and president of the Center for National Interest assured Russian viewers that he, having been present recently numerous times at high-level meetings of the top American military-political brass, had never heard anyone assuming that any attack on Russia would not lead to a devastating response.[38]

Remarkably, in a few words Simes captured not only the essence of Russia's concerns, which have been translated into a set of doctrines, strategies, technologies and actual forces, but also explained why the United States finds itself militarily where it is today—the other big geopolitical players do not want and are not going to try to eliminate the United States, unlike America, which has turned its largely exaggerated military might into a machine for the murder, inter alia, of millions of innocent children, making mockery of the Pentagon's official title of Department of Defense, which has never fought in defense of its country, let alone against a real enemy.

This state of the affairs in America's military was long coming and is a result of failed policies, both on the government and DoD levels, and of corruption. It is the result of a culture in which war has become a business, or a racket, in the words of General Smedley D. Butler, and profiteering and greed remove any considerations of actual national interest and realistic defense requirements. Professionalism and competence in such an environment thus become secondary to politics and greed, and at the end of the day create a demand for people such as Douglas J. Feith—a lawyer, a politician, a man who never served a day in any armed forces capacity, and a man who became an architect of the Iraq War debacle. A man whose moral and intellectual qualities made him a perfect fit for the U.S. political elite or, as he was characterized by General Tommy Franks, "The fucking stupidest guy on the face of the earth."[39]

* * *

The U.S. Naval War College publication *NWCR* (*Naval War College Review*) has been known for decades for projecting wonderful introspective articles known as *Newport Papers* (Newport, Rhode Island, being a location of the Naval War College) into American military thought. Fascinating collections of thoughts and reports on war gaming were and continue to be included. One such, Newport Paper 20, submitted in 2004, was titled *Global War Game. Second Series 1984-1988*. It is a monograph on global war-gaming between NATO and Warsaw pact and the foreword to this paper states that it:

> ...recounts a uniquely interesting and challenging period in the Naval War College's engagement with naval and national strategies through the war-gaming process. The games examined the ability of the United

States to sustain conventional warfare with the Soviet Union until full mobilization of the nation's resources could be achieved. Through a sustained set of sequential and interlocking games, the Global process identified a number of important and controversial findings. ...these games pointed to the importance of offensive action, including maritime operations; the ability of "Blue" (the West, broadly speaking) to win without resorting to nuclear weapons; and the extensive planning necessary to conduct high-intensity combat over a lengthy period.[40]

The monograph is instructive in many important respects, including the fact that it attempted to look at such a massive conflict only within the conventional, non-nuclear framework. It is also instructive in terms of the rather severe constraints which the carrier-centricity of the U.S. Navy imposed on the imagination of American planners, who still could not recognize the unfolding of a new paradigm which would render the carriers obsolete. The most peculiar phrase in the report on the mutual casualties of war is on page 134:

D+38 Red OSCAR SSGN launches only successful ASCM attack of war.[41]

This is an extremely important note which forecasts that on the 38th day of the simulated 1984 war between the USSR and the West, a project 949 Oscar-class missile submarine scored the only hit by the anti-shipping missiles P-700 Granit (NATO: SS-N-21 Shipwreck) on any NATO target of significance.

This brief review of the mutually inflicted casualties by no means showed Western "technological superiority," which was and continues to be the tune du jour since the early days of the Cold War. In the actual war game, the main asset of the U.S. Navy, its aircraft carriers, was being torpedoed left and right and even being heavily damaged by the salvos of cruise missiles by

Soviet long-range *Naval Missile-carrying Aviation (MRA)*. It is peculiar to regard the D+38 Red OSCAR SSGN as the only successful ASCM attack of the war game since, unlike the Soviet MRA which at that time in 1980s carried very high supersonic (Mach=4.6) anti-shipping missile *Kh-22* with active radar homing warhead, its range was around 600 kilometers which was making the mission of Soviet carriers of this missile—Tupolev TU-22—a very calamitous affair against any Carrier Battle Group if it was on alert and had E-2 Hawkeyes and its F-14s Tomcats, in the air and ready to take on those swarms of TU-22s. Soviets did recognize that the early versions of a Kh-22's homing devices were vulnerable to jamming and serious losses were expected among TU-22s. In other words, the U.S. Carrier Battle Groups had better chance of intercepting Soviet long-range aircraft, at least some of them, than the salvo of supersonic long-range anti-shipping missiles carried by stealthy Oscar-II SSGNs.

The first Aegis-equipped *Ticonderoga-class* cruisers began to be deployed in 1983 and instead of being equipped with MK-41 Vertical Launch System *(VLS)*, they carried outdated and slow MK-26 dual-rail launchers for their Standard MR SM *-2* anti-air missiles—systems simply not designed to deal with a massive salvo of anti-shipping missiles. Not until the end of 1986 would the U.S. Navy see new "improved" *Ticonderoga-class* cruisers, starting from *USS Bunker Hill (CG 52)*, entering the fleet. These ships carried much more "productive," meaning higher rate of fire, MK 41 VLS.[42] Arleigh Burke-class destroyers would not appear in the U.S. Navy until 1991. Moreover, the issues with much touted *Aegis* combat control system build around *SPY-1* Radar would not only continue to plague it early on, but the whole system failed to intercept even slow and "one-after-another"—a scenario excluded from real combat—missiles in tests. Out of 16 missiles launched "one-after-another" only 5 were shot down—a dismal and a deadly failure in case of a real war.[43]

Yet, in the 1984 military-technological war game paradigm, while the U.S. Naval War College assumed that some of its carriers would be damaged by torpedo salvos from Soviet submarines, it remained largely impervious to the likely impact of the Soviets'

The reality was, of course, self-evident. Russia's real gross domestic product, or in a broader sense, its real economy, was much larger than that of the United Kingdom or France and was equal to or larger than that of Germany. Nations with economies "smaller than Texas" are not capable of maintaining a state-of-the-art military such as Russia's, let alone gaining a decisive advantage in weapons that will define warfare for 20-30-year period at least. That the size of Russia's economy is routinely demeaned in the U.S. press and academe is only yet another indicator of the quality of the inquiry often conducted there.

The final conclusion on the matter would certainly give chills to proponents of the American exceptionalism and of the American way of war.

> Russian military expenditure, and as a consequence the potential for Russia to sustain its military power, is much more durable and less prone to fluctuations than it might appear. The implication is that even at its current anemic rate of economic growth, Russia is likely to be able to sustain a considerable level of military expenditure, posing an enduring challenge to the United States for the foreseeable decades. While ours is an exploratory analysis, it suggests that Russian defense spending is not prone to wild swings, nor has it been dramatically affected by changes in oil prices or U.S. sanctions. Given the disparity in national budget allocations, even as European allies increase their defense spending, Moscow is not going to struggle in keeping pace."[50]

The issue of how much bang a nation gets for a buck was never more pronounced than for the United States under present circumstances, which at present is not just being challenged by Russia or China or both, as many pundits let us believe, but actually faces a serious lag in military technology.

To be sure, nowadays, the term "hypersonic" is a hot catchword in Washington D.C. What was once laughed at in the United States as a nonsensical technology and operational concept five years ago, today is a center of attention of America's politicians, pundits and military. Suddenly, the United States wants its own hypersonic weapons. Considering the still impressive American technological and industrial expertise, there is little doubt that at some point in time the United States will be able to develop and deploy some sort of a hypersonic weapon, probably of a glider variety. As was reported by the media earlier in 2020, Pentagon did successfully test Common-Hypersonic Glide Body (C-HGB) which, allegedly, should start arriving to the field units in 2023.[51] However, there are many reasons to believe that this is not a realistic date, once one considers the general and well pronounced trend in American procurement to be behind the time-table by years, sometimes by as much as a decade or more. Moreover, America's prospects as it concerns developing a modern, fully controllable, air-breathing, hypersonic anti-shipping and land-attack missiles such as Russia's 3M22 Zircon (Tsirkon) are not very bright, considering the United States' failure to develop and procure even one supersonic anti-shipping missile with a respectable range, such as the Soviet/Russian P-700 Granit, not to speak of its P-800 Oniks.

This fact, however, didn't prevent National Security Adviser Robert O'Brien from declaring that all U.S. Navy destroyers will be armed with hypersonic missiles. Eventually. This statement created confusion even among people who would, otherwise, applaud such a decision. As Defence News noted:

> The Navy has discussed back-fitting some of the older Burke-class destroyers, but putting them on all three flights, including ships dating back to the early 1990s, would be a massive expansion of the capability in the surface fleet. The current launchers are not large enough to accommodate the larger diameter missiles. Swapping out the launchers on all the destroyers would be a significant expense and would likely tie

up shipyards for years to come. An alternative to back-fitting the older destroyers would be waiting for a smaller hypersonic missile to be developed, such as an air-breathing model, as opposed to the boost-glide design."[52]

An air breathing hypersonic missile for now remains merely a concept to demonstrate crucial technologies and is being developed by DARPA for feasibility studies under the title of the Hypersonic Air-breathing Weapon Concept (HAWC) program, which is long years away from becoming a weapon, let alone being procured.[53] NSA Advisor O'Brien, being a lawyer by education, didn't stop with this confusing announcement, however. Speaking at the Hudson Institute on October 28, 2020, he even threatened Russia with a U.S. deployment in Europe of hypersonic weapons— which the United States, actually, doesn't have and who knows when it will.[54] But there has been a dramatic change of the tone in the U.S. around the discussion on hypersonic weapons, which has gone from disbelief and even ridicule to hypersonic weapons being mentioned at every corner in the media and even on the top political level. The Russians were not impressed and released the videos of their air-defense and anti-missile complexes designed to repel attacks of any prospective hypersonic weapons.[55] This real news was obscured, however, by the white noise of the American election cycle.

During Kavkaz-2020 maneuvers which were held in Russia in September 2020, the submarine *SSK Kolpino* launched the 3M14M Kalibr-M land-attack cruise missile. This cruise missile was a deep upgrade of now famous 3M14 which became known for its strikes on ISIS targets in Syria. Unlike its predecessor this version of Kalibr has a range of 4,500 kilometers and a 1-ton warhead. This launch also announced the arrival of the new anti-shipping, M=2.9 on terminal, 3M54 Kalibr M missile which has same 1-ton warhead and a range of 1,500 kilometers.[56] The ramifications are enormous. For evangelists of American sea power the whole notion that a 900-ton-displacement missile ship of the Buyan or Karakurt classes can launch and sink any modern U.S.

Navy destroyer deployed to the Eastern Mediterranean without even leaving its naval base in Sevastopol or Novorossiysk may seem as anathema, but this was and is precisely the point—the rules of the game have changed. The fact that any Russian Pacific Fleet corvette deployed to the Bering Sea under the protection of own aviation can launch land attack Kalibr-M missiles and hit Seattle is a reality few in the U.S. military establishment would have predicted even ten years ago.

There were warnings—but they were dismissed as unimportant, despite the fact that already by the mid-2000s it was clear that advances in electronics, materials, fuels targeting and engine design would be bringing about today's reality. Time cannot be turned back, no matter how many American pundits and ideologues try to promote the utterly false narrative of the American military superiority. Being not the armed forces of the nation, but of supranational economic and globalist ideological interests, U.S. military today is designed entirely to serve only one purpose of colonial policing. The United States military and its military-industrial complex completely forgot that expeditionary warfare has very little to do with an actual defense. As a result, the United States proper has no viable air defense, except for much touted and dubiously effective against modern weaponry, THAAD, the real state of the U.S. Air Force is not known except that much of it is being cannibalized for spares, while much laughed at around the globe, including within the U.S. itself, F-35, in the words of one observer "is still a lemon."[57] U.S. military-industrial complex continues to churn out some ridiculously expensive and ineffective weapon systems which become obsolete before they even leave manufacturing floor. America's lagging behind in serious advanced missile technology is not just huge, it is increasing.

Feeble attempts to move away from carrier-centric navy by means of a timid "distributed lethality" doctrine, based around slow, subsonic, easily detectible and shot down by modern air-defense systems, anti-shipping missiles was dubious from the onset. Venerable *Harpoon* anti-shipping missile has reached its obsolescence long time ago, being slow (M-0.71) and relatively short range. U.S. Navy's new acquisition of the *Norwegian Kongsberg Naval Strike Missile (NSM)* gives the U.S. Navy somewhat better range when compared to *Harpoon* but nowhere near the range of its Russian counterparts. Moreover, *NSM* remains the same iteration of the light subsonic missiles not designed for modern advanced and net-centric battle against peer or near peer. The fact that the United States, after years of fruitless discussion on the fate of a disastrous *Littoral Combat Ship (LCS)* concept, was forced to resort to European FREMM frigate design by Italy's *Fincantieri*, granted, being built in the U.S. is another sign of a serious rot within the U.S. procurement system.[58] By the time first such frigate should be commissioned in 2026, the whole class will be effectively defenseless against advanced modern weapons. It was inevitable for the system which never defended own motherland to sputter and for all intents and purposes grind to a halt. Eventually, the luck was supposed to run out and it did run out.

Among the doctrinal rut and institutional rot which afflicted U.S. military, demoralization and intellectual collapse among its military elites, officers, reached an alarming scale. The letter by the former professor from the United States Military Academy at West Point, Lieutenant Colonel Heffington, himself a graduate of West-Point, class of 1997 was akin to a nuclear explosion, when his letter was published in the American Military News in 2017. Every officer school in the world has its problems, including with a discipline, once in a while. This is true for any military organization in Russia, United States, China or France. It is in the nature of the beast, transgressions are as normal a part of any high-level officer academic institution in the military as is discipline. But what Heffington described was downright disturbing. Apart from ideological and disciplinary issues, revelations about academics were stunning:

> Academic standards are also nonexistent. I believe this trend started approximately ten years ago, and it has continued to get worse. West Point has stated standards for academic expectations and performance, but they

are ignored. Cadets routinely fail multiple classes and they are not separated at the end-of-semester Academic Boards. Their professors recommend "Definitely Separate," but those recommendations are totally disregarded. I recently taught a cadet who failed four classes in one semester (including mine), in addition to several she had failed in previous semesters, and she was retained at the Academy. As a result, professors have lost hope and faith in the entire Academic Board process. It has been made clear that cadets can fail a multitude of classes and they will not be separated. Instead, when they fail (and they do to a staggering extent), the Dean simply throws them back into the mix and expects the faculty to somehow drag them through the academic program until they manage to earn a passing grade.[59]

One could have put these allegations into doubts being driven by loyalty but Tim Bakken, himself a professor at the West Point, dispelled any doubts about academic collapse in the Academy when in 2020 published his *The Cost of Loyalty: Dishonesty, Hubris, and Failure in the U.S. Military* in which he presented terrifying facts. He writes: "The Department of the Army became so concerned with the dropping quality of officer aspirants that it even considered converting the USMA [West Pont] from a 4-year to 3-year institution."[60] This is not an environment conducive to life-forming academic and service experiences which allow transition from a tactical to operational levels with further progression towards strategic level thinking, including across the variety of disciplines ranging from technology, to warfare, to economy to geopolitics. Not only these terrifying facts are the evidence of a disastrous level of American public education; West Point even accepted students who "scored in the Category IV range" on test for ASVAB [Armed Services Vocational Aptitude Battery], which in enlisted recruiting is the lowest allowable qualifying score.[61]

Few years ago, when having a conversation with one of the former combat pilots from Russian Air Force—RuAF Officer

Schools are 5 years, 6 days a week academies, same as Russian naval academies—he complained that throughout his career he never for once needed the course in Differential Equations he had to take while in academy. The response from the group was unanimous—they didn't teach you to use Differential Equations every day, they taught you to develop complex synaptic connections which are applicable for everyday life, including combat flying. He grudgingly admitted this to be true. From the point of view of an old Cold Warrior, in the Cold War 1.0 we all knew that our opponents were great professionals, very capable and smart, academically well-schooled, officers, which Cold War 1.0 in all domains proved to be largely true. Today, when one observes what happens in the so called "defense" field in the United States one cannot get rid off the sense of a complete surrealism, from American servicemen made to wear high heels and pregnancy simulators, "to experience what women experience," to promotion of the most radical racial and sexual theories, to political extremism—this is not the American military which I used to know. No doubt, there are still many first-rate professionals and truly talented and dedicated people in it, but the environment itself becomes increasingly toxic and not conducive for acceptance of the military-technological and geopolitical reality. No amount of preaching will address these increasingly disturbing problems unless the America recognizes and forms itself as a nation and builds her Armed Forces for defense of a motherland, not for enriching the class of globalists who view America as a merely a vehicle on their way to Orwellian reality, which America is becoming with an alarming rate.

Endnotes

1 Michael Hudson, "The Economics of American Super Imperialism: How the US Makes Countries Pay for Its Wars," *Unz Review,* April 24, 2020, https://www.unz.com/mhudson/the-economics-of-american-super-imperialism/.

2 Robert H. Latiff, *Future War. Preparing for the New Global Battlefield* (New York: Alfred A. Knopf, 2017), 131.

3 Roger Thompson, *Lessons Not Learned: The U.S. Navy Status Quo Culture* (Naval Institute Press, 2007), 167.

4 Michael Lind, "The Return of Geoeconomics," *The National Interest,* Oct. 13, 2019, https://nationalinterest.org/feature/return-geoeconomics-87826.

5 Ronald O'Rourke, "The Tanker War," *Proceedings,* May 1988, https://www.usni.org/magazines/proceedings/1988/may/tanker-war.

6 Peter Huchthausen, *America's Splendid Little Wars. A Short History of U.S. Military Engagements: 1975-2000* (New York: Viking, Penguin Group, 2003), 103.

7 Ibid.

8 *U.S. Policy in the Persian Gulf and Kuwaiti Reflagging. A reprint of a statement presented by Under Secretary Armacost before the Senate Foreign Relations Committee,* Washington, D.C., June 16, 1987, 14, https://apps.dtic.mil/dtic/tr/fulltext/u2/a496911.pdf.

9 Richard Pyle, "Navy Learns Many Lessons in Gulf Battle," The Associated Press, *Lakeland Ledger,* October 26, 1988, accessed February 1, 2021 on Google News archive, https://news.google.com/newspapers?nid=1346&dat=19881026&id=0PAvAAAAIBAJ&sjid=A_wDAAAAIBAJ&pg=1191,6109330&hl=en.

10 (Alexey Leonkov—military expert and the editor of a publication "Arsenal of Fatherland"), "Алексей Леонков – военный эксперт и редактор издания 'Арсенал Отечества'" *Men's Magazine,* August 20, 2020, https://natroix.ru/karera/aleksej-leonkov-voennyj-ekspert-i-redaktor-izdaniya-arsenal-otechestva.html.

11 World Bank, *IRAN, ISLAMIC REPUBLIC: Recent Developments,* MPO, October, 2019, http://pubdocs.worldbank.org/en/355601570664054605/EN-MPO-OCT19-Iran.pdf.

12 Carl Von Clausewitz, *On War* (Princeton, NJ, Princeton University Press, 1976), 75.

13 Daniel Larison, "The Inhumanity of 'Maximum Pressure,'" *The American Conservative,* October 16, 2020, https://www.theamericanconservative.com/state-of-the-union/the-inhumanity-of-maximum-pressure/.

14 Iliya Tsukanov, "71 Out of 103 Destroyed: Here's How Syria's Air Defense Repelled West's Missiles," *Sputnik,* April 14, 2018, https://sputniknews.com/military/201804141063558487-syria-air-defense-forces-analysis/.

15 "Trump's Big Flop In Syria by Publius Tacitus," *Sic Semper Tyrannis,* April 15, 2018, https://turcopolier.typepad.com/sic_semper_tyrannis/2018/04/trumps-big-flop-in-syria-by-publius-tacitus.html#more.

16 Rose Lopez Keravuori, "Lost in Translation: The American Way of War," *Small Wars Journal,* November 17, 2011, https://smallwarsjournal.com/jrnl/art/lost-in-translation-the-american-way-of-war.

17 Richard Pipes, "Why the Soviet Union thinks it Could Fight and Win a Nuclear War," *The Defense Policies of Nations: Comparative Study* (The John Hopkins University Press, 1982), 135.

18 Patrick Armstrong, "Americans, War – Slow Learners," *Strategic Culture Foundation,* August 5, 2020, https://www.strategic-culture.org/news/2020/08/05/americans-war-slow-learners/.

19 Ibid.

20 Jim Griffin, "A More Flexible Fleet," *Proceedings,* January 2015, 34.

21 Robert C. Rubel, *The Future of Aircraft Carriers: Consider the Air Wing, Not the Platform*, Center for International Maritime Security, December 3, 2019, http://cimsec.org/the-future-of-aircraft-carriers-consider-the-air-wing-not-the-platform/42469.

22 Ibid.

23 Andrei Martyanov, *The (Real) Revolution in Military Affairs*, (Atlanta: Clarity Press, Inc., 2019), 66–67.

24 "'We don't need aircraft carriers, we need weapons to sink them with' – Russian defense minister," *RT,* September 22, 2019, https://www.rt.com/russia/469353-russia-weapons-aircraft-carriers/.

25 MTCR, *Missile Technology Control Regime, FAQ,* https://mtcr.info/frequently-asked-questions-faqs/.

26 Missile Defense Project, "SS-N-26 'Strobile' (P-800 Oniks)/ Yakhont / Yakhont-M / Bastion (launch systems)," *Missile Threat,* Center for Strategic and International Studies, December 2, 2016, last modified June 15, 2018, https://missilethreat.csis.org/missile/ss-n-26/.

27 "World reacts after Iran fires missiles at US targets in Iraq," *Aljazeera,* January 8, 2020, https://www.aljazeera.com/news/2020/1/8/world-reacts-after-iran-fires-missiles-at-us-targets-in-iraq.

28 Adam Taylor, "Billions spent on U.S. weapons didn't protect Saudi Arabia's most critical oil sites from a crippling attack," *Washington Post,* September 17, 2019.

29 Ibid.

30 "'Панцири' для Абу-Даби" ("Pantsirs" for Abu-Dhabi), *Military-Industrial Courier,* November 22, 2011, https://vpk-news.ru/articles/8384.

31 Ben Wolfgang, "U.N. arms embargo on Iran expires," *The Washington Times,* October 18, 2020, https://www.washingtontimes.com/news/2020/oct/18/un-arms-embargo-on-iran-expires/.

32 "Iran rules out weapons 'buying spree' as UN embargo is set to expire," *France 24,* October 18, 2020, https://www.france24.com/en/middle-east/20201018-iran-rules-out-any-arms-buying-spree-as-it-expects-un-embargo-expected-to-end.

33 David Wainer, Anthony Capaccio, "Iran to Seek Advanced Arms as UN Embargo Expires, Pentagon Says," *Bloomberg,* November 19, 2020, https://www.bloomberg.com/news/articles/2019-11-19/iran-to-seek-advanced-arms-as-un-embargo-expires-pentagon-says.

34 "Министр обороны Ирана заявил о соглашении с Россией по развитию иранской авиации" (Iran's Defense Minister announced an agreement with Russia on a development of Iranian aviation), *TASS,* October 19, 2020, https://tass.ru/mezhdunarodnaya-panorama/9754919.

35 Igor Yanvarev, Rinat Abdullin, "Российские истребители стали для Ирана важнее С-400" (Russian fighters became more important to Iran than S-400), *News.RU,* August 24, 2020, https://news.ru/near-east/rossijskie-istrebiteli-stali-dlya-irana-vazhnee-s-400/.

36 Carl Von Clausewitz, *On War* (Princeton, NJ: Princeton University Press, 1976), 627.

37 Jonah Goldberg, "Baghdad Delenda Est, Part Two," *National Review,* April 23, 2002.

38 Dmitri Simes, *Со скоростью гиперзвука ракета "Циркон" перевернула представления об идеальном оружии сдерживания (With a hypersonic speed "Zircon" missile overturned understanding of an ideal deterrent)*, News at First Channel, October 11, 2020, https://youtu.be/NTtmGDd-1Dc.

39 Chris Sullentrop, "Douglas Feith: What has the Pentagon's third man done wrong? Everything," *Slate,* May 20, 2004, https://slate.com/news-and-politics/2004/05/douglas-feith-undersecretary-of-defense-for-fiascos.html.

40 Captain Robert H. Gile (U.S. Navy, Ret.), *Global War Game,* Second Series 1984–1988, Naval War College Newport Papers, August 20, 2004, Foreword, https://digital-commons.usnwc.edu/newport-papers/34

41 Ibid., 134.

42 Norman Polmar, The Naval Institute Guide to Ships and Aircraft of the U.S. Fleet, 18th Edition (Annapolis, Maryland: Naval Institute Press, 2005), 138–42.

43 Roger Thompson, *Lessons Not Learned: The U.S. Navy Status Quo Culture* (Naval Institute Press, 2007), 176–77.

44 Ibid., 45, 81.

45 "Генштаб РФ: система разведки 'Легенда' давала СССР полную картину Фолклендского конфликта" (Russia's General Staff: reconnaissance system "Legenda" provided USSR with a full picture of Falkland Conflict), *TASS,* January 20, 2020, https://tass.ru/armiya-i-opk/7564843.

46 Stephen F. Cohen, "Distorting Russia," *War with Russia? From Putin & Ukraine to Trump & Russiagate,* (New York: Hot Books Kindle Ed., 2019).

47 Ibid.

48 Richard Connolly, "Russian Military Expenditure in Comparative Perspective: A Purchasing Power Parity Estimate," University of Birmingham & Chatham House, *CNA,* October 2019, https://www.cna.org/CNA_files/PDF/IOP-2019-U-021955-Final.pdf.

49 Michael Kofman and Richard Connolly, "Why Russian Military Expenditure Is Much Higher Than Commonly Understood (As Is China's)," *War on the Rocks,* December 16, 2019, https://warontherocks.com/2019/12/why-russian-military-expenditure-is-much-higher-than-commonly-understood-as-is-chinas/.

50 Ibid.

51 Jen Judson, "Pentagon's major hypersonic glide body flight test deemed success," *Defense News,* March 20, 2020, https://www.defensenews.com/smr/army-modernization/2020/03/20/pentagons-major-hypersonic-glide-body-flight-test-deemed-success/.

52 David Larter, "All US Navy destroyers will get hypersonic missiles, says Trump's national security adviser," *Defense News, Yahoo,* Oct. 22, 2020, https://www.yahoo.com/news/us-navy-destroyers-hypersonic-missiles-141639181.html.

53 Ed Adamczyk, "DARPA's air-breathing hypersonic missiles ready for free-flight tests," *UPI,* September 2, 2020, https://www.upi.com/Defense-News/2020/09/02/DARPAs-air-breathing-hypersonic-missiles-ready-for-free-flight-tests/5321599071903/.

54 "America's National Security Challenges, Today and Tomorrow: A Conversation with Robert O'Brien," *Hudson Institute*, October 28, 2020, https://youtu.be/xWJReyfHSGU.

55 "Пуск новой противоракеты системы ПРО" (The launch of a new anti-missile of the anti-missile system), *TV Zvezda,* October 28, 2020, https://youtu.be/vIMDNSsZt1E.

56 "Новый «Калибр-М» меняет глобальные правила игры" (New "Kalibr-M" changes the rules of the game), *Sonar2050,* October 25, 2020, https://youtu.be/6ogiXBkJLUY.

57 Sean Gallaher, "DOD tester's report: F-35 is still a lemon," *Ars Technica,* January 30, 2020, https://arstechnica.com/information-technology/2020/01/not-a-straight-shooter-dod-review-cites-fleet-of-faults-in-f-35-program/.

58 David Larter, "The US Navy selects Fincantieri design for next-generation frigate," *Defense News,* April 30, 2020, https://www.defensenews.com/breaking-news/2020/04/30/the-us-navy-selects-fincantieri-design-for-next-generation-frigate/.

59 Melissa Leon and Editorial Staff, "Exclusive: Former West Point professor's letter exposes corruption, cheating and failing standards" [Full letter], *American Military News,* October 11, 2017, https://americanmilitarynews.com/2017/10/exclusive-former-west-point-professors-letter-exposes-corruption-cheating-and-failing-standards-full-letter/.

60 Tim Bakken, *The Cost of Loyalty: Dishonesty, Hubris, and Failure in the U.S. Military,* Kindle edition (Bloomsbury Publishing, 2020), 282.

61 Ibid., 278.

8. EMPIRE ÜBER ALLES— INCLUDING AMERICANS

America's Corporatist Military

American nationhood, or rather its historic failure to coalesce into a genuine nation, together with its benefiting from an exceptional geographic location, making America impervious to the weapons of an early industrial age, has played a cruel joke on the American "way of war" and its military thought throughout its history. Almost four years ago I wrote:

> The secret of American weaponry of the 21st century is not really a secret—American weapons are made for sale. They are made for profit as commercial items, be it commerce inside the U.S. or internationally. This was inevitable in a nation which never fought a foreign invader in its history nor, by dint of geography, had much to fear. It is very telling that a small American military-technological idiosyncrasy of using the term "sophisticated" instead of "effective" when passing the judgment on the quality of its weapons systems, took such a profound hold inside American military culture.[1]

This notion that there is something inherently wrong with the American view of warfare and, by implications, geopolitics is not new. In 2016 Benjamin H. Friedman and Justin Logan arrived to a conclusion, a correct one, that:

The vast majority of U.S. foreign policy makers are
devotees of primacy, a grand strategy that sees global
U.S. military exertions—alliances, foreign bases,
patrols, military training, regular wars, and continual
air-strikes—as the only guarantee of national security,
global stability, and free trade. Foreign policy debate
in Washington, when it exists, mostly concerns how
to implement primacy rather than alternative grand
strategies.[2]

The answer to this question is rather simple: to discuss any
grand strategy in the second half of the 20th, let alone 21st century
it is not enough to have what Friedman and Logan describe as
their qualifications:

The U.S. foreign policy establishment—the group
of people typically appointed to security posts in the
federal government, writing for the major opinion
pages, and hired by most prominent think tanks—
barely debates grand strategy.[3]

Far from discussing "grand strategy," as the overwhelming
empirical evidence demonstrates, in matters of operations and
tactics this is exactly the group of people which is utterly unqualified
for passing serious judgements on what is required for any grand
strategy—a balance of real power and its dynamics. Indeed, a body
of overwhelming empirical evidence exists today demonstrating
that not only is the American establishment incapable of debating
the issue, let alone developing any grand strategy, it is absolutely
situationally unaware. Worse, it is simply incapable of developing
global situational awareness, at least publicly, and as such is
forced to pass off pseudo-scholastic semantic play for "strategy,"
which is a fig leaf covering the absence of the only assumption this
establishment can operate on—America's economic, military and
political primacy. This is not to say that there are no people in this
establishment who understand the dramatic and very dangerous
fallacy of such an approach—primarily people with real military

backgrounds and service experiences. It is absolutely legitimate
to state that today the remnants of the American geopolitical
competence rests primarily with the U.S. military and even
there, those remnants continue to evaporate at a very high rate
or are being compromised by connections to military-industrial
complex. That should give us all a pause.

The U.S. military has not been like the classic militaries of
nation-states since the post-WW II period. The reason is because
it is not operating as a nation to start with. The United States,
as a powerful and large country, certainly, has vital interests but
how many of those interests are truly national—for the good of
the nation, including the wellbeing of its people, its infrastructure,
etc.? This question doesn't have a straight answer. Bonnie Kristian
is entirely justified in her anger:

> For nearly two decades and over three administrations,
> U.S. foreign policy has assigned American soldiers
> to reckless, counterproductive, miserable and even
> impossible tasks. It has asked them to act well outside
> their rightful purpose and oath of enlistment. It has
> tasked them with battles unconnected to U.S. interests
> and neglected constitutional safeguards. It has asked
> our troops to kill and be killed as instruments of
> aggression rather than defense.[4]

But she makes a mistake; the United States has been involved
in wars of aggression since the Korean War, and even before the
two world wars. This is more than a century-long record of doing
anything but defending national interests. And whose interests
were they, indeed? Assumptions are not good tools for sound
foreign policy and prosecuting a war. U.S. elites have proved
themselves incapable of learning this for far longer than "nearly
two decades." But does the U.S. military represent the American
nation or is it merely a tool of transnational corporations and
global financial institutions for furthering their agenda?

Today, the answer to this is obvious, it is the latter. Not
only are American wars a racket, they are wars that are conducted

contrary to real American national interests—if one assumes that there is an American proto-nation still in existence and its overriding proto-national legitimate interests are security, guaranteed survival that is, and prosperity.

Here is a conundrum: the official title of the Pentagon is the Department of Defense. As was noted sarcastically by many over the years, the term "Defense" is an odd qualifier for a department which has never defended its homeland once in its history and has distinguished itself primarily by fighting in distant lands which could not threaten the United States. It seems absolute madness to consider the constant and reckless wasting of the national resources through the wars America conducts as serving any kind of national interest, unless those wars are conducted on behalf of supranational interests, who merely use the United States, with its dwindling economy and social disintegration, as a vehicle, because the United States Armed Forces are not designed or structured for a defense of motherland anyway. The only rationale for their existence is for servicing the well-known machine of threat inflation, as Daniel Larison defines it.[5]

It is precisely this never-ending threat inflation which passes for a debate of grand strategy in Washington D.C. As Colonel Lawrence Wilkerson summarizes it: "America exists today to make war."[6] Remarkably, America makes wars which it cannot prosecute competently on any level above the tactical, let alone win, and even there, it is merely an issue of America's overwhelming technological superiority over her opponents. Making war in America's case is tantamount to self-suffocating in order to make an armed robber's job easier, rather than fighting back or at least running away. Dwight Eisenhower's 1961 warning about the powerful interests of the Military-Industrial Complex are known even by those whose acquaintance with America's history is very brief. It is one of the most important political speeches in American history. Few would doubt that nation of such size and capability as the United States needs its own military-industrial complex. Russia has its own, so does China or, for that matter, France, which, among Western nations, is second only to the United States in producing and maintaining its independent nuclear deterrent and building a large share of its military technology based on French know-how.

France, while hardly exemplifying successful social, cultural, or economic policies, still maintains a military capability which provides for a reliable national defense in case of just about any type of attack on French territory, including by a global power, since France deploys a robust naval nuclear deterrent, also known as a Strategic Oceanic Force, all of which, from strategic nuclear power submarines to sea-launched ballistic missiles, are of French origin. The British Royal Navy, while having its own naval nuclear deterrent, uses American-designed Trident SLBMs and is not allowed to modify them, despite the British prime minister having the authority to launch.[7]

Both the United Kingdom and France have regional and global aspirations while the latter has military means for some power projection in the Mediterranean on its own. Unlike the Royal Navy, however, which commissioned two aircraft Queen Elizabeth-class carriers which are useless without U.S. designed and produced F-35B fighters, the French Navy, aka *Marine Nationale*, operates not only a fully French-designed and built nuclear powered aircraft carrier, the Charles de Gaulle, but de Gaulle's air wing consists, with the exception of two U.S.-made E-2 Hawkeye early warning aircraft of French-designed and made Dassault Rafale M fighters, which gives France a degree of flexibility and independence, which no other NATO member, including the United Kingdom has. But what is important about French defensive posture, once one removes France's aggressive attempts on regime change in Libya and Syria, force structure-wise, is that France looks like a well-balanced defense-wise nation and the term "nation" is crucial here, since French military views evolved as that of an independent nation which was able to formulate its national interest, which included its agreeing, after a bloody war, to the independence of Algeria, letting go French colonial possessions and establishing the Fifth Republic. Quitting NATO de facto, including by means of removing all U.S. troops from French territory in 1966, was one of the more prominent endeavors of a national interest undertaken by de Gaulle, who also clearly understood that an indigenous and comprehensive military-industrial complex and ability to deter the enemy was at the foundation of national sovereignty. France, being a true continental power unlike the United States, certainly had had its own history of war and invasions, both as aggressor and as a victim, and was able to arrive to such conclusions. In developing a comprehensive French military-industrial complex, de Gaulle was acting as a true national leader.

Eisenhower, warning "against the acquisition of unwarranted influence, whether sought or unsought, by the military-industrial complex" was also acting as a true national leader.[8]

Today neither France nor the United States are nations in a full meaning of this word, with France descending into the chaos of globalist multicultural orthodoxy, while the United States is completely subverted by ethno-religious and corporate interests, which run U.S. military-industrial complex like a cash cow, which must provide profit margins, and not the effective elimination of an enemy which actually fights back. Such circumstances do not require an exhaustive study of history, operational planning or developing situational awareness. As long as a fairly defenseless country can be targeted for aggression and openly false, threat-inflated rationales can be presented for the delivery of American-made munitions and platforms, the going should be really good.

What National Interest?

This is anything but the pursuit of national interests. It is corporatism on a grand scale. Charles Erwin Wilson, President Eisenhower's nominee for defense secretary, and at that time the General Motors CEO, reluctantly agreed, when facing the Senate Armed Services Committee in 1953, to sell his GM stockholdings to avoid a conflict of interest. Wilson explained that he honestly saw no problem in holding on to his stock "because for years I thought what was good for our country was good for General Motors, and vice versa."[9] Wilson, at least, had some point—General Motors of 1953 was making a tangible product which was in demand, and making it in America. Today, apart from exporting inflation and shoving increasingly inferior American military technology down the throats of the U.S. "allies" in NATO and elsewhere, the United States acts not as a nation but as a corporation and financial Ponzi scheme and money laundering organization. Modern America's military doctrine was encapsulated in headlines on the morning after Donald Trump ordered missile strikes on the Shayrat military base in Syria on April 7, 2017:

> Investors seem to be betting President Trump's decision to retaliate against Syria after the chemical attack on Syrian citizens earlier this week may mean the Pentagon will need more Tomahawks. The Department of Defense asked for $2 billion over five years to buy 4,000 Tomahawks for the U.S. Navy in its fiscal 2017 budget last February. Nearly five dozen Tomahawk cruise missiles were launched at military bases in Syria from U.S. warships in the Mediterranean Sea late Thursday. Raytheon (RTN) wasn't the only defense stock rising Friday either. Lockheed Martin (LMT), which partners with Raytheon on the Javelin missile launcher system and also makes Hellfire missiles, gained nearly 1%.[10]

The main objective of this "doctrine" is not winning wars—it is starting them. The longer those wars continue, the better it is for the bottom line of defense contractors and subcontractors. For a country whose officers and soldiers never fought against an enemy in direct defense of their motherland the whole surrealism of the situation may not be as immediately obvious but the chronic, debilitating effect on military thought cannot be denied, once one delves into the particulars of American warfare views' evolution for the last 30-40 years. As the late Richard Pipes noted in 1977 about the U.S. approach to war: "We have no General Staff; we grant no higher degrees in 'military science'; and except for Admiral Mahan, we have produced no strategist of international repute."[11] Pipes may have ulterior motives for arriving at this conclusion: to fan the flames of the Cold War, as he was one of the more outspoken not only anti-communists but Russophobes. Yet, in doing so, Pipes pretty much described the state of the American strategic thought which since then declined dramatically, if not precipitously, and missed almost completely what was then already emerging as a main vehicle of the real revolution in military affairs which was merely delayed by the collapse of the Soviet Union and resulting chaos of Russia in 1990s. When it ultimately arrived in the 2010s it overturned the American view on war and strategic balance completely.

It is worth noting that empires—and the United States is an empire—by their very nature are supranational constructs which by no means insulate the nation at the heart of the metropole from the influences of the colonies. The British Empire was a testament to the multinational nature of the empire business; so were the Roman and the Russian empires, as were the other European colonial empires. The United States, which proclaims its interests to be global in nature, is no exception. Obviously, the fact that multinational empires do not endure and end up in the agony of collapse is not a geopolitical truism many in the United States want to keep in mind. But, as the decline of the metropoles of former empires such as Great Britain or France demonstrate, Enoch Powell's warning was prophetic. As recent events in France, such as Arab-Chechen violence in the French city of Dijon demonstrate, Western nations are incapable of assimilating other peoples.[12] In so doing, the majority ethnicity in the empire-building nation, be they French, English or, what are called "whites" (people of European descent) in the U.S., are subjected to what they regard and resent as reverse discrimination and suffocating political correctness and censure.

Thus, Steve Sailer's famous dictum expressed in the title of his 2005 book, *Invade-the-world-Invite-the-World*, came to fruition in the West which sees no inhibitions in destroying nations abroad by invading them, then admitting as refugees those fleeing the destruction they have wreaked, thus simultaneously destroying the cultural homogeneity and sense of national ownership of their domestic majorities, who increasingly reject what they regard as suicidal immigration and multicultural policies.[13] This degradation of the West not in relative, but in absolute terms is a final result of the globalist agenda of neoliberalism which views a nation as "no more than so many human atoms who happened to live under the same set of laws."[14] The combined West wants to maintain an imperialist posture, while simultaneously homogenizing its own population into the gray mass of consumers devoid of passions and attachments that cultural affinities provide. The clockwork of globalism is anti-national in principle and indeed anti-multinational as it concerns other states.

It cannot be otherwise within the framework of free trade orthodoxy and full penetration of other economies to the advantage of the dominant corporations' bottom line. One of the unpleasant things white Americans are beginning to learn nowadays is the fact that for many corporations, their bottom line is by far more important than maintaining a coherent American culture of whatever passes today for the American nation, or indeed the wellbeing of those comprising it. John Derbyshire, formerly of *The National Review*, may produce some well-written fumes regarding lack of any principles in the American political class but nothing can change the trend which is woven not into the political mechanism of the United States, which is primarily a derivative, but into the economic DNA of American corporatism—the nation doesn't matter as long as the margin of profit grows while costs decline. As Derbyshire writes:

> Outrage of the week was surely Utah Senator Mike Lee getting his S.386 bill through the U.S. Senate. S.386 means a massive loosening of the rules for foreign workers to take up white-collar jobs in the U.S.A. ... Lee didn't have to break much of a sweat to get his bill passed. He used a Senate rule called "Unanimous Consent," which allows the chamber to pass legislation with no hearings or debate, so long as no Senator objects. No Senator did—not one.[15]

S.386 is but the latest of many other measures, not the least of them NAFTA, which seek to remove any significance of the needs and rights of American workers, the majority of whom are of white European stock, from consideration as it concerns the management of the American economy. With the ongoing dilution of the visible and numerical role of the white majority that has been historically known and recognized as representing it, the American national identity is simply disappearing. Balanced off against its warts and crimes, so many of which are now coming to light in waves of revisionist history, America's white European population still deserves recognition as having played a crucial role in contributing to America's legitimate greatness and the values of liberty and law which had made America attractive to so many.

In his important 2009 treatise on the Islamization of Europe, Christopher Caldwell, somewhat hastily and presumptuously concluded, when comparing immigration policies of Europe and the United States that:

> Immigration *is* Americanization. …America maybe open in theory, but in practice it exerts Procrustean pressures on its immigrants to conform, and it is its pressures, not its openness that have bound America's diverse citizens together as one people. Yes, you can have a "hyphenated identity" if you insist on it—but you had better know which side of the hyphen your bread is buttered on.[16]

Caldwell's conclusions that the pressures of conformity could create one people seem in train to be debunked, undone by the extremities of the initial relationships. Founded as a state by settler colonizers whose southern states operationalized slaveholding, then apartheid, Americans never were one people in the past, and as a wave of racially and politically charged violence rolled over U.S. cities in 2020, it seems likely that there never will be "one people" in America in future. Indeed, even the whites seem to be bifurcating on ideological lines, as those supportive of America's globalist elites line up against its disparaged white "deplorable" majority. In the current and forthcoming economic crisis, could violence reach a critical threshold unleashing a full-blown racial and economic warfare?

Under such circumstances one is forced to question whether the United States is even capable of formulating any national interest when it already is composed of several nations, no matter how one insists on denying their existence. Whose interests, African American, WASP, Latino or maybe Jewish ones, do America's military operations in Iraq defend? The influence of Israel lobby in the United States is an established fact and, these were and are primarily, albeit not exclusively, Israeli interests that are served by American involvement in the Middle East. As John Mearsheimer and Steven Walt note:

> The overall thrust of U.S. policy in the region is due almost entirely to U.S. domestic politics, and especially to the activities of the "Israel Lobby." Other special interest groups have managed to skew U.S. foreign policy in directions they favored, but no lobby has managed to divert U.S. foreign policy as far from what the American national interest would otherwise suggest, while simultaneously convincing Americans that U.S. and Israeli interests are essentially identical.[17]

Both Mearsheimer and Walt, while admitting that both Israel and other ethnic lobbies effectively subverted U.S. foreign policy, still refer to some "American national interest," but never define it. Nobody is trying. At least, nobody within the political and governing elites is speaking to the interests of the average Joe or Jane, who are being robbed and run into the ground by policies which do not serve the shrinking American, primarily white but not exclusively, middle and working class. It is being slaughtered as a sacrificial lamb on the altar of globalism and multiculturalism whose only beneficiaries are transnational corporations which care not about right or wrong, about ethics or morality as long as the mechanism of military and economic aggression provides for their bottom line. America's foreign policy and military machine are built around this idea. As Bronislaw Malinowski noted in 1941: "Another interesting point in the study of aggression is that, like charity, it begins at home."[18]

America today is a torn country in the process of evolving into an existential and, most likely, terminal and losing struggle to overcome the historical, psychological, and anthropological centrifugal forces of disintegration. Under such circumstances any talk about the national anything, least of all interest, of the United States is an exercise in futility. The American interest today, as it was to a large degree over the last hundred years, is the interest of corporations, foreign and internal ethnic and religious lobbies, and other special interests, none of which really cares of American nation, whether it exists or perishes with the latter being the most likely outcome.

Nobody's minding the shop.

Endnotes

1 Andrei Martyanov, *Losing Military Supremacy: The Myopia of American Strategic Planning* (Atlanta: Clarity Press, Inc., 2018), 179.

2 Benjamin H. Friedman and Justin Logan, "Why Washington Doesn't Debate Grand Strategy," *Strategic Studies Quarterly,* Winter 2016, https://www.cato.org/sites/cato.org/files/articles/ssq_1216_friedman.pdf.

3 Ibid.

4 Bonnie Kristian, "The Biggest Insult to the American Military Is Our Foreign Policy," *Military.com,* September 16, 2020, https://www.military.com/daily-news/opinions/2020/09/16/biggest-insult-american-military-our-foreign-policy.html.

5 Daniel Larison, *Even a Pandemic Can't Kill Threat Inflation*, The American Conservative, April 20, 2020, https://www.theamericanconservative.com/larison/even-a-pandemic-cant-kill-threat-inflation/.

6 Lawrence Wilkerson, "'America Exists Today to Make War'": Lawrence Wilkerson on Endless War & American Empire, *Democracy Now,* January 13, 2020, https://youtu.be/JYHRlK3VYbI.

7 Freedom of Information Act, ref. 21-06-2005-094719-001, Directorate of Chemical, Biological, Radiological and Nuclear Policy – Assistant Director (Deterrence Policy), July 19, 2005, https://webarchive.nationalarchives.gov.uk/20121109140513/http://www.mod.uk/NR/rdonlyres/E2054A40-7833-48EF-991C-7F48E05B2C9D/0/nuclear190705.pdf.

8 Dwight D. Eisenhower, "Eisenhower's Farewell Address to the Nation, January 17, 1961," *Dwight D. Eisenhower Presidential Library, National Archives,* https://www.eisenhowerlibrary.gov/sites/default/files/research/online-documents/farewell-address/reading-copy.pdf.

9 Dan Ponterfact, "What's Good for Our Country Was Good for General Motors," *Forbes,* November 26, 2018, https://www.forbes.com/sites/danpontefract/2018/11/26/whats-good-for-our-country-was-good-for-general-motors/#6cc140d52075.

10 Paul R. La Monica, "Tomahawk maker's stock up after U.S. launch on Syria," *CNN Business,* April 7, 2017, https://money.cnn.com/2017/04/07/investing/syria-raytheon-tomahawk-missiles/index.html.

11 Richard Pipes, "Why the Soviet Union Thinks It Could Fight and Win a Nuclear War," *Commentary Magazine,* July 1, 1977, https://www.commentarymagazine.com/articles/richard-pipes-2/why-the-soviet-union-thinks-it-could-fight-win-a-nuclear-war/.

12 "French city of Dijon rocked by unrest blamed on Chechens seeking revenge," *France 24,* June 16, 2020.

https://www.france24.com/en/20200616-french-city-of-dijon-rocked-by-unrest-blamed-on-chechens-seeking-revenge.

13 Steve Sailer, "Invade-the-World-Invite-the-World Personified," *ISteve,* February 24, 2005, https://isteve.blogspot.com/2005/02/invade-world-invite-world-personified.html.

14 Corelli Barnett, *The Collapse of British Power* (New York: William Morrow & Company, Inc., 1972), 91.

15 John Derbyshire, "U.S. Senate (INCLUDING Republican Senators) to U.S. Citizen Tech Workers—Drop Dead!" *Unz Review,* December 5, 2020, https://www.unz.com/jderbyshire/u-s-senate-including-republican-senators-to-u-s-citizen-tech-workers-drop-dead/.

16 Christopher Caldwell, *Reflections on the Revolution in Europe* (New York: Anchor Books, 2009), 276-277.

17 John Mearsheimer and Steven Walt, "The Israel Lobby and U.S. Foreign Policy," HKS Working Paper No. RWP06-011, Harvard Kennedy School Faculty Research Working Paper Series, March 2006, https://research.hks.harvard.edu/publications/getFile.aspx?Id=209.

18 Bronislaw Malinowski, *An Anthropological Analysis of War: War Studies from psychology, sociology, anthropology* (New York: Basic Books, Inc, 1964), 251.

9. TO BE OR NOT TO BE

Internal Divisions

Today, the United States is not a nation, certainly not in the traditional sense of having a dominant ethnic nationality, while the foundational American meme and myth of a "Melting Pot" has turned out to be exactly that—a myth. America's many ethnicities have not been assimilated to form a single nation, but rather are more aptly regarded as a salad bowl comprised of descendants of the majority "white" European settlers and the "colored" (Native American, African American, and Latin and Asian immigrant) minorities, all maintaining to varying degrees their original cultural identities.[1] But even the salad bowl analogy is too weak to reflect the multicultural disaster the United States has become.

The country is utterly divided and not merely by political views. Divisions along political and ideological lines are nothing new in human history. The United States fought a Civil War over those divisions, but it was a civil war for a reason—people of the same culture and largely of the same ancestry (European, Anglo-Saxonized) were fighting each other over states' rights, the structuring of economic activity and, among other divisions, over slavery. At that time, America seemed to be firmly on its way to becoming a nation. But it never happened.

There is no longer a distinct American identity because whatever that might have been hasn't been allowed to settle. An indication of a possible resolution to this peculiar American self-immolation now taking place came, paradoxically, from Russia. While the Western media, predictably, were spinning the "Putin-the-autocrat" narrative during Russia's preparation for voting on amendments to its Constitution in 2020, one amendment to article 68 of what is effectively a new Russian Constitution would give the modern American polity an aneurism.

Article 68 of Russia's Constitution para 1. states that: "The State language on all the territory of the Russian Federation is the Russian (*Russkii*) language, *the language of the State-founding people.*"[2] In fact, nowadays in America anything even remotely comparable to acknowledging that Euro-Americans represent the core nationality of the United States would be an anathema for the primarily globalist establishment—not the minority groups who legitimately seek recognition as being among the founding peoples, but from the majority of the Euro-American media to the majority-dominated political parties—which run America today.

The significance of Article 68 is not in declaring the Russian language an official State language, it is in recognizing the role of the Russian people—not in the English-language political tradition of calling anyone born within the territory of the state a citizen, but rather by designating the ethno-cultural features of that founding group, ranging from race, blood, language and common heritage, among many other things, as the core of the nation.

The response of Russia's internal Chechen nationality was expressed by the reaction of Chechnya's minister of communications, Dzhambulat Umarov, to the 2018 Russian language law:

> "I have no doubt that the nations of the Russian Federation had, have and will have the right and desire to learn their own languages. It is understandable why people do not want to learn the language because our subjects are multinational, and representatives of other nationalities do not want to learn additional languages of the indigenous peoples of the subject. This is their right. The law does not violate the rights of the nations of the Russian Federation. They only reaffirm their commitment to the leadership of the Russian Federation on democratic principles," says Umarov.[3]

Such an orientation is at the present time antipathetic and impossible to propose in the United States—even though it points the way out of this American dilemma. Such a recognition of the majority would of necessity require its recognition of the other founding peoples within the territory of the United States when it emerged as a state—the African Americans, Native Americans and Chicanos—irrespective of their status within the legal system of the U.S. at that time. And similar to adjustments made in Russia to resolve the extreme discord with the Chechen nationality, would include systemic adjustments as may be required to enable America's national minorities and internal peoples to maintain their distinct ethnic identities within the context of also being Americans, and enjoying all civil rights of American citizens.

After shedding and letting go of its empire in the wake of the Soviet collapse, Russians recognized that living peacefully in a multicultural country is possible only by recognizing the significance of the majority of its people. In the case of the Russian Federation an overwhelming majority among the different nationalities populating Russia are ethnic Russians, as in *Russkie*, who constitute 81 percent of Russia's population.[4] The rights of all other ethnicities populating Russia are protected and nobody is persecuted or ostracized in Russia for saying that without specifically Russian people there would have been no Russia.

But today in America, it would be regarded as racist and inadmissible to state in any Western media that without the primarily white Christian settlers of European descent, the Euro-Americans, there would have been no modern-day America—the very media that presumptuously regard themselves as agenda-setters for America's African American minority. David North's analysis of recent *New York Times* coverage provides critical insight into how and why it has been not only so divisive for America, but also so very off the wall:

> The "financialization" of the *Times* has proceeded alongside another critical determinant of the newspaper's selection of issues to be publicized and promoted: that is, its central role in the formulation and aggressive marketing of the policies of the Democratic Party. This process has served to

obliterate the always tenuous boundary lines between objective reporting and sheer propaganda. The consequences of the *Times'* financial and political evolution have found a particularly reactionary expression in the 1619 Project. Led by Ms. Nikole Hannah-Jones and *New York Times Magazine* editor Jake Silverstein, the 1619 Project was developed for the purpose of providing the Democratic Party with a historical narrative that legitimized its efforts to develop an electoral constituency based on the promotion of racial politics. Assisting the Democratic Party's decades-long efforts to disassociate itself from its identification with the social welfare liberalism of the New Deal to Great Society era, the 1619 Project, by prioritizing racial conflict, marginalizes, and even eliminates, class conflict as a notable factor in history and politics.

The shift from class struggle to racial conflict did not develop within a vacuum. The *New York Times,* as we shall explain, is drawing upon and exploiting reactionary intellectual tendencies that have been fermenting within substantial sections of middle-class academia for several decades.

The political interests and related ideological considerations that motivated the 1619 Project determined the unprincipled and dishonest methods employed by the *Times* in its creation. The *New York Times* was well aware of the fact that it was promoting a race-based narrative of American history that could not withstand critical evaluation by leading scholars of the Revolution and Civil War. The *New York Times Magazine*'s editor deliberately rejected consultation with the most respected and authoritative historians.[5]

In fact, as the recent rioting by globalist brown-shirts—the white but radically anti-white domestic terrorist organization, ANTIFA and the highly foundation-funded anti-Western Black

Lives Matter (BLM), whose followers appear to be primarily white—has demonstrated, the assault on white Euro-American heritage has started in earnest and may well continue with different degrees of intensity well into America's future irrespective of the Trump presidential loss, until the United States is fully Balkanized.

America's remaining vestiges of freedom of speech may not just give way to the intimidations of the "cancel culture," but actually be eradicated by a strong push in favor of laws banning hate speech which—even as they purport to be seeking to give voice to the painful historical experience of the dispossessed Native and enslaved African peoples—seek in actuality to deconstruct and background the role of white people and the actual historical and statistical data that backs that up. As America's media, universities and colleges have already demonstrated, the process is well underway. This process takes on grotesque forms, such as declaring math "racist" by the Seattle Public Schools Ethnic Studies Advisory Committee (ESAC) which released a rough draft of notes for its Math Ethnic Studies framework in late September, which attempts to connect math to a history of oppression. "The committee suggests that math is subjective and racist, saying under one section, 'Who gets to say if an answer is right?' and under another, 'how is math manipulated to allow inequality and oppression to persist?'"[6] Not to be outdone in race-baiting was a recent article appearing in *The Nation* magazine proposing to count voices of black Americans twice in what was defined as "vote reparations."[7] The fact that this ludicrous, not to mention openly discriminatory towards the white and other minorities' population of the United States, idea was even worthy of presenting in what amounts to the herald of Democratic party's left wing is a troubling sign, showing the extent of destructive racialist radicalization on what passes in the United States for the largely white "left wing."

America's disintegration rests squarely on the foundation of post-modernism whose effect and perhaps aim is infinite cultural fragmentation and the promulgation of hatred of those traditions rooted in the acceptance of the fact that the truth is knowable and can be agreed upon. Post-modernism rejects the notion of universal truth as such and clears the pathway to wholesale bifurcations in the society which is constantly subjected to the pressures of satisfying each and every narrative—as long this process of satisfaction serves the foundational purpose of globalism, the destruction of nationhood and of any nation's building block, the family, whether nuclear or extended.

Corelli Barnett saw liberalism and its role in disintegrating the community as the main driving force behind the decline of British power.[8] But Barnett was talking about liberalism of the 19th-early 20th century variety. That liberalism wasn't post-modernist; far from it, it did operate, however imperfectly, and on the basis of many false assumptions, with reality, or, at least, it tried to grasp it. It definitely had a relatively free exchange of the ideas and it was industrial capitalism, capitalism born in the crucible of steam, steel, oil, massive construction, printing presses and radio, whose ideas led to some of the most consequential political, economic and scientific revelations for humanity. This is not the case with post-modernism, practiced in the Western world *en masse*, manifested in attention span-shrinking social networks, mass exhibitionism, self-absorption, and instant propagation of the most bizarre and unnatural dopamine-dependent social practices. It is a doctrine which rejects a common perception of reality as such, overcoming facts by swamping them with counter-narratives. Once truth becomes muddied by a storm of perspectives, it ceases to exist in any operational sense.

Modern culture has fallen victim to this state of affairs; it cannot be actualized as a reality without commonly accepted truths as its basis. Modern reality is increasingly ugly, because it lacks truth in multiple sectors, not just political and economic, but cultural and artistic. While admittedly beauty is in the eye of a beholder it is impossible to deny that this potentially exclusionary truism works only so far. If there were no common understandings, we wouldn't have had classics, from art to architecture, which are a reflection of beauty as humanity has defined it for millennia. There is very little argument, if any, across the world about the beauty of the Taj Mahal or Notre Dame or, for that matter, of European classical music or the second great globally embraced music, jazz—they are universally accepted as standards of beauty. Even some scientific concepts are beautiful in an almost aesthetic, mathematical and physical sense. No longer in the Anglo-Saxonized or WASP world. High fashion today largely consists of grotesque and ugly ensembles, as the industry turns to oddities in order to contrive something "new." The only thing which matters is the new human—a consumer of "content," much of it virtual, not real that is, with this consumer's feelings designated by whatever narratives the media chooses to advance. A mental disposal of the existing building blocks of civilizational memory has begun, followed by the destruction of its physical representations.

* * *

The late John Lord, a keyboard player for a legendary British hard rock group, Deep Purple, once famously noted in his interview to *New Musical Express* in 1973: "We are as valid as anything by Beethoven."[9] At that time, one could have easily dismissed it as an arrogant boast designed to attract the attention of the public in order to sell more records. As history has proved, John Lord was not arrogant, he was prophetic. Today, Deep Purple's music is known globally and a famous riff from *Smoke on the Water* is known around the world, even in the most backward places, certainly as well known as the famous four opening notes of Beethoven's Fifth Symphony. Beethoven is one of the cornerstones of the Western Classical Art, but so is Deep Purple of the Western pop-art, in the time when pop-music was not only played by musical virtuosos such as Deep Purple's legendary lineup throughout the 1970s, but had memorable music and a melody, which provided a standard on which generation after generation of people was brought up. In other words—it was marked by true creative talent.

This started to change at the time of the great pseudo-intellectual upheaval in 1970s and came to a head around early 2000s when things changed in a revolutionary and worrying way. Just as the Big Band orchestras of the 30s gave way to smaller groups in ensuing decades for financial reasons, so too were the latter reduced to one plus synthesizer with disco, on the same premise. Not surprisingly, as one 2012 study by a Spanish researcher concluded, in the last 50 years, music started to sound all the same.[10] In fact, much of what constitutes today's pop-music is primarily a collection of primitive progressions, beats, and noise lacking any truly talented composing. And then, of course, the "music industry" began to near collapse.

Modern art in paintings has led to a palette of ugly exhibits which are touted as valuable art, with some of those items fetching astronomical sums in art auctions, where the moneyed class is engaged directly in the honorific investments, paying hundreds of millions of dollars for "art" pieces which are nothing but a collection of disjoined lines and spots and brush strokes, the like of which might be sold as abstract home art in any chain store such as Ross or T.J. Max. at prices ranging from $19.99 to $49.99—a much better deal than paying $87 million for Malevich's *Supremacist Composition* or *Black Square*, or the even more expensive "numbered" paintings by Pollock or Rothko.

Of course, it is very naïve to expect the ability to accurately render human or natural reality—or even their less representational depictions of human emotional realities—to receive accolades in what has become the art business in the modern day West, despite the fact that a vibrant realist art scene still survives in America. Such works wouldn't even be noticed by the hype-infused, tasteless and uncultured American upper-class and its large following among new Western in general and American in particular younger generations, where innovations in form hold sway, and the explanation of the work is its predominant value. This prevents them from grasping even basic principles of beauty and real aesthetics, not to speak of appreciation of classics, which today, as reflective of European imperial culture is being construed as oppressive and not worthy of studying and preserving. Representational art is no longer regarded as "art" by the art and culture businesses, which impose on the American culture aesthetic forms characteristic of underdeveloped primitive societies, albeit delivered with all the hyper-glitz of modern electronic communications technology. Hype, amplified by broadband, while requiring no true talent, still sells, while true talent without that does not.

This process has been underway for a long time. It marks the death of American meritocracy and demolishes the crucial filters and fail-safe mechanisms societies create and impose in order to preserve their coherence. In the world of post-modernism and fuzzy abstracts meritocracy cannot exist because talent, ethics, and morality cannot be defined. It is a perfect environment for financial capitalism because it relegates humanity to a status of human consumer-financial energy units not unlike as depicted in the cult classic *Matrix*. In fact, de-humanization becomes an ultimate goal, as long as a certain level of consumption and cash flow is sustained.

Societies like these do not require liberties and merit in any professional field, as long as one adheres to a "consensus," which itself is primarily shaped by the media—for now, before fundamental constitutional changes are attempted. And if so conforming, one can expect higher chances to advance along the career path. If anyone thinks that this description is eerily reminiscent of the realities of the *Ninety Eighty-Four* by Orwell, they are correct.

In fact, this new reality is being introduced as I write. Threats to people based solely on their political views are already a norm. No matter how one may view Donald Trump or his political base, the ideological infrastructure for declaring and identifying those people as bigots, racists, thought-criminals and, in general, as people who do not fit into the new American narrative—"deplorables" as Hillary Clinton demeaned them by that enduring skillful epithet—is already in place. This is not just consistent with the regular nauseating and tasteless name-calling for which United States "democracy" has become known around the world; this time it is different. People are being specifically threatened not just with the loss of their current livelihood as a result of their political views—but with an exclusion that is projected into the future. Jennifer Rubin of the *Washington Post* is on record with the threat:

Any R now promoting rejection of an election or calling to not to follow the will of voters or making baseless allegations of fraud should never serve in office, join a corporate board, find a faculty position or be accepted into "polite" society. We have a list.[11]

Rubin, far from being an exception, is supported by the much heavier legislative "artillery" of Congresswoman Alexandria Ocasio-Cortez, who together with some allies from Obama Administration, foresee actual political purges of people who worked with Donald Trump. Cortez and others propose compiling lists of people who worked in or with the Trump Administration to make sure that they are "held responsible for what they did"[12]—a far cry from the preceding American tradition of never holding accountable America's practitioners of torture or instigators of illegal and unjustifiable foreign wars.

Blacklisting people is a fine American tradition, but unlike during the McCarthy era paranoia, where even George C. Marshall was accused of associating with "enemies," the modern iteration of America's paranoia, inflamed by lies and baseless accusations by the primarily Democrat-controlled media of collusion with Russia—which failed to be substantiated by their own much-touted and prolonged Mueller investigation—has a much grimmer underside to it. The process no longer resembles how Communist activities of 1950s were targeted as "anti-American" in order to keep domestic capitalism in place. Now it is about reshaping the United States into a one-party dictatorship and using the United States as a main driver of the ongoing attempt to globalize the world based on economic and cultural "values" which are antithetical to most of the rest of the world and cannot survive in any reality other than that of America's intellectually sterile and economically declining large coastal cities—all of which are hotbeds of post-modernism and its first derivative, neo-liberalism.

The belief by many that the Republican Party offers some kind of an antidote to the increasingly obvious totalitarianism promoted by the Democrats is naïve and absolutely baseless. Both American political parties are neoliberal globalist entities tightly connected to different wings of the American oligarchy. Both are deeply complicit in the events which are leading to a condition where the United States implodes economically, and its political institutions disintegrate with an astonishing speed. The only difference between the Democrat and Republican "elites" is that some segments of the GOP tend to use more catch-phrases and buzz-words about America's greatness and some even timidly venture toward American nationalism. As Seth Kaplan tried to define American "nation" recently:

> To understand nationhood, we need to define "nation." Ernest Renan provides a definition in his classic lecture on the subject: "a soul, a spiritual principle... the desire to live together, and desire to continue to invest in the heritage that we have jointly received.... a great solidarity constituted by the feeling of sacrifices made and those that one is still disposed to make." This may require "forgetting... even historical error." A product of long, shared history, involving both bottom-up organic evolution and top-down state-led socialization, nationhood creates a strong sense of togetherness and common destiny and identity—an "imagined community," in the words of Benedict Anderson. This sentiment of nationhood is upheld in, as Renan said, "a daily plebiscite, just as an individual's existence is a perpetual affirmation of life." It requires continuous reinforcement, especially in large populations, in order to maintain its force. This is especially true as the baton of leadership is passed on from generation to generation.[13]

After that, Kaplan proceeds to ignore humanity's many centuries' experience in forming nations and mistakes the state's territorially-enforced cohesion for nationalism. America, certainly, knew some periods of natural cohesion but the warnings about the threat of America's balkanization are nothing new. In 1996 Robert Bork warned:

What needs to be said is that American culture is
Eurocentric, and it must remain Eurocentric or
collapse into meaninglessness. Standards of European
and American origins are the only possible standards
that can hold our society together and keep us a
competent nation. If the legitimacy of Eurocentric
standards is denied, there is nothing else. ...We are,
then, entering a period of tribal hostilities. Some of
what we may expect includes a rise in interethnic
violence, a slowing of economic productivity, a
vulgarization of scholarship (which is already well
under way).[14]

Bork was prescient but he was not original in warning that
rejection of American Eurocentricity will lead to the ideational
disintegration which we all observe today. In fact, Democratic
National Committee policies, despite their fluffy pro-European
platitudes and tropes about democracy, seem unaware that modern
Europe itself retains practically nothing from what made European
civilization, at some point of time, a center of scientific, artistic
and economic achievement on an historically unprecedented
scale. Today, Europe is disintegrating even faster. One can only
imagine what utterances such as those by UK MP Enoch Powell
in his 1968 speech strongly criticizing mass immigration from
the Commonwealth would have created today in the modern
U.S. or European mainstream media. European social sciences
academia today is in a complete state of epistemic closure and
provides anything but education as it is supposed to be: making
students knowledgeable and able to think logically. A French-
Russian scholar, the Chief Editor of the Paris-based magazine
Glagol, Elena Kondratieva-Sagliero, speaking to Israel's *Iton TV*
company, didn't mince her words when describing the process of
non-stop dissolution of the French national identity—identifying
the constant reproduction of guilt that was being used to remove
any vestiges of the historical national consciousness and academic
and artistic standards while promoting politically correct and

largely anti-scientific points of view on race, gender, and culture in general.[15]

Considering the nature of the modern West's ideology-driven social science fields it is not surprising that some suggested reading lists used by many universities and colleges are nothing more than compilations of writings often by minimally educated "writers," very many of them from minorities, describing the horrors of slavery or imperialism by the West as if this kind of behavior was inherent in and specific to the nature of Western man.[16] Under such conditions any mentioning of Islam's bloody expansion, or slavery as facilitated by Africans themselves, not to speak of open genocide, such as was the case in Rwanda in 1994, becomes taboo and even could be construed as hate speech in many European countries. Eventually, the same laws will be forced on the United States, and the First Amendment to the Constitution protecting free speech will either be "modified" or removed altogether, thus placing the United States on a par with Europe, which increasingly looks like it is on its way to complete epistemic closure and the triumph of a totalitarian ideology in which a thought-crime will become a reality fairly soon in historic terms.

Remarkably, the main visible engines promoting these changes are the media. In the United States these media outlets are primarily associated with the DNC and stuffed with people with minimal education and experiences in practically any field requiring actual professional skills such as geopolitics, international relations, the military or science, which in the modern United States are becoming distorted by their need to conform to an ideological consensus. Once people can even raise questions of bias where big data and algorithms are concerned, then the validity and the need to have "freedom from oppression" for any field of knowledge could be questioned, be that Newtonian Mechanics, Chemistry or Theory of Operations. It's not surprising then, that bizarre ideas immediately penetrate the more amorphous modern humanities and social sciences fields in the West and coalesce into political ideologies and slogans which are as "reliable" or reality-based as the American economic or polling data, known by the meme of GIGO: Garbage In-Garbage Out. Of course, the bottom line of this whole process lies in the fact that real scientific fields and disciplines, be they theoretical or applied, are much more complex than anything taught in the social sciences and require a completely different mindset and effort. A degree in aeronautical engineering is much harder to obtain than a degree in journalism or in contemporary Western political pseudo-science. But it is from the latter, not the former, that American political elites emerge.

When a nation chooses a vast majority of its political establishment from the disciplines of law or business there is a problem with that. The deindustrialization of the country may be allowed to happen under the watch of corporatists and what amounts to wrecking countries in many geographic locations around the world may be spun by domestic lawyers as *not* being internationally prohibited war crimes. The lingo of political discourse becomes so complex and obfuscating due to the need to disguise what is really going on, that it prevents even well-educated people from keeping abreast with the events in the country. Furthermore, any event in a fully post-modernist tradition is up for interpretation by parties with different ideologies and by that means, too, lacks clear definitions both from the legal and ethical points of view. The world begins to spin and so does the head of an average Joe, who can make the sense of the world around him only through his wallet, faced with a tsunami of opinion by people very many of whom wouldn't even qualify to run a convenience store, let alone offer their opinions on the subjects of a real economy or international relations.

The dumbing down of America proceeds apace not only in its educational establishment, including what passes for the elite segment of it, but also through self-proclaimed intellectuals, including Hollywood celebrities, most of whom are uneducated people who, in the words of Ricki Gervais, have spent less time in school than Greta Thunberg.[17] But this is precisely the level of education which is required by the modern Woke or Social Justice Warrior culture, because people with serious intellectual abilities developed through in-depth education and life experiences which fortify ethical views on life will always present a serious obstacle to the globalist agenda, one of whose main vehicles is wholesale ignorance by the masses, whose acquiescence is necessary to achieve it.

Many revolutions have had as one of their main objectives the creation of a new man. They seldom succeeded in creating what they envisaged. But what has become known as the Woke revolution in the combined West is enjoying an astonishing success in terms of efficacy of its indoctrination of the young generation, who, while seeking to shed light on past wrongdoing against blacks, are oblivious to the oppression and suffering of the white working class population who still comprise the majority of the nation. As the famous Russian-American specialist in the collapse and implosion of empires, Dmitry Orlov, points out—the American generation of millennials is a "meat generation" slated to be sacrificed on the altar of the globalist dream, categorized as "meat," a terminology used in the cattle business separating cows into milk and meat categories, due to its lacking any resources to be milked for the benefit of globalist elites.[18] It is a terrifying analogy and image, reminiscent of the scene from Alan Parker's screen adaptation of Pink Floyd's *The Wall*, with children serving as a source of meat for the meat-grinder which served as an epitome of the British educational system.

Yet, there is very little doubt that the transformation of the American educational system from knowledge-bearer to indoctrination machine has been remarkably successful in the last 20 plus years and today. With the exception of some elite and primarily private schools, it provides an extremely efficient desensitizing of America's future generation's reactions to crimes, lies and moral decay. This system was at it for more than 20 years and it continues to increase its "productivity" in bringing up "meat generation," or generations to be precise.

Who's Running the Show?

One of the more remarkable manifestations of the complete breakdown of governing in the United States came with the *Defense One* interview of President Trump's Envoy for Syria Ambassador, Jim Jeffrey, who nonchalantly admitted that he had lied to the U.S. Supreme Commander about U.S. forces in Syria, saying, "We were always playing shell games to not make clear to our leadership how many troops we had there." The actual number of troops in northeast Syria is "a lot more than" the roughly two hundred troops Trump initially agreed to leave there in 2019.[19] The fact that the U.S. President was being openly lied to on such an extremely important matter made no real splash in the American media, which implicitly conveyed the notion that disobeying Trump would be saving the nation, nor among the majority of younger Americans, preoccupied with largely contrived gender and race issues and finding jobs, points to the complete demoralization of American society. Moreover, such a public disclosure in a normal country would be considered an act of treason and the people involved in it would be charged accordingly. That Jeffrey felt no compunction in publicly revealing the military's refusal to follow the direction of the president of the United States in itself marks a peculiar turn in America's culture, where the institutions of state act entirely out of their own interest, fraudulently informing the Commander in Chief, who was placed in office by democratic process and who may have been attempting to rein them in. Ambassador Jeffrey will retire and will continue to receive generous pension and other benefits. In fact, he is fully convinced that he did the right thing, as is Lieutenant Colonel Vindman, who took upon himself, contrary to his oath, to decide with regard to Ukraine how the President of the United States must conduct U.S. foreign policy. Vindman was a star witness in a failed Impeachment attempt on President Donald Trump by the Democrats, effectively performing as their asset. As many American servicemen pointed out: "Vindman is a disgrace to all who have served. [In] transcript of his previous closed-door testimony, he clearly admits to undermining President Trump's foreign policy and now he has [Adam] Schiff advising him on how to answer questions."[20] Unsurprisingly, Vindman was praised as a "hero" by the DNC-connected media ranging from the *New York Times* to the *Washington Post*.[21]

Increasingly the title of "hero" is being bestowed upon people who, in a healthy society, would be considered outcasts and shunned, if not prosecuted for treason. American "heroes" today are such as Alexander Vindman, Jim Jeffrey or anyone who enables not just attacks and disobeying a legitimately elected, however personally flawed, U.S. president but on the already shaky American constitutional order as a whole—the last barrier between the United States as a viable state and either its final descent into the chaos or, which seems more likely, its steady transformation into a totalitarian society in which the Constitution and Bill of Rights will be widely publicly recognized as having been disposed of. After all, it's "just a goddam piece of paper," as George W. Bush put it.[22]

America's utility for the pursuit of the globalist agenda today, however, is in serious doubt precisely by virtue of the United States still having not been entirely disassembled, thus not completely prevented from forming something reminiscent of a real nation in which the majority classic European core of the culture is preserved.

If not, the America as we knew it, even 15 years ago, is over, and its fate will be sealed. The nightmarish playground for every human sin, perversion and anomaly will be opened up until it inevitably disintegrates, through violence and bloodshed, into a barren land of proto-state entities held together by well-organized militias whose legitimacy will be ensured by the paramilitary organizations and, yet again, violence.

What happens to America's nuclear weapons arsenal— that should give many a pause, especially when one considers America's non-existent border control sabotaged by globalists. The overwhelming majority of America's modern political class has no grasp of the extent of social forces it is playing with and the possible outcomes. The majority are people whose only difficulty in life was choosing between which Ivy League school to study in, where they studied primarily the humanities and social sciences, or deciding which law firm, bank, newspaper or TV station to work in. Most importantly, these are not people who understand the implications of a breakdown of civil society and law and order, which very many of them advocate. In a dramatic demonstration of utter incompetence and double morality the mayor of Washington

State's capital, Olympia, Cheryl Selbi, was all for anti-police riots and was an ardent supporter of Black Lives Matter until her house was vandalized by this very same Black Lives Matter, which made her call it a case of "domestic terrorism" and even complain that it is "unfair."[23]

The scale of the lack of awareness of the consequences of a radically anti-state, anti-Constitutional and anti-law and order positions that the Democratic Party took is astonishing. As Olympia's mayor found out and shared it with Seattle's *KIRO 7 News*: "It's pretty traumatic when somebody comes to your home." When those somebodies come to your home armed and with the intent to harm or kill you and your family—that is a whole other game altogether and this is what the U.S. political class, especially its so-called "left" wing, cannot grasp yet. This infantilism is a defining feature of the American political class, especially on its "left" wing, which is as globalist as its Republican counterparts.

The entropy in American political life grows, as it usually does, with some militant right-wing groups already active. While the plot to kidnap Michigan governor Gretchen Whitmer was busted by the FBI and the conspirators were brought to justice, there is very little doubt that this is just the start of a further radicalization of the U.S. population.[24] While anti-government plots and militias are nothing new for the American cultural landscape, it is the unprecedented delegitimization of governmental power per se in the United States which represents a clear and present danger. If the U.S. media feed clearly false and malicious information and leaks to the public for four years, who can say whether, in such an environment, the radical ideas and sentiments that it has fomented among both left and right will not perpetuate, even after their need (to unseat Trump, from the DNC perspective) has passed and what passes for normal has returned? They will. Eventually it may come to the point that no number of informants, FBI or police forces will suffice to contain the explosion of the powder keg of American dissatisfaction that is ready to blow, even now. As the astonishing statistics of weapons sales in the last year attests, very many Americans have lost faith in the U.S. establishment's ability to provide even basic law and order. The sales of handguns in the U.S. more than tripled in March 2020 when compared with the year earlier and were up almost two times for long-guns.[25] This is all one needs to know about how "safe" Americans feel themselves in their homes—those who have them—when seeing the dramatic and grim transformation of their country into a third world political and economic circus. It couldn't have been otherwise in a culture which today is almost entirely based on lying—which also is being praised as a virtue and, in fact, is encouraged.

> "When I was a cadet, what's the cadet motto at West Point? You will not lie, cheat, or steal or tolerate those who do. I was the CIA director. We lied, we cheated, we stole. We had entire training courses. It reminds you of the glory of the American experiment," Pompeo boasted as the audience laughed and celebrated the statement.[26]

The source of this encouragement today is very clear—it is America's globalist mafia which has metastasized into the political, media and educational systems in order to prepare generations of Americans to become faithful bearers of the globalist orthodoxy. Their covert goal is to see human society abort fundamental human aspirations ranging from faith, love, family, and the pursuit of truth and justice to form uniform, atomized global economic units designed for consumption only and having no concept of normality and morals. This will ensure the dying out of large portions of humanity which, in the eugenicist globalist view, is a good thing. It will ensure that the earth's resources last longer, to be consumed by globalist elites who themselves are slaves to meaningless capitals, much of which are nothing more than collections of digital zeros on the hard drives of computer servers, and not tied to anything materially significant or beneficial.

A lot has been achieved already in driving American society towards dystopia. Moral decay has become manifest in the physical realm, and abnormality, ugliness and ignorance have been turned into the virtues. Western society as a whole, led by the

United States, suffers today from a serious mental illness which is a consequence of the systemic crisis of modern liberalism, a term which today is completely contradictory to its social reality, since the society this decaying ideology seeks to establish is anything but liberal. Modern liberalism, especially as espoused by the United States Democratic Party and its adherents, is an intolerant, fascist dictatorship, a totalitarian ideology which seeks to destroy everything positive which has been achieved in the last several centuries since the start of the age of Enlightenment and with it, the rise of the West.

Paradoxically, modern globalism is effectively anti-Western insofar as it seeks to achieve its aims via the destruction of Western civilization. It is also anti-human, and an anathema to human civilization. It is a moribund ideology born out of the American establishment's arrogance, ignorance and inability to learn. It is also an ideology which, considering its proponents' utter ignorance of the ramifications of its technological and scientific deployment, primarily through the medium of exhibitionist social networking, is simply incompatible with the new emerging global economic, industrial, military, scientific and moral paradigms and as such is being rejected all around the world, which has already moved on, not waiting to see the final result of America's disintegration— which is now a fait accompli no matter who will be the next U.S. president or which party will continue to front the disastrous economic and cultural policies, any change to which the system itself is preventing.

Endnotes

1 Bruce Thornton, "Melting Pots and Salad Bowls," *Hoover Digest,* October 26, 2012, https://www.hoover.org/research/melting-pots-and-salad-bowls.

2 *"Новый текст Конституции РФ с поправками* 2020" (New text of the Constitution of Russian Federation with 2020 amendments), State Duma of Federal Assembly of Russian Federation, http://duma.gov.ru/news/48953/.

3 Aruuke Uran Kyzy, "Why did Russia's new language bill draw flak from the Caucasus?" *TRTWorld,* December 31, 2018, https://www.trtworld.com/magazine/why-did-russia-s-new-language-bill-draw-flak-from-the-caucasus-22975.

4 "Russian Demographics, 2020," *World Population Review,* https://worldpopulationreview.com/countries/russia-population.

5 David North, "Introduction to *The New York Times' 1619 Project and the Racialist Falsification of History,*" *World Socialist Web Site,* December 4, 2020, https://www.wsws.org/en/articles/2020/12/04/intr-d04.html.

6 Ben McDonald, "*Seattle Public Schools Say Math Is Racist,*" *Daily Caller,* October 21, 2019, https://dailycaller.com/2019/10/21/seattle-schools-math-is-racist/.

7 Brandon Hasbrouk, "The Votes of Black Americans Should Count Twice," *The Nation,* December 17, 2020, https://www.thenation.com/article/society/black-votes-reparations-gerrymandering/.

8 Corelli Barnett, *The Collapse of British Power* (New York: William Morrow & Company, Inc., 1972), 91.

9 "Organist's classical influence defined Deep Purple," *Irish Times,* July 21, 2012, https://www.irishtimes.com/news/organist-s-classical-influence-defined-deep-purple-1.541563.

10 Sean Michaels, "Pop music these days: it all sounds the same, survey reveals," *The Guardian,* July 27, 2012, https://www.theguardian.com/music/2012/jul/27/pop-music-sounds-same-survey-reveals.

11 Bronson Stolking, "A Vengeful Jennifer Rubin Wants Republican Party to 'Burn Down' and 'No Survivors,'" *Townhall,* November 7, 2020, https://townhall.com/tipsheet/bronsonstocking/2020/11/07/jennifer-rubin-calls-for-republican-party-to-be-burned-down-and-no-survivors-n2579673.

12 Sam Dorman, "*AOC, others pushing for apparent blacklist of people who worked with Trump,*" *Fox News,* November 9, 2020, https://www.foxnews.com/politics/aoc-blacklist-trump-supporters.

13 Seth Kaplan, "America Needs Nationalism," *The American Conservative,* November 10, 2020, https://www.theamericanconservative.com/articles/america-needs-nationalism/.

14 Robert H. Bork, *Slouching Towards Gomorrah: Modern Liberalism and American Decline* (New York: Regan Books, 1996), 311-313.

15 "*Чем гордятся "полезные идиоты" Европы?*" (What Europe's useful idiots are proud of?), *Iton TV,* September 8, 2020, https://youtu.be/YlCMuoveDFE.

16 Ibid.

17 "Ricky Gervais' Monologue - 2020 Golden Globes," *NBC,* January 5, 2020, https://youtu.be/LCNdTLHZAeo.

18 Dmitry Orlov, *The Meat Generation* (Club Orlov Press, 2019), 3

19 Katie Bo Williams, "Outgoing Syria Envoy Admits Hiding US Troop Numbers; Praises Trump's Mideast Record," *Defense One,* November 12, 2020, https://www.defenseone.com/threats/2020/11/outgoing-syria-envoy-admits-hiding-us-troop-numbers-praises-trumps-mideast-record/170012/.

20 Samantha Chang, "Benghazi hero and Navy SEAL in bin Laden-kill torch 'traitor' Vindman: 'A disgrace to all who have served,'" *BPR,* November

20, 2019, https://www.bizpacreview.com/2019/11/20/benghazi-hero-and-navy-seal-in-bin-laden-kill-torch-traitor-vindman-a-disgrace-to-all-who-have-served-854909.

21 "Multiple War Heroes Slam 'Prissy' and 'Disgraceful' Lt. Col. Vindman Following Testimony," *Ohio Star,* November 21, 2019, https://theohiostar.com/2019/11/21/multiple-war-heroes-slam-prissy-and-disgraceful-lt-col-vindman-following-testimony/.

22 "Bush administration vs. the U.S. Constitution," *Sourcewatch,* https://www.sourcewatch.org/index.php/Bush_administration_vs._the_U.S._Constitution.

23 Leo Brine, "Olympia mayor's home, downtown vandalized during Friday night protest," *The Olympian,* June 14, 2020, https://www.theolympian.com/news/local/article243516852.html.

24 Cole Waterman, "What we know about the militia members charged in kidnapping plot against Michigan governor," *Michigan Live,* October 17, 2020, https://www.mlive.com/crime/2020/10/what-we-know-about-the-militia-members-charged-in-kidnapping-plot-against-michigan-governor.html.

25 "Monthly unit sales of firearms in the United States from 2019 to 2020, by type (in thousands)," *Statista,* https://www.statista.com/statistics/1107651/monthly-unit-sales-of-firearms-by-type-us/.

26 "'We Lied, Cheated, and Stole': Pompeo Comes Clean About the CIA," *Telesur,* April 24, 2019, https://www.telesurenglish.net/news/We-Lied-Cheated-and-Stole-Pompeo-Comes-Clean-About-CIA-20190424-0033.html.

CONCLUSION: NOT EXCEPTIONAL, NOT FREE, NOT PROSPEROUS—NOT AMERICA?

As British tabloid *Daily Mail* reported in November 2020, Megyn Kelly, the famous U.S. media personality who passes for a journalist decided to move out of New York. This decision came about not because New York somehow is dying, which has been the case for some time now, but for ideological and political reasons. As the *Daily Mail* states:

> Kelly revealed she snapped after a letter was sent around to faculty in her sons' school that claimed "white school districts across the country [are] full of future killer cops." It added that "white kids are being indoctrinated in black death" and are "left unchecked and unbothered in their schools."[1]

The *Daily Mail* characterizes this private school thus:

> Collegiate School is ranked as one of the best private schools in the country and also claims to be the oldest. It counts JFK Jr., his nephew Jack Schlossberg, and Game of Thrones co-creator David Benioff among its alumni.[2]

This development signifies a trend which is very pronounced in the United States today and which will spread all over the land. Yet, one peculiar feature of this whole tempest in the teacup is especially remarkable. Megyn Kelly is very well off, which is usually the case with the talking heads who make it to the mainstream media, especially TV, and can easily afford to move elsewhere—unlike most Americans all over the country, who are tied by their property and family to a particular locality. But that is not what is remarkable. What is remarkable is that Megyn Kelly's sons, whose mother paid $56,000 a year for them to attend this private and allegedly very elite school, were then confronted with the statements above.

As *The Hill* clarifies, the letter was in actuality a blog post written by Orleans Public Education Network Executive Director Nahliah Webber, but was circulated within the school's diversity group.[3] Insofar as Webber is in Louisiana and not a staff member, it demonstrates the extent to which its subsequent distribution to the faculty (one wonders by whom and to what intent?) in an elite primarily white school reflects the problematic of how to include the African American experience within Americans' historical understanding without enflaming enmity between groups concerned. One can only imagine the seriousness of the cognitive dissonances these white students face, as their traditional historical understanding encounters that reflecting the African American experience when the latter, while trying to achieve acknowledgment in the historical record, is expressed in exaggerated, emotive and indeed even racist terms while trying to set that record straight. Kelly's reaction is indicative of how that is working out.

Of course, there are myriad other reasons for wanting to leave New York—as indicated by the recent exodus of some 800,000 persons, clearly not similarly motivated.

This New York school is not an exception. The so-called neo-left progressive agenda is being implemented wholesale all over the United States. Future American generations may end up completely intimidated by this radical orthodoxy which already has a baneful effect on America's social cohesion, with fear reigning supreme. Even today, up to 40% of the UK university students are scared to voice their opinions out of fear for their future careers or for being judged by their peers.[4] Woke and cancel culture seem to have won.

Paradoxically, the freedom of speech and expression which enabled that is already largely dead in Europe, with its death in the United States pending, prevented for now only by a thin tubing of the First Amendment's life support in an increasingly irrelevant U.S. Constitution, already under assault from all directions, especially from America's so-called progressive left—wittingly or not doing the heavy lifting for totalitarian globalist forces which have been in the business of socially reengineering the United States into the Anglo-Saxon version of South Africa, where African faces front for the Anglo elites who still control the economic levers of power.

The scaffolding of the American society is collapsing. After the scandalous fabrications of the Russiagate hysteria, the corrupted election process and the paranoia of COVID-19 lockdowns, modern American "democracy" is revealed as a political spectacle financed by the American oligarchy seeking to legitimize its hold on political power while avoiding by all means any reforms to the economic system, which is both anti-American and moribund. If it takes ANTIFA and BLM to provoke violent release of the steam pressure building up in America's increasingly pressurized salad bowl, so be it. No price is big enough for maintaining the status quo or at least what is perceived as a status quo by powers that be.

This oligarchy, realistically, is not very bright, despite being rich, with many of them having Ivy league degrees. They have proved this beyond the shadow of a doubt. Clausewitz' dictum that it is legitimate to judge an event by its outcome for it is the soundest criterion remains true even after two centuries.[5] American politics was always tawdry, now the whole American political system, with its allegedly "free" media and establishment academe, have been paraded around the world as one huge tawdry blob, whose functionaries continue to perceive it as a global superpower, which it no longer is. Of course, the United States still can blackmail foreign politicians, here and there; the United States still can send a couple of its Carrier Battle Groups to intimidate some third world country, but increasingly, as Pat Buchanan noted recently, "nobody is quaking in their boots."[6]

This sentiment was echoed in 2019 by the excellent Russian journalist, Irina Alksnis, who, when reviewing the unconcealable American agony at losing its exceptionalist status, pointed out that the only people in the world who can understand that experience are Russians. Alksnis is on target here, the Soviet Union being the culmination of Russia's millennium-old empire-building, a super-power next to the United States, but under conditions no nation has experienced, let alone the United States, which was blessed with geographic insularity. The USSR bore the brunt of the war against the Axis powers and was a demolished country by the end of the World War Two. The United States emerged from that war as a superpower because it benefited from that war immensely. The collapse of the Soviet Union and the economic catastrophe which followed taught Russians a lot, and also left an aftertaste of the humiliation of losing power—a process the United States is going through right now. Speaking in a layman's lingo, the Russians get it. They, unlike any other people in the world, can relate to what the United States is going through right now. Russians can read the signs extremely well, while the U.S. elite not only has no experience with it but is completely insulated from understanding it. This is America's tragedy unfolding before our very eyes. Not only is America's crisis systemic, but its elites are uncultured, badly educated and mesmerized by decades of their own propaganda, which in the end, they accept as a reality.

They are also arrogant and corrupt. Thus, no viable ideas or solutions to the current unfolding economic, social and cultural catastrophe can originate within these elites, who see the world only through Wall Street and *New York Times* lenses. Real intellect, courage and integrity are simply not there; they all have been traded for the perks and sinecures of what many correctly describe as Washington D.C. blob, whose only purpose for existence is self-perpetuation.

Alksins, when describing America's reactions and the flow of the pathos-ridden statements and declarations coming from D.C., suggests the United States should simply recognize the continuity of world history, in which the United States is merely a newcomer, and recognize its defeat, not in general, but for this particular moment, in order to learn the lessons for the future. She writes:

> However, to hear this simple advice—not to mention following it—the United States needs to stop, at least for an instant, and silence themselves. To stop shaking the air with statements, declarations, demands, and threats, which come across as either strange, or outright silly because of their obvious inability to ever be carried out in reality. But it is precisely, it seems, what the U.S. is not capable of doing. As a result—the continuation of a never-ending declaratory carousel: Moscow, Assad must go! Russians, we will provide for freedom of navigation in the Kerch Strait! Russians, we will punish you for support of Maduro. But the most insulting for Americans is that only Russia can understand them. Because we remember the pain behind those words.[7]

Of course, the United States is still capable of starting a war with Russia, but if it does so, this will mean only one thing—the United States will cease to exist, as will most of the human civilization. The horrific thing is that there are some people in the U.S. for whom even this price is too small to pay as long as it satisfies their addiction to power. Considering that no American soldier, let alone politicians, ever fought *in defense* of their country and that U.S. Armed Forces don't know what it means to be on the receiving end of high-tech stand-off munitions capable with a single salvo to obliterate a battalion-size force, it is difficult to explain to them that the times of America's main defense—two oceans—are long gone. In the end, how do you even talk to people who believe that they are invincible, even in the face of overwhelming empirical evidence that militarily they are not, or that the United States is deindustrialized to such a degree that the only path it can take is further financialization and deindustrialization of the country, merely postponing the inevitable collapse?[8] This will continue to increase the level of misery in the already miserable country but these self-anointed "elites" are one-trick ponies—they simply do not know how to do anything else. As is the case with sociopaths—they lack the ability to self-assess and see their situation in perspective.

But surely, to control the population of deplorables, especially those anguished white ones, American elites will deploy their propaganda machine known as U.S. media which can lead an attack on what's left of America's genuine, not talked up fake, greatness—the U.S. Constitution and its Bill of Rights. Attacks on its freedom of speech and expression, attacks on its Second Amendment, shaky guarantees against the final imposition of tyranny, will continue and increase. The shutting down of free thought is number one on the agenda of the American coastal urban self-proclaimed masters of discourse, who are ready to demolish the country if they can't rule it.

It is difficult to properly react to the surrealism of their fixations occurring in the context of the approaching American multi-leveled collapse. We have provided just a small indicator of what are purported to be, driven home as, and perhaps now are the concerns of the new totalitarian-inclined, brain-washed American generation coming to take the controls of its political, economic, cultural and intellectual life. It is an unhinged generation. Poor American millennials, who are primarily white, face a grim future. As *Newsweek* reported:

> The millennial generation, people born between 1981 and 1996, make up the largest share of the U.S. workforce, but control just 4.6 percent of the country's total wealth. Baby Boomers, people born between 1946 and 1964, currently control ten times more wealth than millennials, whose 72 million workers make them the most represented group in the workforce. Although it's not unusual for younger age groups to have less money than their elders, the average Baby Boomer working in 1989 during their

early 30s had quadruple the wealth of what millennials have at that same age today.[9]

This generation has become the hostage of the debauchery in economics, foreign relations and culture that the Baby Boomers' generation, most of whom never experienced any kind of serious difficulty in life other than boredom, unleashed on both the United States and the world, the minute they found themselves off balance due to trends in the world which originated in the scientific and technological revolution, which also globalized the world through the electronic mass-media.

This was the downfall of what has become commonly known as the *Davos Culture*. The expanding freedom of exchange of ideas and information (now being curtailed), disclosed to many that for all the glitz and glamour of the dot.com billionaires and the "green" evangelicals, the world was and is still operating based on energy, machines, real production, and what amounts to basic physics and mathematics. IPhones do not grow on trees. They require gigantic resource extraction and processing cycles, which involve millions of people still getting every day into the coal mines somewhere in China. They require an electrical grid, the CNC and lithography machinery, which is being built around the world; they require massive metal ships and aircraft made out of aluminum, requiring bauxite to be extracted from the ground, they require the millions upon millions of engineers, designers, workers, doctors, and teachers who run the actual wheels of modern civilization. America has forgotten how it all works.

It couldn't have been otherwise. An increasingly porno-graphic culture dominated by celebrities, sports stars and media personalities, most of whom are barely educated in any practical sense but are nonetheless enabled to pontificate on subjects they have no clue about—such a culture was inevitably destined to crash. It was also destined to ignore the most important features underpinning modernity—the proper valuation of labor and the distribution and control of the national treasure—while focusing on fake intricacies of the "equality" of races and genders.

In fact, the new gender discovering field is a lucrative business. With that comes the increasing deconstruction of the family without which no nation can survive. Families procreate, educate, and bring up children. Increasingly less so in the United States, while in Europe the declining birthrate is a matter of concern.

But is the United States even a nation? The U.S. demonstrates, at least at present, very weak survival instincts and, most likely, the split deep in the core of what once was called the American nation, has already been made manifest. Indeed, there is nothing in common between a white WASP farm worker from Iowa and Jewish lawyer from Manhattan, or the black rapper from the Bronx. They view the world, America and their place in it differently and those visions are irreconcilable. Economic calamity has brought those contradictions to the surface.

What is in store for America, then? If, hopefully, the United States avoids massive violence and complete disintegration into separatist territories, the only way for the American "elite" to maintain any kind of control over generations increasingly woke or desensitized by drugs is tyranny. Oregon has already legalized hard drugs.[10] Other states will soon follow. For the American oligarchy fearing rebellion, this is good news. While drug dependent people cannot work in complex, hi-tech manufacturing, that is not the plan anyway. Continued American deindustrialization will go hand in hand with the removal of large segments of the American youth from a qualified labor pool. Their life expectancy is declining and their dying out is viewed as "helping" the U.S. economy.

The political tyranny will start with demolishing the U.S. Constitution and transitioning the country to a de jure one-party state with political purges following this transition. Initially those purges will be in the form of firing people from their jobs or preventing them from getting employment, but eventually the social score system will be introduced officially and the "rehabilitation camps" may become a reality. One may say that this is too dystopian and fantastic to even consider. If it is, it is all for the better. But for a country where half of the population believed that the president of the United States was Russia's Manchurian Candidate, with all the media singing in a single voice promoting this fantasy, or where most universities define human nature as a social construct, or where people who have zero background in such fields as physics, mathematics or chemistry are driving the "green energy" field—in such a country nothing is impossible.

Such a country will disintegrate, inevitably, because it is unsustainable, The United States as it used to be known, has no future, especially with its current "elites" running foreign policy under the heavy influence of lobbyists and think-tanks funded by and pursuing the interests of foreign countries.

* * *

I recall how, in the early-to-mid 1990s, whenever I flew between Russia and the United States, each time I returned from Russia, which at that time was a ruined country run by criminal gangs, my routine upon arrival, was always the same. I would get to a nearest airport bar and, having usually very little luggage with me, would order fried chicken wings, beer and then light my cigarette. For some reason, most of the time, and there were many of those times, whenever I get to those bars, the TVs hanging there would show *Cheers*. I never got into *Cheers*, but the opening tune and the whole aura of *Cheers* was at that point in time so counter to my Russian life experiences —many of which were terrifying, to put it mildly—that it captivated me, with its peacefulness and good nature. It was pleasant to feel oneself in the safety and peace of an America which still was experiencing the high of the 1980s. American television projected a free and decent people, a pop culture but a culture nonetheless, and very American. It was idiosyncratic to an America that doesn't exist anymore—most TV shows or films, or music, today have no moral to their story, nor often the sign of any talent or basic likeability—now they have an agenda. It is this agenda which ruins the remnants of that America. A long time has passed since my *Cheers* transitions from one world to another. America is different today. The country has lost the spirit which made it so attractive and this loss is even more menacing than its catastrophic deindustrialization. In the end, in theory, manufacturing capacity can be restored, but the restoration of the spirit of a divided and disintegrating country which holds conflicting images of what it is, cannot. America today is dysfunctional, deeply unhappy and not a free country.

David Hackett Fischer once noted about the famous Cathedral at Chartres:

> The great cathedral was both a religious and an economic institution. At the same time, it was vital to its community in another way. Every great work of architecture is a cultural symbol. Chartres was a case in point. The beautiful cathedral perfectly symbolized an era that Charles Homer Haskins called the Renaissance of the twelfth century.[11]

In May 2020 Russia finished the construction of the Main Cathedral of the Russian Armed Forces. I have been to churches in my life, but what was erected is more than just a stunning Russian Orthodox Church. Some people say, justifiably, that it is more than just a cathedral, it has a mystical quality to it, it is a place of enormous spiritual energy which has revivified Russia's history. Everyone is welcomed to this Cathedral—Christians, Jews, Muslims, atheists, anyone. It reflects a common history, symbolic of Russia's unparalleled unity when defending the motherland from invading enemies. Rod Dreher of *The American Conservative* wrote on this occasion:

> What an overpowering work of architecture. What troubles me about it, a bit, as an Orthodox Christian, is that it is dedicated to military might. ...Unlike many American Christians, I am divided internally about mixing nationalism with religion—but I do recognize that that view is massively ahistorical. I don't judge the Russians on this; their cathedral is also a memorial to those who died in defense of the Russian homeland. No one who knows even the slightest thing about the way the patriotic Russians fought the Nazis, and how they suffered, can begrudge them something like this.

I don't bring it up in this context to argue about its appropriateness. Rather, I want to say that a nation that can build a monument like this to its God and to its greatness is a nation of immense depth and power. Could we build anything like this in America? Don't be absurd. We don't have the internal strength and imagination to do so. And therein lies a tale. We are a nation that allows scum to throw red paint onto statues of our Founders, and to pull down a statue of Union soldiers who died in a war to end slavery, and few if any of our leaders say a word.[12]

As many noted, not for once, the nation that doesn't want to venerate its founders, its first president George Washington, has no future, nor deserves one. Nations which rewrite their history to accommodate a political trend end up losing all sense of who they are, as did, as paradoxically it may sound, the Russia of the 1990s—undergoing a debilitating experiment in historical revisionism and debauchery of a libertarian grim utopia which cost millions of lives and an economic dislocation which makes the Great Depression pale in comparison. It took Russia twenty years to return to being a normal state with a vibrant economy, powerful armed forces and self-respect, but Russians still had a nation, even in those horrifying times of the 1990s so called "liberal" experiment.

The United States doesn't have a nation anymore. Not even close, and if the magnificence and power, through visual representation, of the nation's cathedrals is any indication, the United States has become as a tasteless boxy post-modernist mega-church preaching prosperity gospel. It is fake, it always was, and it cannot stop the disintegration. Because in the end, it is the spirit of the nation, of its people, which decides the outcome, even when everything seems to be lost. Whether America will find this spirit remains to be seen, but in the end, it is the only way America will be able to preserve itself as a unified country and stop its disintegration.

Everything else will follow from there.

Endnotes

1 Frances Mulraney, "Megyn Kelly says she's leaving New York City and taking her kids out of their 'woke' $56k-a-year school after letter circulated saying 'white kids are being indoctrinated in black death' and will grow up to be 'killer cops,'" *Daily Mail,* November 18, 2020, https://www.dailymail.co.uk/news/article-8963261/Megyn-Kelly-says-shes-leaving-New-York-far-left-schools-gone-deep-end.html.

2 Ibid.

3 Celine Castronuovo, "Megyn Kelly says she's leaving New York City, cites 'far-left' schools," *The Hill,* November 18, 2020, https://thehill.com/homenews/media/526537-megyn-kelly-says-shes-leaving-new-york-city-cites-far-left-schools

4 "UK students feel censored on campus, poll finds," *ADF International,* November 18, 2020, https://adfinternational.org/news/uk-students-feel-censored-on-campus-poll-finds/.

5 Carl Von Clausewitz, *On War* (Princeton, NJ: Princeton University Press, 1976), 627.

6 Patrick Buchanan, "Nobody's Quaking in Their Boots, Anymore," *The American Conservative,* November 7, 2017, https://www.theamericanconservative.com/buchanan/nobodys-quaking-in-their-boots-anymore/.

7 Irina Alksnis, "Америка превращается в бессмысленного говоруна" (America is turning into a senseless windbag), *Vz.ru,* April 4, 2019, https://vz.ru/opinions/2019/4/4/971492.html.

8 Michael Hudson, "Financialization and Deindustrialization," *Unz Review,* November 2, 2020, https://www.unz.com/mhudson/financialization-and-deindustrialization/.

9 Benjamin Fernow, "Millennials Control Just 4.2 Percent of US Wealth, 4 Times Poorer Than Baby Boomers Were at Age 34," *Newsweek,* October 8, 2020, https://www.newsweek.com/millennials-control-just-42-percent-us-wealth-4-times-poorer-baby-boomers-were-age-34-1537638.

10 Sam Levin and Agencies, "Oregon becomes first US state to decriminalize possession of hard drugs," *Yahoo News,* November 3, 2020, https://news.yahoo.com/oregon-becomes-first-us-state-065648932.html.

11 David Hackett Fischer, *The Great Wave: Price Revolutions and the Rhythm of History* (Oxford, England: Oxford University Press, 1996), 12-13.

12 Rod Dreher, "America's Monumental Existential Problem," *The American Conservative,* June 30, 2020, https://www.theamericanconservative.com/dreher/america-monumental-existential-problem-symbolism-architecture/.

INDEX

Printed by Printforce, United Kingdom